Intersubjectivity in Psycho

In this book, Lewis Kirshner explains and illustrates the concept of intersubjectivity and its application to psychoanalysis. By drawing on findings from neuroscience, infant research, cognitive psychology, Lacanian theory, and philosophy, Kirshner argues that the analytic relationship is best understood as a dialogic exchange of signs between two subjects—a semiotic process. Both subjects bring to the inter-action a history and a set of unconscious desires, which inflect their responses. In order to work most effectively with patients, analysts must attend closely to the actual content of the exchange, rather than focusing on imagined contents of the patient's mind. The current situation revives a history that is shaped by the analyst's participation.

Supported by numerous case studies, *Intersubjectivity in Psychoanalysis: A Model for Theory and Practice* is a valuable resource for psychotherapists and analysts seeking to refine their clinical goals and methods.

Lewis Kirshner has worked as a Harvard professor and training psychoanalyst in Boston and been visiting professor in Lyon, France, and a Fulbright senior fellow in Ghent, Belgium. His numerous publications have treated developments in French psychoanalysis and the work of Lacan, Winnicott, and Ferenczi. His book, *Having a Life: Self-Pathology after Lacan*, received high praise from reviewers.

Intersubjectivity in Psychoanalysis

A Model for Theory and Practice

Lewis Kirshner

Routledge
Taylor & Francis Group

LONDON AND NEW YORK

First published 2017
by Routledge
2 Park Square, Milton Park, Abingdon, Oxon OX14 4RN

and by Routledge
711 Third Avenue, New York, NY 10017

Routledge is an imprint of the Taylor & Francis Group, an informa business

© 2017 Lewis Kirshner

British Library Cataloguing in Publication Data
A catalogue record for this book is available from the British Library

Library of Congress Cataloging in Publication Data
A catalog record for this book has been requested

ISBN: 978-1-138-93807-6 (hbk)
ISBN: 978-1-138-93808-3 (pbk)
ISBN: 978-1-315-67588-6 (ebk)

Typeset in Times New Roman and Gill Sans
by Florence Production Ltd, Stoodleigh, Devon, UK.

Contents

Acknowledgements

This book represents the fruit of many long conversations with friends and colleagues. Numerous people have been generous with their time and thoughtful in their comments to me. Valued readers of earlier drafts include: Ti Bodenheimer, Werner Bohleber, Jack Foehl, Allannah Furlong, Jaap Jubbels, Peter Lawner, Alfred Margulies, Jon Palmer, Jose Saporta, Murray Schwartz, and David Sherman. Without their frank responses and suggestions, my work would not have advanced beyond its scattered beginnings. Extended discussions with Nicolas Georgieff in Lyon enabled me to think through the interplay between neuroscience and psychoanalysis. Peter Lawner's deep knowledge of relational and Freudian literature helped me clarify my position on these theories. Alec Morgan taught me about the Boston Process of Change Group, and Jose Saporta has never flagged in encouraging me to apply semiotics to psychoanalysis. Presentations at the Université de Paris, René Descartes, in dialogue with Alain Vanier and François Villa; at the Amsterdam Psychoanalytic Society with Jaap Jubbels; at the International Psychoanalytic University in Berlin with Andreas Hamburger; and with the Vermont Study Group, led by Sharon Dennett, stimulated my thinking on intersubjectivity. Stijn Vanheule encouraged my teaching at the University of Ghent and introduced me to contemporary Lacanian texts. Kim Boyd invited my "academic lecture" at the Boston Psychoanalytic Institute on Intersubjectivity, which produced a stimulating exchange with colleagues. Our panel at the meeting of the American Psychoanalytic Association in January 2015, organized by Janine Vivona, on How the Talking Cure Works stimulated me to refine further my ideas. Staci Rosenthal and Waite Worden Jr. were diligent proofreaders and commentators. Major credit for my book belongs to Dawn Skorczewski, editor par excellence, whose rigorous readings, challenges, encouragement, and steady support were essential ingredients of my project. I owe her special gratitude.

Introduction

This book presents an integrative perspective on the meaning and clinical applications of the concept of intersubjectivity in psychoanalysis. As my primary objective, I propose a model that takes into account the diverse sources of intersubjectivity, including contributions from philosophy, neuroscience, and infant research. Psychoanalysts have interpreted the concept of intersubjectivity in several ways, and I offer a critical review of their major approaches. Throughout, I emphasize the field of semiotics, which provides a common foundation for different models of psychoanalytic practice, all of which involve the exchange of signs between subjects. The speaking relationship holds the central place in psychoanalysis, but is often overlooked in ongoing debates over the correct theoretical approach or regarded simply as an instrument of clinical process. Subjectivity depends on speech, taking shape within specific contexts and interactions that are structured within a social framework of roles and symbols, not reducible to biological or intrapsychic mechanisms. I use case examples to illustrate intersubjectivity in clinical relationships.

As a clinician practicing for forty years, I have experienced the productive evolution of analytic thinking from the classic Freudian model of mental function and conflict in which I was trained, through revisions by interpersonal, object relations, self-psychological, and modern relational schools that have culminated in the inclusive, but rather ill-defined notion of intersubjectivity. These changes constitute a paradigm shift for psychoanalysis. Yet, despite many outstanding contributions, we are far from benefiting from a substantial theory of what the concept means and how it works clinically. Many traditional ideas about therapeutic action, the value of formulation and interpretation, and the role of countertransference need to be revised or discarded in the light of post-modern insights into the effects of language and culture. A central focus of disagreement between schools concerns the nature of subjectivity and the experience of self. I argue against a naturalistic conception of the human subject as an object who can be known or explained by scientific methods of observation.

Interdisciplinarity

My first objective in writing this book is to trace the concept of intersubjectivity from its historical developments in several disciplines, each viewing human interaction through different frames. The fields of neuroscience, philosophy, semiotics, and infant research offer substantial, but in many ways incompatible, contributions to understanding human relationships. Their varied methods and findings have influenced psychoanalysis, however, resulting in what often seems a hodge-podge of inconsistent ideas about what actually takes place in treatment. I see a tendency both in the psychoanalytic literature and in the humanities and social sciences to explain human interaction narrowly by causal mechanisms in the brain or self-enclosed psychological systems that dispense with personal intentions and meanings. No single set of observations or research suffices, but a cross-disciplinary perspective can maintain the humanistic and scientific legacy of psychoanalysis and can enable us to construct a broadly based theory.

In many respects, controversies around the meaning of intersubjectivity trace their origins to philosophical arguments going back at least to the time of Descartes over the famous "mind body problem." Splits between the physical and the mental or between cognition and emotion constitute the Cartesian legacy that has influenced subsequent thinking in many fields. The conflict between phenomenology and structuralism in mid-twentieth-century philosophy illustrates another aspect of this dichotomizing tendency, as do recent controversies about applying neuroscience research to explain human behavior. In psychotherapeutic practice, how we conceptualize the experiential, unconscious, and physiologic underpinnings of mental–emotional life influences our way of listening to patients. Likewise, applications of infant research to practice cannot escape the practical and conceptual problems of differentiating biological from symbolic–cultural determinants of behavior. How much of human development unfolds "naturally" and how much depends on learning and internalization of messages from others? A dichotomous model that separates the role of inherited capacities built into a newborn's brain from the effects of symbolic learning coming from its social environment vastly oversimplifies the ways in which biology and culture interact; yet this split has been difficult to avoid, at least in the Western tradition.

I strongly believe that psychoanalysis must remain open to the results both of neuroscientific research and the phenomenological study of human behavior. These neighbor disciplines have a lot to say to us and can greatly enrich our understanding of our patients. We can be interested in mechanisms of the brain that produce mental functions without confining explanations of behavior to a physiologic level, and we can value conscious experience without rejecting the unconscious. Advances in the neurosciences have led to a reevaluation of many psychoanalytic ideas, notably about emotion and about the nature of self. As an attentive outsider, I find reports of this work fascinating and challenging to prior assumptions, and I attempt to take the science into account at several points in my discussion. Nonetheless, I am concerned that a neuroreductionist approach to emotions and actions supported by some scientists and philosophers has taken contemporary psychiatry on a dehumanizing turn and begun to influence psychoanalytic theories. Although the debate about whether behavior, especially psychopathology, derives primarily from essentially impersonal processes in the brain or can be attributed to psychological causation has become conceptually out of date, this duality still permeates clinical training, as in decisions about indications for psychotherapy. In my view, psychological and physiological explanations reflect inescapable forms of dualistic thinking that cannot be reduced one to the other, but are interwoven as a unitary substrate of mental life. By substrate, however, I do not intend the brain itself, but the interplay of brain plasticity and function with external symbolic interactions. The new fields of cognitive social neuroscience and neuropsychoanalysis, as well as recent work by analytically informed philosophers, attempt to integrate the different perspectives of the biological and social sciences, and have influenced my thinking about intersubjectivity.

Semiotics

My second objective focuses on the dialogic process of intersubjective communication that constitutes the subject matter for any viable theory of psychoanalytic practice. Above all, psychoanalysis involves a talking relationship between two subjects and cannot be reduced to impersonal, behavioral, or biological mechanisms. The crux of my argument boils down to the fact that human beings are speaking creatures and, whatever innate capacities they are endowed with to be able to function as social animals, require words to live and work together in groups. The individual subject arises not simply as the product of temperament or basic emotional and cognitive proclivities, which may indeed be hardwired in the brain, but as the product of relationships with specific others who have named and linked him to an inheritance of meanings and symbols. As the French psychologist Rene Kaës (1973) has written, paraphrasing Freud, human beings are subjects of a double unconscious: one rooted in a particular body and physiology, the other anchored to the symbols transmitted along the chain of generations into which they are born. Subjects are created through the incredible transformation of infants from physical bodies into speaking persons through exchanges of affect, gesture, and language with a few important people, woven into a social and cultural context.

From a semiotic point of view, the process of becoming a human subject (sometimes called subjectivation) consists in the gradual internalization of discursive elements (key cultural and familial terms, metaphors, images, affective expressions, and texts) into an embodied consciousness. These assemblages of signs circulate between subjects within the semiotic systems that constitute human societies. Whether some are universal or biologically based remains in dispute, especially around questions about affect, and the issue merits discussion. Whether innate, learned, or a combination of the two, however, signs are communications that represent something for someone and always evoke responses from their recipients[1] (Peirce, 1932, 2.228). From the beginning of life, they carry meanings, albeit enigmatic ones for the child, for whom they become part of an emerging self-consciousness. In addition, symbols like words have the combinatorial property of being available for rearrangement ad infinitum to create new meanings (or new ways of being a subject). Clinicians can listen to individual speech as a polyphonic self-presentation derived from different sources. A patient expresses a diversity of signifying messages, as though voiced by different subjects.

Semiotics itself can present as an impersonal system of units of communication, which make it very difficult to grasp the actual human subject. A strictly semiotic approach can suggest a programmed, schematic exchange of signs, without recognizing the personal nature of relationships between already formed subjects. I suggest that discussing the interaction of two persons requires a level of concepts I designate as "beyond semiosis." This level includes socioculturally specific forms of relationships, roles, or nodes in the network of roles that function as organizers for each intersubjective encounter. I operate from the functionalist assumption in anthropology that regards cultural practices as ways of providing for survival needs like maternal care, developmental supervision and initiation, protection, attachment, and familial bonds. The psychic healer fills a role shaped by his culture to respond to individual suffering and to stabilize or treat disruptions in the lives of its members. The details of this role depend on the relative values the culture places on individual freedom and self-expression, group bonds and loyalties, and spiritual and other beliefs. The healer actively assumes his symbolic position by his presence, willing engagement, and commitment to the welfare of the individual and to the collective. In psychoanalysis, I argue that the basic positions of empathy, responsiveness, and recognition comprise the major features of this role. These allusive, not to be concretized terms refer to vital interactions between individual subjects that are never fully assured. They represent core intersubjective ingredients of an ethical psychotherapeutic practice.

Psychoanalysis and intersubjectivity

Although many analysts from major schools have written about intersubjectivity in recent years, they do not agree on how to define and apply the concept. The common use of the term conceals different assumptions and theoretical positions, as Bohleber's comprehensive review argues. "We find a variety of notions and concepts if the psychoanalytical situation is to be described as a prototypical situation of intersubjective encounter," he states. "However, they are often neither adequately thought through nor properly anchored conceptually" (2013, pp. 800–801). Beebe, Rustin, Sorter, & Knoblauch (2005) argue that there is no single intersubjective theory, but instead "forms of intersubjectivity," partially because of problems integrating the new notion with traditional analytic concepts. Lacan, who first introduced the term into psychoanalysis, made important connections to phenomenology, but later rejected what he considered its inherent assumption of a relationship between complete subjects (Lacan, 1960–61).

Eventually, however, he acknowledged that his attempt to construct a formal system to describe a symbolic subject failed. I suggest that Lacan's later theories, which address the unsymbolizable "real" of the body, can be used to build a revised conception of intersubjectivity without sacrificing his earlier insights. Bion's (1963) efforts to create a symbolic grid and his work on conceptualizing the psychic apparatus bear similarities to Lacan's work and present their own conceptual difficulties. Lacan and Bion are major figures that must be included in thinking about an intersubjective approach to practice. Green, Modell, and Winnicott provide other important contributions.

The historic relationship between the concepts of intersubjectivity, consciousness, and language raises a number of issues for psychoanalysis. First, we cannot ignore the use of signs among animals, whether icons or index signs in Peircian terms. Other animals also communicate, and their communications comprise features that we as humans share, although use of symbols appears not to be one of them. Human language represents a major evolutionary transition from primate signs to symbolic codes. This transition remains a black box, as a recent review by an impressive group of animal researchers and linguists admits:

> Based on the current state of evidence, we submit that the most fundamental questions about the origins and evolution of our linguistic capacity remain as mysterious as ever, with considerable uncertainty about the discovery of either relevant or conclusive evidence that can adjudicate among the many open hypotheses.
>
> (Hauser et al., 2014, p. 1)

The evolutionary continuities and parallels between humans and other social animals can blur the meaning of intersubjectivity by its application to other species and, by implication, construing it as an intrinsic function of the brain. This hypothesis naturalizes (biologizes) intersubjective processes at a presymbolic level. The corollary concept of primary intersubjectivity in infants raises analogous questions about development, close to the arguments of phenomenologists like Merleau-Ponty, which touch on the non-verbal and implicit dimension of human interaction. These issues relate clearly to differences between psychoanalytic theories of subjectivity, affect, and therapeutic action, which I raise throughout the book.

Intersubjectivity forces us to rethink the relationship between the individual subject and the sociocultural field of language and symbolic roles in which he is embedded. On one hand, we reject the notion of a unified or core self as an internal psychological or biological structure in favor of a more fluid and field-dependent subjectivity. The individual emerges from and remains in constant interaction with the groups into which he is born and presents himself in many voices. At the same time, we cannot lose sight of the private subject with its irreducible qualia of personal experience and a unique neurological make-up. This inescapable tension reappears throughout the book.

What follows is a personal work growing out of my intellectual and clinical interests from my undergraduate studies in anthropology and training as a practicing psychiatrist and psychoanalyst. Over the years, I have come to see intersubjectivity as the central concept of a psychoanalytic anthropology that seeks a broader understanding of human behavior. The individual is born into a structure that precedes him and provides his named identity, which is a function of speech. The theory of semiotics, originally developed by C.S. Peirce, best explains the working of this fundamental process and holds the advantage of being applicable to a wide range of analytic theories. Yet the paradoxical focus of therapeutic activity remains the individual subject, which lies at the intersection of the intra and interpsychic realms and calls for another conceptual level of understanding. Each subject is the carrier of many voices, private-life experiences, and historical events that psychoanalysis at its best can address most comprehensively of any discipline.

An outline of the book by chapters

In Chapter 1, I examine the major historical sources of the concept of inter-subjectivity. A crucial problem concerns the meaning of the term "subject" itself, which varies considerably within and between disciplines. The range of denotation extends from referring to a natural aspect of human endowment to signifying an ephemeral social construction and from seeking a neural substrate as the basis of subjectivity and selfhood to a one-sided emphasis on the abstract properties of language. I emphasize that subjectivity is embedded in personal interaction, co-presence, and cultural context. For this reason, the relationship between subjects—intersubjectivity—cannot be studied solely in terms of the isolated physiology of the brain or the operation of a putative "psychic apparatus."

The concept of intersubjectivity originated in philosophy, but later infant researchers took it up; most recently, it has captured the attention of neuro-scientists. Lacan applied it first to psychoanalysis. We cannot speak about their ideas without immediate recourse to highly abstract terms that retain an ambiguity with which I struggle. No doubt, contemporary analysts have little choice but to become more tolerant of the different ways that key concepts have been defined respectively by phenomenologists, Lacan, infant researchers, and neuroscience. Nonetheless, we should remain alert to their implicit logical, evidentiary, and conceptual problems, while pursuing consistency and clarity in using them.

Chapter 2 presents a clinical case to illustrate the development of my thinking "intersubjectively" as a psychoanalyst and introduces concepts that I elaborate throughout the book. I highlight the tension between objectifying, third person formulations and a more open listening to the patient. I argue that treatment primarily involves the process of enabling an expanded subjectivity, rather than a search for explanations or causes.

In Chapter 3, I describe major versions of intersubjectivity within American psychoanalysis. I sketch a brief history of the appearance of the word in psychoanalytic publications, and discuss its use by different theorists. Intersubjectivity was first emphasized by the interpersonal school and then elaborated by relational analysts. It influenced self-psychology, culminating in the rigorous model of intersubjective psychoanalysis of Stolorow. Many authors working in this area have been strongly influenced by observations from infant research, which have been applied to the adult encounter by the Boston Change Process Study Group and many relational analysts. The frequent tilt to an emphasis on the "here and now" of interaction and to concepts of enactment raises questions about the relevance of the past, reconstruction, and the unconscious to psychoanalytic therapies. The role of language is often slighted in many contemporary writings, as if secondary to the non-verbal, implicit relationship. The work of Aron and Benjamin may be an exception to these relational trends. I highlight their attention to concepts of mutual recognition, the pitfall of complementary relationships, and the value of "the third" as a means of modulating countertransference.

Chapter 4 focuses on the crucial question of affect as the area in which different approaches clash most intensely. Reciprocal emotional expression is clearly a fundamental part of intersubjective relations from birth onward and a large part of the therapeutic process, yet the nature of affect and emotion is contested within psychoanalysis, and in philosophy and neuroscience. I attempt to sort out some of the conflicting claims and suggest that different perspectives have to be held concurrently as parallel approaches possessing independent validity. Discoveries of the evolutionary neurobiology of emotion and its expression do not negate important studies of the cultural shaping of affect as a carrier of personal meaning. As with other aspects of intersubjectivity, the biological and psychosocial domains of emotion should not be dichotomized but conceived as intertwined in the communication of affects.

Chapter 5 presents three case vignettes that illustrate intersubjective functions of affect in clinical situations. The pursuit of affect as an analytic goal can lead to enactment and repetition; either flooding with affect or its non-communication can stymie clinical progress. Affect is intrinsic to semiotic communications, even if often difficult to read, but putting it into words remains necessary.

Chapter 6 has two parts. In the first, I review the semiotic approach and explain its key concepts, primarily using the work of C.S. Peirce. A semiotic model of intersubjectivity in clinical relationships focuses on exchanges of signs, including the reciprocal influence of words, affects, and gestures on both participants. In psychoanalysis, the conscious and unconscious dialogue of signs determines speech and even subjectivity itself. To what extent the signs (or signifiers) operate outside the domain of personal meaning, as Lacan and perhaps Bion held, remains an important question. In the second part of the chapter, I unpack Lacan's 1953 under-appreciated paper on "The Function and Field of Speech in Psychoanalysis," and explain the value of this attempt to link phenomenology and semiotics with analytic theory and practice. I argue that Lacan erred by abandoning intersubjectivity in his later seminars and suggest ways in which the phases of his work might be integrated.

Chapter 7 explores the recurring question of whether psychoanalysis can be compared productively to the study of a text. While impersonal in its connotations, the textual analogy raises important issues that ought not to be dismissed by analysts, and I review its strengths and weaknesses. Subjects, like literary texts, resist rigid categorization and definitive interpretation, but are open systems influenced by their social and personal contexts. Rather than functioning as the reader of a text, the analyst might be more usefully viewed as supporting the conditions for an ongoing process of writing one. This metaphor suggests a patient's capacity to produce evolving narratives and new figurations of self through the dialogic process of psychoanalysis. Semiotic concepts often impart an abstract and schematic tone to clinical processes, however, and need to be supplemented by attention to the personal level of interaction between formed subjects.

In Chapter 8, I argue that working intersubjectively in practice involves conceptualizing a personal level of the analytic dialogue that I designate as "beyond semiosis." I include in this category culturally shaped forms of personal engagement and responsiveness to the other that are necessary components of an analyst's role. I highlight the core phenomenological notions of empathy, recognition, and responsiveness to refer to an intentional stance and ethical commitment by the analyst, rather than a specific process or technique. The application of these difficult-to-define terms in practice deserves reflection and exploration by students and candidates training to assume the role of analytic psychotherapist.

Note

1. "A sign is something which stands to somebody for something in some respect or capacity. It addresses somebody, that is, creates in the mind of that person an equivalent sign, or perhaps a more developed sign" (Peirce, 1932, 2.228).

References

Beebe, B., Rustin, J., Sorter, D., & Knoblauch, S. (2005). *Forms of Intersubjectivity in Infant Research and Adult Treatment*, New York: Other Press.

Bion, W. (1963). *Elements of Psychoanalysis*, London: Karnac.

Bohleber, W. (2013). The concept of intersubjectivity in psychoanalysis: Taking critical stock, *International Journal of Psychoanalysis*, 94:799–823.

Hauser, M., Yang, C., Berwick, R., Tattersall, I., Ryan, M., Watumull, J., Chomsky, N., & Lewontin, R. (2014). The mystery of language evolution, *Frontiers in Psychology*, 5: article 401.

Kaës, R. (1973). *Transmission de la Vie Psychique entre Générations*, Paris: Dunod.

Lacan, J. (1953). The function and field of speech and language in psychoanalysis, in *Écrits*, trans. B. Fink, pp. 32–106. New York: W.W. Norton, 2002.

Lacan, J. (1960–61). *Le Seminaire, livre VIII, Le Transfert*, Ed. J.A Miller, Paris: Éditions du Seuil, 1991.

Peirce, C.S. (1932). *Collected Papers of Charles Sanders Peirce*, Ed. C. Hartshorne & P. Weiss, Cambridge, MA: Harvard University Press.

Chapter 1

What is intersubjectivity?

Intersubjectivity as a concept cannot be defined precisely. It may be one of those words whose sense becomes clearer in the negative, like "empathy," to which it is related. Different disciplines with their own independent histories and literature have applied the term to deal with concerns specific to them. While originally a product of philosophy and a cornerstone of phenomenologic thought, perhaps most notably explored by Husserl, it was adopted by pioneer infant researcher Colin Trevarthen in the form of "primary intersubjectivity" to characterize early mother–infant communications. It entered psychoanalysis through Jacques Lacan during his Hegelian period and was subsequently taken up independently by the Interpersonal School in the United States. Rather rapidly, the use of the term spread through different psychoanalytic groups, even gaining a school of its own: the "intersubjective psychoanalysis" of Stolorow and colleagues (discussed in Chapter 3) (Stolorow, Brandchaft & Atwood, 1987). Finally, cognitive neuroscience arrived on the scene, attempting to naturalize intersubjectivity through systematic research. The discovery of mirror neuron systems in the brain gave impetus to this approach. Neuroscientists argue rightly that, if the close intrication of the individual subject with other subjects is a fact of human life, then this state of affairs must have evolved like other traits and originate from processes in the brain that can be studied. Social cognitive neuroscience builds on this approach, looking at two-person interactions by empirical measures (Hari & Kujala, 2009).

In this chapter, I proceed by summarizing the conceptual approaches of phenomenology, Lacan, and neuroscience from the perspective of their own geneologies and problematics without attempting an integrated or unified theory. Although it is correct to say that intersubjectivity deals with the complex processes that go on in the relationship between two persons or subjects, each discipline has its own vocabulary and set of assumptions, so that one cannot equate them without distortion or oversimplification. When advocates of one approach—phenomenology is a good example—turn to other disciplines like neuroscience or infant research, they tend to use them to support their particular model, rather than pursue a true synthesis. Given their considerable differences, a synthesis is not feasible in any case. The goal of establishing a basic definition of intersubjectivity by incorporating evidence from different sources assumes that such an entity exists as an object that can be studied. It is always useful to remind ourselves that concepts like intersubjectivity in human affairs use highly abstract language to construct alternative ways of speaking about personal interactions, not to identify an object independent of the words employed. The extensive findings of empirical research as well as conceptual analyses in philosophy and the humanities all contribute valuable perspectives to a psychoanalytic understanding of human behavior.

The problem of pseudo-consistency across disparate theories occurs within psychoanalysis more broadly. For example, Bohleber et al. (2013) have documented the very different ways a commonly used technical term like "enactment" is employed and the assumptions behind it in different theories. Greenberg (2015) has made a very similar point with his concept of a "controlling theory" that creates a context for specific interpretations, even when the language of description suggests a common atheoretic understanding. In the case of intersubjectivity, tolerating the ambiguity resulting from multiple ways of conceptualizing interpersonal interaction may be the optimum method of dealing with the phenomena of greatest interest to psychoanalysts.

Why is there such a profusion of tongues around definitions of the word intersubjectivity? Apart from the politics of analytic schools, the reason seems quite basic. The interpretation of the concept depends on how one thinks about the nature of the human subject: of which subject is it a question? And this remains a real problem for psychoanalysis, which tolerates a wide discrepancy around how terms like self and subject are actually employed. On a broad scale, there remains a tension across psychoanalytic theories between the assumption of a field-independent subject, with a discernible internal structure of unconscious fantasies or desires, and a field-dependent, malleable subject that arises out of intersubjective messages and contextual interplay. The "naturalized" subject as a product of normal operations of the brain, as proposed by some neuroscience researchers, offers another model, and each holds implications for defining psychopathology.

The subject/the self

A focus on human subjectivity in psychoanalytic practice, so prevalent today, has not always been obvious. Freud, in his pioneering explorations, sidestepped the thorny philosophical problem of subjectivity as irrelevant to psychoanalysis as a science. Through the first half of the last century, his followers approached the psyche as a system dealing with the channeling and discharge of energies through its structural model of drives, conflicts, and defenses. The terms "subject" and "self" were not part of the major concepts of classic analysis, and Freud tolerated the ambiguity of his term *Ich*, referring to the system ego, the self, and the speaking subject in different contexts (of course, literally meaning "I" in German). For him, raising the problematic of the subject belonged to purely philosophical speculation.

He looked instead to a more scientific view of the mind as the product of internal forces, without the humanistic concept of a personal self, an approach that persists in many disciplines. Over the past decades, however, the emphasis of analytic thinkers of different schools has turned toward the agentic self and the old concept of a desiring subject as the objects of therapeutic concern.

Phenomenology

As traditionally defined, phenomenology refers to the branch of philosophy that studies experience from the standpoint of individual consciousness. Philosophers who pursue this discipline have been associated historically with the concept of intersubjectivity, especially as it relates to basic structures of conscious experience. Phenomenology takes the perspective of a subjective or first-person point of view on behavior, with its intrinsic "intentionality" (which means simply that experience always pertains to an external object in the world to which attention is directed). It then analyzes the conditions for the manifestations of personal agency—for example, what kinds of properties of consciousness are necessarily involved in organizing actions, relationships with other subjects, and using language.

Phenomenology carries important implications for how analysts approach and address patients in clinical practice. The assimilation of the phenomenologic tradition into contemporary psychoanalytic models represents in part a reaction to classic theories of an objectified mental apparatus and a medical stance that sees patients as clinical objects. The paradigm of subject-to-subject relations that emphasizes recognition of the other as a primary ethical obligation has rightly become an influential component of clinical thinking. Strictly speaking, of course, both subject-to-object and subject-to-subject relations are "intersubjective" in that participants in each version are equally subjects. A phenomenologic use of the term focuses on the "second person" approach of an "I–you," subject-to-subject perspective. Rather than supporting a specific theory or school of psychoanalysis, intersubjectivity represents a vantage point, a conceptual frame, and a position to occupy.

For psychoanalysts, inviting first-person accounts of experience, along with undertaking a second-person dialogue of inquiry, provides access to another person that would be otherwise unobtainable. When we ask the other to tell us about his experience or what he is seeking from therapy (saying "you"), we invite a direct address (from an "I") that calls on us immediately and, at least for the time of the exchange, creates a relationship, an entanglement, which can decenter us from our usual postures.[1] We don't know what the other will say, and the spontaneity can surprise and disturb. As Freud discovered, the unpredictable flow of speech provides unique access to the life of the subject. Although several ways of knowing another person, including different theories and applications of empirical knowledge, play their parts in a typical psychoanalysis, the intersubjective turn over the past twenty-five years has shifted the balance of clinical listening toward the I–you register.

The Hegelian influence

The philosopher G.F. Hegel's famous parable of the encounter between master and slave has frequently been interpreted as a metaphor for the development of individual self-consciousness and has served as a starting point for numerous philosophers, political scientists, and ethicists dealing with human relationships. In psychoanalysis, Lacan was the first to discuss the parable on several occasions in his early work. Among others, Jessica Benjamin and Arnold Modell have also explored its implications, emphasizing the subject's search (and need) for recognition from an intersubjective counterpart. Blunden (2005) comments that the dialectic of recognition portrayed in the parable is today by far the most famous passage of Hegel's works, despite the fact that it makes up just 19 of the 808 paragraphs of the phenomenology and was never mentioned by Marx or Engels in their entire *oeuvres*.

Hegel portrays an imaginary encounter between two consciously aware but reflectively unconscious subjects in what can be regarded as both a stage in the moral progress of humanity and a personal crisis in individual development. For each subject of the parable, the confrontation with the existence of the other is a mortal threat to his own self-definition.[2] Hegel's original German phrase, *Herrschaft und Knechtschaft*, has been translated as lordship and bondage, which sets up a bipolarity of positions. The confrontation between the two consciousnesses inevitably sets up a struggle for dominance—hence the terms master and slave, each subject seeking to impose its desire for an absolute confirmation of self on the other. Their contest takes the form of a "struggle to the death," since everything seems to be at stake. In brief, in Hegel's scenario one subject saves his life by surrendering to become the slave, but the master soon realizes that a slave cannot provide the freely given affirmation he seeks. Neither subject can yet grasp that self-affirmation requires a recognition by another subject belonging to a social reality of which they both are part. Hegel asserts: "Self-consciousness exists in and for itself when, and by the fact that, it so exists for another; that is, it exists only by being acknowledged" (Hegel, 1807, p. 111).

In taking the phenomenology of consciousness as his reference point, Hegel remained within the Cartesian tradition with its idealist orientation. Like Kant, he renounced the notion of an introjected self that views representations of the world from "inside," by proposing that the world as experienced is essentially constructed by an active consciousness. An important difference from Kant was his rejection of a transcendental self existing a priori. Instead, he proposed that self-consciousness—the experience of having a self—requires engagement with another subject. The self comes to be, as Ver Eecke (1983) summarizes, through an intersubjective relationship in which each subject must discover in another entity a quality of being it possesses itself but of which it is not yet aware (p. 121). The French scholar Jean Hippolyte (Wilden, 1968) interpreted Hegel's rather obscurely worded passages as an attempt to show that "self-formation is only conceivable through the mediation of alienation or estrangement. Self-formation is not to develop harmoniously as if by organic growth, but rather to become opposed to oneself through a splitting or separation" (p. 372). In other words, man splits himself into a subject, recognizing himself in another, and an object, viewed through the eyes of another. In the Marxist philosopher Alexandre Kojève's interpretation of this process (Wilden, 1968), consciousness presses for a kind of absolute recognition from the other, a recognition of its desire for the other to attribute "an absolute value to his free and historical individuality or to his person-ality" (p. 292). This dialectic involves a kind of mirroring process, a passage back and forth from self-objectification in the eyes of the other to self-aggrandize-ment in obliterating the separateness and freedom of the other subject.

The Hegelian themes of the subject's search for recognition, of a mirrored consciousness that founds the subject, of the always problematic encounter with the other, and of a mediating system that transcends both subjects have permeated philosophical and psychoanalytic thinking since his time. We might see Freud's own parable of the meeting with the first object, the *Nebenmensch*, in his Project for a Scientific Psychology (1895) as a commentary. Winnicott, however, was the first to situate the encounter at the level of the newborn's relationship with the mother. Stepping away from the encapsulated, representational tradition of regarding the interpersonal dynamic as a matter of projections and introjections, Winnicott began his story with the mother–baby relationship, prior to any con-ception of the infant as a separate subject. In his well-known paper on the mirror role of the mother (Winnicott, 1956), he discussed the self-formation of the infant within the matrix of affective exchanges communicated by facial expressions, so that when the child looks at the mother's face, it sees itself, while the mother's communication depends in turn on what she sees of herself reflected in the baby. Winnicott famously summarizes this phenomenon: "When I look I am seen, so I exist. I can now afford to look and see. I now look creatively and what I apperceive I also perceive" (p. 114). Here, he affirms that recognition by the other as a self—one might say, by the other's desire to receive an affirming response from one's own self—is more basic than drive or need satisfaction in permitting the active emergence of an infantile subject that can construct a perceptual world, not merely passively receive one.

The fundamental shift in perspective or paradigm brought about by Winnicott's views on the formation of the self has been recognized most consistently by Modell, whose summary of the matter is clearly a version of Hegel's dialectic:

> The psychology of the self is embedded in this fundamental dilemma, namely, that the sense of self needs to be affirmed by the other, and yet a response from the other that is nonconfirming or unempathic can lead at best to a sense of depletion or at worst to the shattering of the self. This results in a defensive quest for an illusory self-sufficiency which is in conflict with the opposite wish to surrender the self to the other, to merge, to become enslaved.
>
> (1984, p. 131)

The notions of recognition or affirmation become quite complex in this formulation. How they are conceived will influence the analyst's therapeutic behavior.

Phenomenology and intersubjectivity

The universal desire to gain recognition underlines the inseparability of intersubjectivity from the ancient philosophical question of what it means to be a subject among other subjects. The problem runs through the writings of the great phenomenologists—Hegel, Husserl, Heidegger, Sartre, and Merleau-Ponty to name the most important. Merleau-Ponty asserted in his *Phenomenology of Perception* that we do not begin our lives immersed in a private self-consciousness encased somewhere inside the skull but in the experience of being with others. This undeniable truth about human life was richly developed by Husserl and Heidegger well before the beginning of infant research and psychoanalysis. Subjectivity is inconceivable without intersubjectivity.

The phenomenologists refer to two apparently contradictory intuitions that form our experience of the other. The other is immediately present to us in its expressive behavior, while at the same time it escapes our understanding in a fundamental way. The paradoxical familiarity and strangeness of the other has been addressed in different ways by philosophers (also by Freud in his Project (1895)). For Heidegger, the human subject, the *dasein*, is by essence and from its very beginning social, hence his term *mitsein*. The subject is in the *we* already, not alone in a precarious position confronting an unknown other. Husserl's position is similar; as subjects, we have implicit knowledge of the other. By contrast, for Sartre, it is only through the concrete encounter of the subject with *l'autrui*, the unknown other who can perceive me and objectify me, that I discover the intersubjectivity of my individual existence. Levinas holds a yet more radical position on the encounter; it is "the *absoluteness* of the other's alterity that Levinas draws from the face-to-face relation" (Bergo, 2015, p. 3).

Phenomenologists agree, however, that the constitution of the subject is given (uniquely) in consciousness, not determined by extrinsic structures. In his version of existential psychoanalysis, Sartre (1943) emphasizes the absolute freedom of consciousness (the *pour-soi*, the for-itself) and the attempt to escape this lack of essence by becoming a reified "me" (an *en-soi*, the in-itself). This is the origin of his analysis of bad faith or inauthenticity, which concerns the fantasy of possessing a substantive identity that defines the self. Consciousness lacks the substance that the ego (the "me"), as a unity of states and actions, appears to possess. In this way, Sartre does not bypass the dilemma of the Hegelian encounter as an existential threat unrelieved by a third.

Despite his rejection of the unconscious in mental life, Sartre's conception of the "for-itself" consciousness seeking to objectify itself as an "in-itself" strikes a persuasive note. Attempting to define an identity and resisting threats to it from others (the Hegelian encounter) describes a familiar clinical situation, often explicit with so-called narcissistic personalities, but with most people at times. Because we cannot circle around the "me" that we sense in ourselves, we are left with the inescapable problem of needing to turn to others to find out what kind of "me" we are. "To really know oneself is inevitably to take toward oneself the point of view of others, that is to say, a point of view which is necessarily false," says Sartre (1936–37, p. 87). The mirrored self, he might argue against Kohut, is an alienated self, an object which the *pour-soi* must negate to achieve authenticity. Both he and Lacan cite Rimbaud's celebrated phrase *"Je est un autre"* (" 'I' is another). Possibly no other thinker has insisted as much as Sartre on the pain of human consciousness; he aphorizes that "the *pour-soi* is a hole in the heart of being" (p. 711).

Lacan praised his contemporary Sartre and shared (or possibly adopted) his position that the self is absent in the Real (as taught by Eastern religions as well), but he could not accept the rejection of a Freudian unconscious. "This philosophy," he says (Lacan, 1966, p. 96), remains within "the limits of a self-sufficiency of consciousness." He regards consciousness "as irredeemably limited . . . a principle, not only of idealization, but of *méconnaissance* (misrecognition)." "For us," he continues, "consciousness matters only in relation to what . . . I have tried to show you in the fiction of the incomplete text" (Lacan, 1964, pp. 82–83). With the master and slave struggle clearly in mind, he asserts that existentialism reduces the subject to a violent encounter of wills (1964, p. 8), an "active annihilation" of the other, the "Hegelian murder" (1966, p. 96).

To be fair, Sartre's position does not entail an observing self in the way that Lacan portrays, but insists rather on an inherent subjectivity in every perception, without any act of reflexion. Among contemporary phenomenologists, Zahavi (2006, 2011) has been a strong proponent of the Sartrian view that rejects any notion of a subject outside of consciousness (thus, one acting upon or structuring the form of consciousness). Consciousness, he summarizes, "is characterized by a fundamental selfness or selfhood precisely because of this pervasive self-givenness, self-intimation, or reflexivity" (Zahavi, 2011, p. 57). The experiential core self is "an integral part of the structure of phenomenal consciousness" (Gallagher & Zahavi, 2008, p. 227). In response to the question of whether the self exists independent of experience or is only the sum of ever-changing experiences, he proposes "a ubiquitous dimension of first personal self-givenness," which he identifies with "the experiential core self" (p. 59). In this way, he hopes to avoid the either-or dilemma of an enduring self versus self as illusion (as in Hume's argument).[3]

Zahavi's discussion does not refer to psychoanalysis (although he lists numerous other disciplines), but the issue of how the self is conceived has been a recurring one for analysts (Kirshner, 1991; Mitchell, 1991; Modell, 1993[4]). Like the phenomenologists, Mitchell observes that "we generally spend most of our time being conscious, not self-conscious, being aware of ourselves as an ongoing process, without objectifying ourselves in an active effort to grasp or understand or communicate" (1991, p. 121). He too is wary of reifications of the self as an entity, which he finds in self-psychology, but emphasizes a view of self as relational, multiple, and discontinuous. In the end, however, discussing his patient "L." who presents with issues of identity and disavowed aspects of herself, Mitchell supports a multiplex analytic approach leading to an enlarged experience of self, including a dependable sense of the self "as functionally integral and continuous" (p. 139). Similar to contemporary analysts, Zahavi advocates a multidimensional view of the self: "We are dealing with a culturally, socially, and linguistically embedded self that is under constant construction" (2011, p. 71). But how phenomenology can deal with these omnipresent elements within the exclusive notion of an experiential self is not obvious.

Many patients seek psychoanalytic therapies because of an uncertain sense of who they are and their place in relationships with others. Certainly in such cases, the different kinds of techniques that Mitchell summarizes (he describes examples derived from object relations, self-psychology, and relational models) will have clinical consequences for the outcome, but it may be unrealistic to expect an analyst to move flexibly across them. In particular, seeking to affirm or restore an inner core of self as something to be found and responded to can conflict with the goal of using the intersubjective process to foster the expansion of senses or versions of self. Likewise, pursuing unconscious fantasies disguised under conscious preoccupations may be incompatible with the affirmation and recognition Kohut promoted, as well as constituting a self to object (third person) method. For this reason, a "naive" phenomenological view of interactions may be a healthy antidote to theory-laden constructions about the supposed inner world of the analysand, as one finds often in some Freudian and Kleinian methods of interpretation. If an analyst concentrates his attention on what may be going on inside his patient's mind, he may have difficulty balancing this effort with observation of his own participation in creating the content of their interaction.

Although some phenomenologists have been accused of being solipsistic, interested only in the mental life of the isolated subject (as perhaps Sartre might exemplify), Gallagher and Zahavi (2008) have taken up the Husserlian case for the immediacy of intersubjective awareness of others. Thus they criticize mentalization concepts, theory of mind (TOM) approaches, and the model of implicit simulation of others' mental states (MS) as unnecessary, overcomplicated explanations for how we acquire knowledge of other minds. Instead, they assert, others are known immediately and implicitly in awareness (Gallagher, 2008), a position consistent with their rejection of a determining unconscious behind experience. They agree with Merleau-Ponty that our implicit perception of others' mental lives belongs to the ordinary context of bodily interactions. For example, the phenomenon of empathy, which they explore at length (also a major part of Husserl's work), does not consist in feeling one's way into other minds or an active process of trial identifications, as self-psychologists have proposed. Instead, knowing others derives from an intrinsic "ability to access the life of the mind of others in their expressive behavior and meaningful action" (Gallagher & Zahavi, 2008, p. 213). They support this conclusion by citing the well-known research of Rizzolatti and Gallese on mirror neurons as demonstrating "an enactment of intersubjective perception" (p. 199). That is, mirror mechanisms are part of a total bodily perceptual process, rather than offering a vehicle for hypothetical implicit simulations (imitative neural sequences that match the observed behaviors), as advocated by simulation theories (ST) of intersubjectivity. This position appears consistent with Ammaniti and Gallese's notion of "embodied simulation" (ES): "ES theory provides a unitary account of basic aspects of intersubjectivity by showing that people reuse their own mental states or processes represented in bodily format" (2014, pp. 16–17).

Gallagher and Zahavi (2008) additionally support their perceptual model of understanding meanings of interactions by referring to Trevarthen's theory of primary intersubjectivity. The interactions of babies and their caretakers are spontaneous and immediate, as though innate and unmediated. This reference parallels currents in relational psychoanalysis that link intersubjectivity to mirror neuron and infant research studies (these trends are discussed further in Chapter 3). Following the pattern of early childhood, they insist, "others are not given primarily as objects, or as entities in need of explanation" (2008, p. 211). Rather, as Merleau-Ponty (1945) proposed, we make sense of the behavior of others because it is expressed by actions in contextualized situations. For example, we can see that someone is sad or angry by his facial expressions or we understand her intention to carry out a specific act from reading posture and movement. Merleau-Ponty's apparent radical behaviorism asserted that the human body is comparable to a work of art whose expression becomes indistinguishable from that which is expressed.

Gallagher (2012) puts the matter quite unequivocally. He writes:

> In most situations we are not trying to mind read the other person; we are not concerned about the other person's mental states, although such concerns may be motivated by relatively unusual behaviors, or by attempts to give reasons or justify actions reflectively. Even in response to questions about why someone is doing something (as opposed to simply what is happening), . . . narrative accounts in terms of actions often suffice.
>
> (p. 193)

His discussion brings out the extent to which, by necessity, primary inter-subjectivity and infant research rely upon a behavioral, phenomenological methodology. Yet he also seems to acknowledge the presence of non-experiential, learned determinants of subjectivity by quoting Merleau-Ponty's comment that the infant is born into a "whirlwind of language" and Rakoczy et al.'s conclusion that the actions children learn "are not just individual, idiosyncratic behaviors, but cultural conventional forms of action. And many of these forms of action are rule-governed and normatively structured" (Gallagher, 2012, p. 192). These quali-fications complicate any notion of implicit knowledge by direct perception that dispenses with concepts of mentalizing or a theory of mind to make sense out of experience (see Noë, 2007, for a balanced discussion of these issues).

A psychoanalyst might also observe that the meaning of perceived behavior is more idiosyncratic than Gallagher suggests and that actions represent symbolically structured carriers of unconscious meaning that can powerfully influence the subject without his knowledge (the subject may not actually "feel" sad or angry). At least in the case of personally important behaviors and messages, meaning is complex and even enigmatic, as Laplanche (1987) has presented at length in his theory of the human anthropological situation.

Many analytic philosophers, including Dennett (1991), have criticized phenomenology on the basis that its explicitly first-person approach to behavior is incompatible with a scientific third-person approach. Phenomenologists might respond that natural science makes sense only as a human activity that presupposes the fundamental structures of a first-person perspective. Searle (2008) has criticized what he calls the "Phenomenological Illusion" of assuming that what is not phenomenologically present is not real and that what is phenomenologically present is in fact an adequate description of how things really are. The content of this debate holds relevance for theories of psychoanalytic practice influenced by intersubjectivity, which depend to a great extent on "here and now" interactions to achieve their goals.

Lavelle contests the direct perception theory on two grounds. First, he takes the "establishment view" in which "'Epistemic Seeing' just isn't possible without a process of inference" (2012, p. 222). Although phenomenologists sometimes refer to the operation of the mirror neuron system to answer this philosophical objection, neuroscience cannot dispense with a theory of inferential rules. Even if it does map goals of actions in the premotor cortex, Lavelle comments, "one must be able to explain how the mirror neuron system organizes and accesses the relevant contextual information" (p. 225). Understanding the goals and motivations of most actions requires complex cognitive processes that depend on learning and previous experiences. Second, he continues, "visual stimulus alone does not give the mirror neuron system sufficient material to ascertain an intention. The additional information required is not 'direct' visual information, but information about culture, context, and expectations" (p. 227). For psychoanalysis, the latter information (again pertaining to personally important situations like intimate relationships or questions of identity) depends on links to associative chains and images that are far from universal givens in an intersubjective exchange.

Returning to Mitchell's ideas about expansion of self-knowledge through analytic dialogue and relationship, analysts know that understanding the beliefs, memories, and intentions that influence perceptions of others constitutes an exceedingly lengthy and uncertain process, one that is at the heart of clinical process. Change that occurs in psychoanalytic therapies derives from unconscious effects of an intersubjective field that influences expression of new sets of words and feelings and from a conscious process of shared reflection and working through. For these reasons, I conclude that we must be wary of being captivated by the phenomenology of clinical experience. Without a concept of unconscious processes, we have only a partial avenue to gaining psychoanalyic understanding.

Lacan and intersubjectivity

It was probably Jacques Lacan who introduced (or at least foregrounded) the concepts of the subject and intersubjectivity in psychoanalysis. He insisted that even for Freud the true object of psychoanalysis was the human subject. The patient on the couch is not the manifestation of a psychic apparatus that one might study objectively, but a subject who speaks, listens, and reacts. Lacan's rejection of biological explanations of subjectivity in favor of experiential presence seems close to a phenomenological view of a subject who is present in its own consciousness and with whom the analyst can interact. During his "Hegelian" phase, he taught that the subject seeks recognition from the Other as a fundamental desire.

In Lacan's treatment of Hegel's master–slave parable, the crucial element in resolving the death struggle is the presence of "a third," referring in his formulation to the symbolic order of language and the rules of using signifiers in speech to which all subjects are subservient. By sharing a symbolic matrix that founds their subjectivities, the dyadic (dialectical) confrontation unto death is lifted to another level that subsumes both adversaries. Lacan's initial conception of therapeutic action relied heavily on a transferential demand for recognition that is obliged to pass through speech. In bringing this demand to the surface, the analysand passes through the stages of his own history of becoming a subject. The Lacanian analyst does not bestow recognition but supports the unfolding of the analysand's past and, like Winnicott, exposes where it became derailed (see Julien, 1981, for a discussion of the development of Lacan's theory of therapeutic action).[5] The human desire to be recognized by the other has implications for a theory of narcissism, and may represent one of the rare points of intersection between Kohut and Lacan. We want to be seen for who we are, and this usually means a preferred self-image or identity. How we look represents a central narcissistic concern. For Lacan, however, "mirroring" describes a phase in the evolution of treatment that must be surpassed to avoid repetition of the dyadic fantasies. Whether recognition and affirmation by the analyst represent a necessary step in resuming a developmental process, as Winnicott and Kohut believed, or instead only lead to consolidation of resistances in the ego, as Lacan contended, has divided analysts. But the oppositional aspect of these models may be only a historical fact. Many Lacanians now incorporate a Winnicottian approach (Kirshner, 2011) and many relational analysts recognize that a symmetrical dyad can operate to block change (Aron, 1991, 1999). The themes of recognition and the importance of the third to avoid dyadic repetition became central to Benjamin's work, which I discuss in Chapters 3 and 8.

Lacan's use of the Hegelian expression, Man's desire is the desire of the Other, may have subtly changed in its implications over time. The encounter between two subjects as the primal scene of intersubjective recognition, elaborated by Benjamin, beginning with the infant's reciprocal exchanges with the mother, comprises one direction (principally pursued in this book). The construction (m)Other emphasizes this developmental aspect of intersubjectivity. By contrast, the structural or logical relationship between a split or barred subject and the Other (an abstraction representing the universal field of signifiers) leads away from a relational, phenomenological view toward a more impersonal formulation of this desire. Lacan's rejection of intersubjectivity (summarized by Fink, 2007, pp. 148–149) derives from this perspective. "Is not intersubjectivity what is most foreign to the analytic encounter?" he writes (Lacan, 1960–61, p. 21). I take up this issue again in Chapter 6.

In his early seminars, Lacan also spoke about another subject, the subject of the unconscious, a concept suggesting Freud's famous metaphor of the mind functioning as if two separate persons were vying for control, a conscious one with definite beliefs and values, and an unconscious one pursuing a pleasure-seeking agenda. The Hegelian desire to be recognized turned toward pursuit of an unrealizable fantasy (as unconscious and unrepresentable). With his theory of the symbolic register, Lacan specified that the subject in question in psychoanalysis emerges as an effect of discourse, a subject of the signifier (fitting the field-dependent model of a malleable subject). The division or split in the latter conception refers to the unbridgeable gap between a verbally represented but evanescent subject using a code of signifiers and the silent, unconscious, unrepresented domain of "the real" of organic life.

Lacan gradually left phenomenology and its inherent intersubjectivity behind in favor of a linguistically determined subject, arising from and persisting only for the duration of a speech act, and deriving its transient identity from the chain of signifiers in play. Influenced by his readings of the linguists Benveniste, Jacobson, Peirce, and Saussure, he pursued a semiotic approach, teaching that the subject transforms itself along the moving chain of spoken words, which constantly revises prior self-definitions. The familiar vacillating subject of post-modern philosophy exists only during the time of the words at its immediate disposal for expressing itself, to be modified continuously by further enunciations. Lacan assigned notions like the self, the ego, and ego identity to the imaginary register; they are impermanent images or fantasies that attempt to reify complex, ephemeral processes, not substantive entities. He proposed, however, that the illusory construction of self-consciousness, the object "me," becomes tied to specific memories and cultural labels that provide points of reference, halting the constant slippage of meaning along the unending chain of words.[6] Through these *pointes de capiton* (a kind of upholstery button), the signifiers "subject" or "self" accumulate links to signifieds in the social world.[7] The signified meanings that define the self lack a precise content, but are socially shared, like transitional objects, supporting a representation of individuality endorsed by the culture. Subjects are structural products of the culture that creates them, which suggests a return to intersubjectivity in another form (the culture consists of a collection of speaking subjects).

Reading Lacan, who is far from explicit on many of these points, raises the question of whether one must speak of multiple subjects, as in Proust's famous phrase, "I was not one man; I was a crowd of men" or, perhaps, of different subjective positions or voices. This polyphony of the subject seems to me the most important conclusion of Lacan's structural analysis. On the other hand, by referring to "Being" as a property of the Real and thereby linked to the body, Lacan (1962–63) implies a uniqueness and continuity of subjective existence, albeit represented in a kaleidoscope of changing forms.[8] These speculations remind me of Winnicott's conception of the "true self," for which he also employed the term "being" and which certainly antedates the development of any symbolic identity in words. Perhaps the two men shared the notion that a primal intuition of *being* as the living substrate of the subject underlies all the subsequently evolving selves of later interactions (Eigen, 1981). This interpretation suggests a sense in which "self" precedes intersubjective existence, at least for Winnicott, before any apprehension of the existence of a separate other. The developmental researcher Rochat (2009) has written of an intrinsic property of sentient "aware-ness" that is not yet "self-awareness," and the neuroscientist-analyst Solms (2013) argues that this basic awareness includes a capacity for emotional responsiveness as a common mammalian property, originating in lower brain stem centers, prior to any reflexive, intersubjective consciousness of self and other.

Lacan did not indicate a clear position on early subjective life. Although he saw the infantile subject as living in the unsymbolized "real," he increasingly emphasized the overarching presence and function of the Other (the mother for all practical purposes) from the very beginning. To the extent the being of the infantile subject can be psychically represented in awareness, the Other as a back-ground or precondition is necessarily present as something impinging on this awareness.[9] Infant researchers would probably agree that becoming organized (psychically and neurocognitively) as a self-system depends on the presence of the mother. From this highly speculative perspective, self with Other precedes subject with other (as in Winnicott's "baby is always baby with mother" paradigm). As noted above, the first "other" (a parent) is often confounded with the Other, the overarching human cultural field of signifiers into which the child is born (sometimes written as mOther to convey this).

Unfortunately, Lacan never integrated his initial advocacy of intersubjectivity in psychoanalytic practice with his later ideas about the real and desire. After a certain point, he no longer spoke about intersubjectivity, having concluded that the use of this concept by philosophers assumed a complete subject capable of a full relationship, an integrated (imaginary) subject who engages his peers in an endless quest for recognition following the Hegelian paradigm. He took the position that the premise of a unified subject, which he found in phenomenology, reified an imaginary construction. In his seminar on the transference (1954–55), Lacan pointed out that the analytic relationship lacks reciprocity and symmetry as a basic feature, the two subjects not interacting on the same plane. The analyst does not occupy the place of another subject but of the Other. Yet, even accepting these qualifications, does the Lacanian analyst not consciously and unconsciously express signs like any subject, manifest in the flux of his language and gestures?

The asymmetry in the transference does not preclude (and may actually heighten) the influence of the analyst on the patient's subjective position within the intersubjective field. Already in the 1930s, the social psychologist G.H. Mead (1934) observed that the self takes its form within the context of current interpersonal relationships,[10] and we can easily verify this dimension of subjectivity for ourselves. One feels almost imperceptibly or even enormously different in each encounter with another person, especially if magnified in imaginary fantasy. Harry Stack Sullivan (1953) elaborated Mead's observation in his theory of interpersonal psychoanalysis, countering the exclusively intrapsychic focus of Ego Psychology. How to preserve the analytic focus on the individual subject while recognizing its dependency on a bi- or multipersonal field has become a problem for analytic theory. Lacan's increasingly abstract course away from intersubjectivity and the humanistic ethics of his beginnings removed him from this dialogue.

Intersubjectivity without a subject

Consistent with his emphasis on the interpersonal field, Sullivan (1953) did not have much use for the notion of an inner self, unlike Winnicott, Modell, or Kohut (in their varied ways). On this issue, he joins the diverse group of classic Freudians, Ego Psychologists, French structuralists, and the skeptical philosopher David Hume in relegating the concept of a discrete subject or coherent self—what Kohut called a psychic center of initiative—to a retrospective illusion of consciousness,[11] a "ghost in the machine" (in Ryle's phrase, 2002). Perhaps the notion of a substantial self embodies the residue of a Western religious belief in an immortal soul. Yet something like this concept remains part of the thinking of many psychoanalysts who hold to the concept of an authentic or core self that needs to be affirmed or restored.

If philosophy and neuroscience cannot find a justification for the notion of an interior agentic self, psychoanalysts must face the question suggested above: Is there a subject of intersubjectivity, a durable center of some kind that retains its singularity across varied contexts?[12] If not, are we then left with a version of intersubjectivity that dispenses with the unique individual subject? To take the argument a step further, could what we call the subject merely represent the consequence of having a position in an intersubjective network, a node in the structure of human relationships as Levi-Strauss or Foucault understood the term? The fact that many human beings have the capacity to narrate a reasonably integrated story of their selfhood may only reflect the social imperative to give a credible account of oneself or, perhaps, to internalize the assorted labels, categories, names, and relational positions that a person is allotted within a designated familial network as if they amount to an internal identity.

With few exceptions, the absence of the subject except as a formal term of reference is typical for both psychiatry and the neurosciences. Of course, the term "subject" is applied to the object of research when neuroscientists study the brain with the fMRI or its equivalent to determine, for example, which cerebral centers function during an act of empathy. Yet the notion of a phenomenal subject is put aside during this activity, unless the researcher opens a conversation after the experiment is completed. For the physician, as well, the subject has a medico–legal status, but does not constitute the true object of clinical work, which works on systems and diagnoses. Contemporary psychiatry similarly targets the symptoms or dysfunctions of a patient as more or less correctable malfunctions of the biological organism. The psychiatrist would like his patient to feel better and especially to function better, but the psychoanalytic principle that a symptom in some ways best represents the singularity of the subject, that it constitutes a sign of a trouble touching the very being of the subject, is put aside. Increasingly, the modern psychiatrist treats the diagnosis, not the subject, and his evaluation consists of an algorithm that leads to identifying one or more disorders. Psychopharmacologic interventions take him inside the gears and switches of the nervous system, not the structures of personhood. Because of the necessary isolation of the chemistry of the brain for psychopharmacologic purposes, the subject of psychiatry has become more and more a montage or bricolage of independent functions and systems—hence the famous problem list.

The psychiatric approach is, in fact, a derivative of the scientific materialist position of the neurosciences. Neuroscience research documents the reality that impulses and transmissions in the brain never arrive at a central point of synthesis and decision; nor does "information" flow to an internal judge. The brain contains no executive center to direct its operations. No one is at home, even if some researchers anthropomorphize the results of their studies. As many philosophers of science have pointed out, the brain has no desires or motivations, doesn't send messages, and carries no burden of guilt (properties of persons). The vocabulary of subjectivity translates very poorly to the laboratory, which at best can discover the mechanisms or processes enabling these personal phenomena to occur. To talk about the subject from a scientific perspective amounts only to a way of speaking, a retrospective footnote, a familiar term evoked to reassure ourselves that the neurologic mechanisms producing our behavior have a transcendent feature and cannot be reduced to the operations of an automatic and impersonal machine.

We find ourselves here in a paradox. Certainly, the subject is not the ego, nor any conscious agent that emerges, in a more or less fleeting or stable manner, from our mental activity. On this point, traditional psychoanalysis and the neurosciences are in accord. Yet at the same time, human beings do have a sense of enjoying or bearing an enduring nature of self or, I prefer to say, of a subjective organization that represents who they are—what Winnicott saw as a private center of self that is nurtured and protected from impingement. Moreover, a psychology that dispensed with subjectivity, with the sense of a continuity of existence in time and a set of private feelings rooted in the past, would be absurd. We seek a personal psychoanalysis to understand our specific lives more fully and to become better able to pursue our private desires. Perhaps these impressions of enduring selfhood derive, as Lacan suggested, from possession of a desiring, appetitive body that is the permanent reference point of being an individual subject. Yet entering an intimate relationship, with its implicit transitionality (in which it is not questioned whether perceptions are objective or subjective), immediately blurs the boundaries of the self. In psychoanalysis, we learn that our cherished individuality is interwoven with the voices and messages of others who seem to reincarnate themselves in internal conversations and our actual relationships. We are left with a version of the uncertainty principle: human subjectivity retains a continuity and identity, yet is protean and contextual.

The contributions of Paul Ricoeur

Ricoeur, perhaps more than any philosopher, has devoted large portions of his work to defining the nature of psychoanalysis as a discipline. His notion of the duality of mechanism (causation) and meaning in psychoanalysis influenced Leavy and Modell (discussed in Chapter 3) in their pioneering reformulations. From his origins in phenomenology, through immersion in Freudian theory, then during a lengthy period of association with Lacan, and finally with his rejection of the classic paradigm in favor of Kohut's self psychology, Ricoeur has grappled with intersubjectivity as the fundamental human situation. In 1970 he wrote:

> The theme of intersubjectivity is undoubtedly where phenomenology and psychoanalysis come closest to being identified with each other, but also where they are seen to be most radically distinct. . . If the analytic relationship may be regarded as the privileged example of intersubjective relations . . . it is because the analytic dialogue brings to light . . . the demands in which desire ultimately consists.
>
> (p. 406)

As I understand him, the distinction turns on the emergence of unconscious desire in the transference, which he sees as requiring technical management.[13] Even in infant development, the desiring relationship with the father and the mother is carried by language,

> because the child is born into an environment of language, meaning and discourse. In this pre-constituted realm, the father and mother are not only the 'beings' or 'parents' that nourish him, but rather also bring him into the community of language, and therefore into the lifeworld.
>
> (cited in Busacchi, 2015, p. 17)

Late in his career, as a professor at the University of Chicago, Ricoeur saw the limitations of Freud's isolated intrapsychic model of the mind and turned to Kohut for an alternative. In the concept of the selfobject, he found the inextricability of subject from other, the dependence of psychic life on interaction with other subjects. As with Husserl, empathy became for him the privileged vehicle of contact between subjects.

> This need for empathy distinguishes the relation between the self and its selfobjects from the relation between the ego and its love objects. Before being the key weapon of the psychoanalytic cure, empathy is the basic structure of the relation between self and selfobject.
>
> (Ricoeur, 1986, p. 440)

At the same time, he addresses the apparent circularity of the empathic relation, especially its assumptions about the nature of the other. With whom does one empathize? Does the structure of a relationship create its own other, a projection of the self? Like many psychoanalysts, Ricoeur finds an answer to this problem in the therapeutic and educational course of professional training, which can free the candidate from countertransference tendencies. I find this a weak argument, however, for justifying the analyst's problematic position of objective judgment.

The analogous question of recognition (of whom) emerges again in the self-object transference. In one of his most significant contributions, Ricoeur (2004) plumbs the historic and linguistic meanings of the term "recognition" (*reconnaissance*), where, in the final part of his work, he touches on the ethics of personal life in the manner of Levinas. "The withdrawal or refusal of approbation," he states, in a form reminiscent of Modell's comment on affirmation cited above, "touches everyone at the prejuridicial level of his or her being with others . . . Deprived . . . the person is as if nonexistent" (2004, p. 191). He uses the metaphor of the gift to speak of the "irreplaceable character of each of the partners in the exchange . . . different from any form of fusional union . . . a just distance is maintained" (p. 263). I explore the important issues of empathy and recognition at length in Chapters 3 and 8.

The Lacanian subject

It is worth pausing for a moment to reconsider the Lacanian perspective, as it is often misunderstood and arguably represents the most thoroughgoing exploration of the problematics of the subject considered above. If Hegel's subject can be defined as that which is other than all possible objects of consciousness (Solomon, 1983), the Lacanian subject can be tentatively described as the product of an unconscious structure of language which has been internalized as a dialogue bridging a primal moment of separation. Lacan's discussion of the famous *fort-da* game portrays this developmental step. In his account of this game, Freud (1920) describes an infant playing at throwing away and retrieving a spool while his mother has gone out. The child has substituted for the relation with the mother the German words *fort* and *da* ("gone" and "here"), the shared language of his world by which he can symbolically master her presence and absence. For Lacan, however, the element of mastery is of secondary importance:

> This reel is not the mother reduced to a little ball by some magical game worthy of the Jivaros—it is a small part of the subject that detaches itself

from him while still remaining his, still retained. How can we fail to recognize here—from the very fact that this game is accompanied by one of the first oppositions to appear—that it is in the object to which opposition is applied in the act, the reel, that we must designate the subject. It is the repetition of the mother's departure as cause of a *Spaltung* (splitting) in the subject.

(1964, pp. 62–63)

Later, in fact, Freud observed the child turning to the mirror to play at his own imaginary disappearance, confirming that he has taken the perspective of the mother. In the child's solitude, Lacan proposes that his desire has become the desire of another, "of an alter ego who dominates him and of whom the object of desire" (i.e. what the mother desires) will be henceforth "his affliction" (*peine*) (1966, p. 203). She is elsewhere, wants something that is not him, and thereby evokes by this "want" the child's desire, born of separation.

In this little drama, the sense of being a member of a disrupted pair is expressed by the phonemic opposition of the sounds *fort* and *da*. Already the product of a physical separation, the incipient infantile subject is split again by language, which forces him to become what Lacan calls an incomplete text, struggling to express through signifiers his inexhaustible desire for wholeness and reunion with the mother. Zahavi surprisingly evokes similar terms in speaking of episodic memory as involving "some kind of doubling or fission; it does involve some degree of self-division, self-absence, and self-alienation" (2011, p. 74). Yet he does not modify his support for a prereflexive, unitary experience of selfhood (*ipseite*) by this admission. Sartre debunked the psychoanalytic concept of a divided self on logical and common-sense grounds (by appealing to an intuitive experience of self-awareness and by his critique of the Freudian "homuncular" unconscious with its own intentions and desires as requiring a non-existent locus of decisions about repression or expression).

Lacan's conception of the basic splitting of the subject relies on the centrality of speech in human life, the "whirlwind of language" expressed by Merleau-Ponty (Gallagher, 2012). Speech permits the child to enter the symbolic order that enables it to reach the mother through the power of words, but this power belongs to a structure that preexists the child and mother, and presents an impassable step away from the preverbal oneness (or its fantasy) he desires. Both mother and child take their positions as subjects within the rules and logic of culture, which rest upon the symbolic distinctions that provide their historical identities as persons. The phonemes *fort* and *da* represent a prototypal structure of the symbolic order within which the subject emerges as figure to ground. Lacan stated that this order is represented by the father (or, more precisely, by the name of the father as a third party), the one to whom the mother goes when leaving the child and to whom she speaks her desire. The patriarchal model adopted by Lacan (and widely criticized since) does not preclude another "third" who disrupts the enclosed world of the dyad.[14]

By grounding both "self" and other in the third term of the symbolic order, implicit in their shared language, Lacan attempts to bypass the problematic

Hegelian encounter. For Hegel, resolution of the dual desire for recognition by the other depends on a dialectical unfolding of consciousness (of which the struggle of master and slave represents an early form). The system of language, however, lies outside the realm of conscious experience. More specifically, the child's identity as subject, to use a very unLacanian term, originates in the desires of the parents and the words they use to speak about and to him. Lacan depicts the construction of the subject in its formative encounter with others in his schema L, a quadrangle whose four corners represent the egos of the subject and the other and their dual unconsciouses, which he describes as a couple in their "reciprocal imaginary objectivization." By this model, he illustrates the attempt by the ego to confirm its imaginary unity as a complete self, while by speaking the subject acknowledges the impossibility of such total affirmation, since language coming from the Other implies absence, the possibility of being thrown away like the reel. This "genetic moment," he writes, "is reproduced each time that the subject addresses himself to the Other as absolute, that is to say, as the Other who can nullify the subject himself" (1966, p. 67). This formulation carries a theological ring. Although Lacan refers to the position in the transference held by the analyst as Other, he does not consider this an intersubjective relationship (which he equates with a kind of co-presence). Speech never succeeds in presenting a whole self, and other persons' responses never quite match the longed-for recognition, as though somewhere in the background lies an unreachable interlocutor.

Lacan finds an exception to this limitation of gaining satisfaction in the symbolic gift of love (Fink, 2016). Lacan differentiates imaginary infatuation, a form of the narcissistic illusion of the mirror stage, from a symbolic love based on lack and incompleteness. Imaginary or mirror love seeks sameness, completion, and ideal selfhood, while symbolic love opens the possibility of a non-narcissistic relationship that recognizes the other subject as a fully separate being. He writes:

> We all know that to say one loves someone has only a slight connection to what is meant by this love as experienced bodily. Whatever may be said on this topic, everything indicates a gap which exists between affect as interiorised bodily emotion, as something which has its own profound source in that which by definition cannot be expressed in words.
>
> (Lacan, 1961–62, p. 192)

Lacan poetically alludes to "the miracle of love" when one desire reaches out to another who reciprocates (Fink, 2016, pp. 44–45). Symbolic love implies acceptance of human limitation, of the impossibility to represent fully the content of desire, in which the beloved must be pursued through the structures of language and culture, rather than by enacting private images and fantasies.

Lacan's treatment of love suggests Winnicott's concept of the crucial developmental step between constructing subjective objects, which are imaginary, and finding real objects that possess independent existence outside the sphere of the child's omnipotence. Imaginary love evokes fusional oneness, rather than full acceptance of a separate other. It demarcates extreme situations like the intense infatuations of adolescence or delusional passion, which tend to be short-lived states of feeling and can quickly reverse to their opposite. Actual relationships are obviously a compound of imaginary, symbolic, and bodily ("real") qualities in shifting proportions, as depicted by Lacan in a later seminar ("RSI"). The combined interplay of these components suggests a more accurate way to conceive of intersubjectivity for psychoanalysis—the body, fantasy, and symbolic representation combining as inextricable strands woven into intimate relationships.

Neuroscience of intersubjectivity

During the past decade, intersubjectivity has gained a new perspective through the research of cognitive social neuroscience, which studies the brain basis of second-person interaction. Review articles by Hari and Kujala, 2009, Georgieff, 2013, and Przyrembel et al., 2012 explore the scope of this work, usually without mentioning psychoanalysis. As Hari and Kujala summarize (p. 18), "The mind, with its many levels, is socially shaped and reconstructed dynamically by moment-to-moment interactions." The integrative volume *The Birth of Intersubjectivity* by Ammaniti and Gallese (2014) is an exception in attempting to integrate developmental research and neuroscience with psychoanalysis. Yet, as Przyrembel et al. (2012) observe, there are significant problems translating between different disciplines, which can use the same term in much different contexts. This difficulty is magnified when the kinds of abstractions employed in psychoanalytic theory are in question.

Georgieff's approach (2011, 2013) builds on the author's collaborative research with Marc Jeannerod in France, using models of neuroscience to address issues of concern to psychoanalysts—for example, taking the perspective of cognitive theories of action to study desire and motivation. He contends that neuroscience can investigate the operations in the brain that produce effects recognized by psychoanalysis, without recourse to phenomenologic concepts like subjectivity or psychological ones like a dynamic unconscious, but this depends on finding common objects between disciplines. Georgieff (2011, 2013) and Jeannerod (2006, 2011) identify the cognitive neuroscience of how actions are generated in the brain as offering a shared object with the psychoanalytic notion of the drive (a force which pushes toward action). Similarly, social interactions that evoke conscious feelings, empathy, and recognition of motives can be studied as effects of mirroring operations of neural networks that produce them. "Social neuroscience," Georgieff writes (2011, p. 5), "focuses on the mechanisms through which a person's psychic activity can be occupied, induced, and modified by another psychic activity."

Studies of mechanisms like mirror neurons or pathways of action generation that produce the phenomenology of intersubjectivity, Georgieff maintains, demonstrate a type of influence between the brain processes of two subjects, now susceptible to scientific explanation. Neuroscience confirms Freud's observation that one unconscious can influence another unconscious, and obviates subsequent attempts by analysts to explain this phenomenon by metapsychological theories. He notes that neuroscience research does not tarry over the question raised earlier in this chapter of the nature of the subject. Most of its findings pertain to impersonal, "asubjective" levels of neural processes where questions of subjectivity become almost irrelevant. The studies merely confirm at a biological level the obvious social reality of human behavior.

Social cognitive neuroscience attempts (and in some respects has succeeded) to resolve the old philosophical problem of the existence of other minds. How do we know that our fellow humans have inner psychic lives just like ourselves? Georgieff along with many others working in different fields (phenomenology was mentioned earlier) argue that the problem was resolved with the discovery of mirroring operations in the brain, which extend beyond the pre-frontal motor activation originally found by Gallese, Rizzollati, and their colleagues (Gallese, 2001; Rizzollati, Fogassi, & Gallese, 2001). What Jeannerod (1997, 2011) terms "mental physiology" seems to provide a biological basis for what phenomenologists have long characterized as an immediate knowledge of the other—a kind of hard-wired intersubjectivity that does not need to be constructed by any cognitive process (Brunet-Gouet & Jackson, 2013). As reviewed in the previous section, however, this conclusion claims too much for mirroring systems. Understanding the actions or emotions of other people relies on several systems in the brain and (with the possible exception of a few extreme situations) is closely linked to symbolized, cultural meanings without which most human behavior would not make sense.

Like other neuroscience approaches, the interdisciplinary model of common objects pursued by Georgieff and Jeannerod does not entirely escape the problem of reduction of meaningful intersubjective behavior to asubjective brain processes that underlie them. Although they confirm the value of clinical observations for therapeutic purposes, psychoanalytic hypotheses carry no explanatory value for science. Because there is no wizard behind the screen making decisions, no internal entity in the brain who chooses, the notion of a subject deciding what actions to take lacks meaning. Instead, the narrative of decision making and the conscious sense of willing an event come after (or during) its completion. "The role of consciousness should rather be to ensure the continuity of subjective experience across actions which are—by necessity—executed automatically," Jeannerod argues (2006, pp. 36–37). While the logical and empirical bases of this conclusion seem irrefutable and the research strategy of searching for the relevant pathways that lead to particular behaviors makes scientific sense, conceiving of the subject as a belated narrative remains problematic. Can the cognitive neuroscience of intersubjectivity truly dispense with a form of dualism—at least one that accepts the need for the two languages of causality and intention to understand human behavior?

The case of mirror neurons as an apparently naturalistic explanation for knowledge of other minds and immediate intersubjective communication exemplifies the problem of reductionist thinking in many disciplines. Phenomenologists, relational analysts, and scholars in the humanities have used this discovery of neuroscience to support claims for a hard-wired perception of meaning, as though understanding others can derive directly from implicit biological processes. Leys notes a "fascination in the humanities and social sciences with the neurosciences resulting in an often naive and uncritical borrowing from the work of scientists such as Antonio Damasio" (2010, p. 666). She sees a widespread tendency to short-circuit cognitive and intentional explanations of action and behavior, which are held to be determined by "material-corporeal affective programs or dispositions or systems that are independent of the mind" (p. 668).

From a psychoanalytic vantage point, unconscious fears, fantasies, and wishes subtly or hugely distort subjective interpretations of behavior. Reciprocal dialogue and explicit assessment of context are required to sort out some part of these influences. Moreover, although there are fascinating correlations between the cerebral activities of interacting persons, the accuracy of reading other minds is highly debatable. Although the brain regions active in a behavior may be similar in two experimental subjects, their actual experience cannot be accurately inferred from the data. In a study by Hasson et al. (Hari & Kujala, 2009, p. 458), subjects were studied with an fMRI scan while watching a film. "Significant inter-subject correlations occurred not only in the visual and auditory projection cortices, but also in association cortices as a sign of collective ticking." Yet other brain areas failed to show this synchrony, in accord "with many imaging studies that have demonstrated the existence of highly individual intrinsic brain networks." Indeed, this result conforms to common-sense observations. Humans share many things in common but are unique in the qualities of their inner experiences. Empathy research likewise reveals the highly contingent and variable success of attempts at understanding the thoughts and feelings of others (Ickes, 1993). Much of what we intuit about others derives from cultural knowledge and personal experience with people.

Major areas of interest to the neuroscience of intersubjectivity include psycho-pathologies of self and other (Feinberg, 2010), empathy (Decety & Jackson, 2004), and communication of affect (Damasio, 1994, 2003). Mirror neuron systems do not fully explain these phenomena, which utilize several brain locations and systems. The lack of consistent correlations of most mental functions with cerebral centers reflects the complexity of the terms under discussion. Psychiatric disorders like misperceptions of the identities of others or of the self in schizophrenia, for example, cannot be localized to specific brain regions any more than the concepts themselves can be precisely specified. How we define and then operationalize terms like self or identity for research purposes limits the conclusions we can draw. As Georgieff (2011) observes, the subpersonal level of cortical processes elucidated by research does not in any way eliminate the relevance of psycho-analytic observations of subjective, purposive, and unconscious aspects of intersubjective relationships, which can be independently studied by psychological methods.

Empathy

The intersubjective concept of empathy exemplifies the necessity for retaining a psychological language of explanation. Empathy has been taken up by several disciplines and been studied in numerous ways, to which neuroscience makes a unique contribution, but research has not identified a specific "empathy system" (Ferrari, 2014; Decety, 2010). Similarly, Przyrembel et al. (2012) conclude that neuronal networks, computations, or single cells exclusively tuned to process on-line social interactions have not yet been found. They make the added point that no current social neuroscience paradigm demonstrates "a pattern of actions and reactions in which living and uncontrolled partners engage in behavior that leads to reciprocal impact on each other's behavior" (2012, p. 10). On the other hand, developmental research does focus on mutual interactions over time, confirming the delicate attempts at attunement between infants and mothers (Tronick, 2007). No one would argue that what goes on in this relationship can be explained by mirror systems or any other automatic process, although simultaneous events in the two brains can be studied.

As Ammaniti and Gallese conclude (2014), we cannot dispense with knowledge gained from multiple disciplines, including psychoanalysis, to understand what goes into everyday social interactions. Intersubjectivity is inherent in human life in the sense that we dwell in a social world that includes language, shared symbols, and communication of affects, and our understanding of these highly complex phenomena draws from many domains of cognitive, psychodynamic, affective, and neuroscience research. Some, but not all aspects of human interaction rely mainly on asubjective physiologic processes, but, as Leys (2010) argues, eliminating meaning and intention altogether seems a questionable move. Decety and Jackson state that empathy "is not something one needs to learn. Rather, the basic building blocks are hardwired in the brain and await development through interaction with others" (2004, p. 71). Yet they qualify this comment by subsequently remarking that "empathy is not a simple resonance of affect between the self and other. It involves an explicit representation of the subjectivity of the other" (p. 72). Moreover, they surprisingly conclude, "empathy is a motivated process that more often than commonly believed is triggered voluntarily" (pp. 93–94). As another of Georgieff's common objects shared by neuroscience and psychoanalysis, empathy can be studied at different levels, without being reducible to any single mechanism or process.

The powerful tools of neuroscience enable us to learn a great deal about the human brain and the physiology of social interaction. Research findings arguably impose constraints on psychoanalytic theory, which should accord with scientific facts. I suspect that future studies will begin to make much of analytic metapsychology obsolete. Moreover, the data suggest that in many respects the brain as a whole has evolved as a mirroring organ, oriented to perceiving and responding to the emotions and messages of others (Georgieff, personal communication) —an organ of intersubjectivity. These conclusions do not justify removing the psychological language of personal beliefs and desires from our understanding of behavior. Rather than a reductionist dismissal of the alternative frames of observation provided by philosophy and psychology, psychoanalysis will be best served by maintaining an interdisciplinary dialogue.

Summary

Concepts like intersubjectivity, the self, and subject refer to indeterminate abstractions that can only be clarified by other terms themselves lacking specific referents. To be investigated scientifically, such concepts must be operationalized or redefined in materialist language, which fails to capture their phenomenologic presentation. Neuroscience research tells us about the substrate of behavior but not much about its meaning, which requires a more metaphorical and symbolic way of speaking about people. The insights of phenomenology and psychology do not invoke a Cartesian dualism of mind and body so much as they address different levels of explanation, which carry their own independent validity, yet maintaining a non-reductionist stance remains a significant problem for philosophers of science and researchers in intersubjectivity.

The psychological and linguistic dimensions of intersubjectivity (the second-person perspective of subject speaking to subject) add crucial information to first- and third-person knowledge about the other (i.e. I feel this about him; I know these things about him; psychological tests or scans of his brain suggest possible diagnoses, etc.). Personal interactions cannot be reduced to an automatic set of behavioral responses based on identifiable neurological systems, although they obviously depend on neural processes. Moreover, the physiological events in the brain that cause behavior may be more intertwined with cultural and linguistic symbols than we can conceptualize at this point. Language and culture "program" and colonize the developing brain with signs that begin to shape behavior at least from birth. *Homo sapiens* shares the evolutionary achievement of mirroring with other species, but adds to this process the enormous architecture of higher level semiotic, self-reflective, and affective capabilities on which the discipline of psychoanalysis depends.

Notes

1. The important role of the pronoun in speech relations called "deixis" was developed by the French linguist Benveniste. Muller (1996) has reviewed this literature at length. Litowitz (2014) covers similar issues. Rizzuto (1993) has written of the implications of pronoun use for the analytic process.
2. Parts of the following section are taken from Kirshner, 1991.
3. Zahavi's book, *Subjectivity and Selfhood: Investigating the First-Person Perspective*, which deals with issues of self in philosophic discourse, was favorably reviewed by Stolorow (2008). Stolorow concludes, however, that "Zahavi does not consider the intersubjective contexts that promote or undermine the experience of mineness itself. That is the job of psychoanalysts" (p. 1042).

4. Arnold Modell may be the analyst who has most consistently probed the nature of self. Beginning with his adaptation of the theories of Winnicott and continuing through his studies of infant research and neuroscience, Modell has supported the concept of a paradoxical self, both ephemeral and enduring (see Kirshner, 2010).

5. This anamnestic model of psychoanalytic therapeutics bears similarities to Winnicott's ideas about the freezing of development and the manifestation of this sticking point in the transference. Lacan may have been influenced by his readings of Winnicott, but the apparent similarity of their initial approaches to repeating the history of the patient did not remain, as Lacan vehemently rejected a developmental model. Their relationship is explored in Kirshner, 2014.

6. Lacan spoke of this metaphor in his seminar on the psychoses, 1955–56.

7. The question of "being" in Lacan and Winnicott was first addressed by Eigen (1981); it remained a cryptic leitmotif in Lacan's seminars.

8. See Malabou's discussion of the roots of this conception of "affection" (being affected) as the basis of subjectivity (Johnston & Malabou, 2013).

9. Mead's thinking about subjectivity and consciousness anticipated many subsequent contributions by philosophers and psycholologists. His conception was intersubjective, linguistic, and symbolic. "The process by which the self arises is a social process which implies . . . the preexistence of the group" (1934, p. 164), and "there neither can be nor could have been any mind or thought without language" (p. 192).

10. For Hume (1787), identity is an illusory product of the mind's capacity to remember and to infer causes—"the chain of causes and effects which constitutes our self or person" (p. 262).

11. Ruti's study (2012), *The Singularity of Being: Lacan and the Immortal Within*, takes on this problem from a Lacanian direction. She writes that "singularity is less a nameable quality than an inscrutable intensity of being that urges the subject to persist in its unending task of fashioning or reiterating a self that feels viscerally 'real,' (meaningful, compelling, or appropriate)" (p. 9).

12. A recent paper by Taipele (2015) finds the Huserrlian view of intersubjective relationships incomplete without the Freudian concept of an unconscious transference.

13. The basic prerequisites of the symbolic order structuring the subject are about absolute separation—separate persons and genders, finititude in time and space, and life from death, which all fall under Lacan's conception of castration (see Muller & Richardson, 1982, especially pp. 212–213, 367–368) for a discussion of his use of this loaded Freudian word.

14. Jeannerod (2011, p. 157) writes that each state of mind, desire, belief, preference, will, judgement, etc. corresponds to an experience that can be identified with a concept and studied empirically (the common object of cognitive and neuroscience). This step invites research into the mechanisms subjacent to such concepts.

References

Ammaniti, M. & Gallese, V. (2014). *The Birth of Intersubjectivity: Psychodynamics, Neurobiology, and the Self*, New York: W.W. Norton.

Aron, L. (1991). The patient's experience of the analyst's subjectivity, *Psychoanalytic Dialogues*, 1:29–51.

Aron, L. (1999). Clinical choices and the relational matrix, *Psychoanalytic Dialogues*, 9:1–29.

Bergo, B. (2015). Reading Levinas as a Husserlian might do, online at: www.academia.edu/17068668/

Blunden, A. (2005). Hegel: The subject as self-consciousness, http://home.mira.net/~andy/works/hegel-habitus.htm

Bohleber, W., Jiménez, J.P., Scarfone, D., Varvin, S., & Zysman, S. (2013). Towards a better use of psychoanalytic concepts: A model illustrated using the concept of enactment, *International Journal of Psychoanalysis*, 94:501–530.

Brunet-Gouet, É. & Jackson, P. (2013). Ce que l'imagerie cérébrale nous apprend sur l'intersubjectivité, in *Psychopathologie de l'intersubjectivité*, Ed. N. Georgieff, pp. 141–150, Paris: Elsevier Masson.

Busacchi, V. (2015). Habermas and Ricœur on recognition: Toward a new social humanism, *International Journal of Humanities and Social Science*, 5:11–20.

Damasio, A.R. (1994). *Descartes' Error: Emotion, Reason and the Human Brain*, New York: Putnam.

Damasio, A.R. (2003). *Looking for Spinoza: Joy, Sorrow, and the Feeling Brain*, New York: Harvest Books/Harcourt.

Decety, J. (2010). To what extent is the experience of empathy mediated by shared neural circuits? *Emotion Review*, 2:204–207.

Decety, J. & Jackson, P. (2004). The functional architecture of human empathy, *Behavioral and Cognitive Neuroscience Reviews*, 3: 71–100.

Dennett, D.C. (1991). *Consciousness Explained*, Boston, MA: Little Brown.

Eigen, M. (1981). The area of faith in Winnicott, Lacan and Bion, *International Journal of Psychoanalysis*, 62: 413–433.

Feinberg, T. (2010). Pathologies of self, *Neuropsychoanalysis*, 12: 133–158.

Ferrari, P. (2014). The neuroscience of social relations: A comparative-based approach to empathy and to the capacity of evaluating others' action value, *Behaviour*, 151(2–3):297–313.

Fink, B. (2007). *Fundamentals of Psychoanalytic Technique: A Lacanian Approach for Practictioners*, New York: W.W. Norton.

Fink, B. (2016). *Lacan on Love: An Exporation of Lacan's Seminar VIII, Transference*, Cambridge/Malden, MA: Polity Press.

Freud, S. (1895). Project for a scientific psychology, in *The Standard Edition of the Complete Psychological Works of Sigmund Freud, Volume I (1886–1899): Pre-Psycho-Analytic Publications and Unpublished Drafts*, pp. 281–391.

Freud, S. (1920). Beyond the pleasure principle, in *The Standard Edition of the Complete Psychological Works of Sigmund Freud, Volume XVIII (1920–1922): Beyond the Pleasure Principle, Group Psychology and Other Works*, pp. 1–64.

Gallagher, S. (2008). Direct perception in an intersubjective context, *Consciousness and Cognition*, 17: 535–543.

Gallagher, S. (2012). In defense of phenomenological approaches to social cognition: Interacting with the critics, *Review of Philosophy and Psychology*, 3:187–212.

Gallagher, S. & Zahavi, D. (2008). *The Phenomenological Mind: An Introduction to Philosophy of Mind and Cognitive Science*, London: Routledge.

Gallese, V. (2001). The "shared manifold" hypothesis: From mirror neurons to empathy, *Journal of Consciousness Studies*, 8: 33–50.

Georgieff, N. (2011). Psychoanalysis and social cognitive neuroscience: A new framework for a dialogue, *Journal of Physiology – Paris*, 105: 1–5.

Georgieff, N. (2013). Intersubjectivité et subjectivité en psychopathologie, in *Psychopathologie de l'intersubjectivité*, Ed. N. Georgieff, pp. 3–18, Paris: Elsevier Masson.

Greenberg, J. (2015). Therapeutic action and the analyst's responsibility, *Journal of the American Psychoanalytic Association*, 63:15–32.

Hari, R. & Kujala, M. (2009). Brain basis of human social interaction: From concepts to brain imaging, *Physiology Revues*, 89: 453–479.

Hegel, G. (1807). *The Phenomenology of Spirit*, trans. A.V. Miller. Oxford: Oxford University Press, 1977.

Hume, D. (1787). *A Treatise of Human Nature*, Oxford: Oxford University Press, 1978.

Ickes, W. (1993). Empathic accuracy, *Journal of Personality*, 61:587–610.

Jeannerod, M. (1997). *De la physiologie mentale: Histoire des relations entre psychologie et biologie*, Paris: Odile Jacob.

Jeannerod, M. (2006). Consciousness of action as embodied consciousness, in *Does Consciousness Cause Behavior*, Ed. Pockett, S., Banks, W., & Gallagher, S., pp. 25–38, Cambridge, MA: MIT Press.

Jeannerod, M. (2011). *La Fabrique des idees*, Paris: Odile Jacob.

Johnston, A. & Malabou, C. (2013). *Self and Emotional Life: Philosophy, Psychoanalysis, and Neuroscience*, New York: Columbia University Press.

Julien, P. (1981). *Jacques Lacan's Return to Freud: The Real, the Symbolic and the Imaginary*, trans. D.B. Simiu, New York: New York University Press, 1994.

Kirshner, L. (1991). The concept of the self in psychoanalytic theory and its philosophical foundations, *Journal of the American Psychoanalytic Association*, 39:157–183.

Kirshner, L. (2010). Paradoxes of the self: The contrapuntal style of Arnold Modell, *Journal of the American Psychoanalytic Association*, 58:327–345.

Kirshner, L. (2011). *Between Winnicott and Lacan: A Clinical Engagement*, New York: Routledge.

Kirshner, L. (2014). Winnicott with Lacan, in *The Winnicott Tradition: Lines of Development—Evolution of Theory and Practice over the Decades*, Ed. M. Spelman & F. Thomson-Salo, pp. 85–96, London: Karnac Books.

Lacan, J. (1954–55). *The Seminar of Jacques Lacan, Book II, The Ego in Freud's Theory and in the Technique of Psychoanalysis*, Ed. J.-A. Miller, trans. S. Tomaselli, Cambridge: Cambridge University Press, 1988.

Lacan, J. (1955–56). *The Seminar of Jacques Lacan, Book III, The Psychoses*, Ed. J.-A. Miller, trans. R. Grigg, London: Routledge, 1993.

Lacan, J. (1960–61). *Le Seminaire, livre VIII, le transfert*, Ed. J.-A. Miller, Paris: Éditions du Seuil, 1991.

Lacan, J. (1961–62). *The Seminar of Jacques Lacan, Book IX: L'Identification*, unpublished, trans C. Gallagher, online at: www.lacaninireland.com/web/wp-content/uploads/2010/06/Seminar-IX

Lacan, J. (1962–63). *Anxiety: The Seminar of Jacques Lacan, Book X*, trans. A.R. Price, London: Polity 2014.

Lacan, J. (1964). *The Four Fundamental Concepts of Psychoanalysis*, Ed. J.-A. Miller, trans. A. Sheridan, New York: W.W. Norton, 1978.

Lacan, J. (1966). *Écrits*, trans. B. Fink, New York: W.W. Norton, 2002.

Laplanche, J. (1987). *New Foundations in Psychoanalysis*, trans. D. Macey, Oxford: Blackwell.

Lavelle, J.S. (2012). Theory-Theory and the direct perception of mental states, *Review of Philosophy and Psychology*, 2:213–230.

Leys, R. (2010). Navigating the genealogies of trauma, guilt, and affect: An interview with Ruth Leys, *University of Toronto Quarterly*, 79:656–679.

Litowitz, B.E. (2014). Coming to terms with intersubjectivity: Keeping language in mind, *Journal of the American Psychoanalytic Association*, 62:294–312.

Mead, G.H. (1934). *Mind, Self, and Society, Volume 1*, Chicago: University of Chicago Press.

Merleau-Ponty, M. (1945). *The Phenomenology of Perception*, trans. C. Smith, London and New York: Routledge, 1962.

Mitchell, S.A. (1991). Contemporary perspectives on self: Toward an integration, *Psychoanalytic Dialo*gues, 1:121–147.

Modell, A.H. (1984). *Psychoanalysis in a New Context*, New York: International Universities Press.

Modell, A.H. (1993). *The Private Self*, Cambridge, MA: Harvard University Press.

Muller, J. (1996). *Beyond the Psychoanalytic Dyad: Developmental Semiotics in Freud, Peirce, and Lacan*, New York: Routledge.

Muller, J. & Richardson, W. (1982). *Lacan and Language: A Reader's Guide to Écrits,* New York: International Universities Press.

Noë, A. (2007). The critique of pure phenomenology, *Phenomenology and Cognitive Science*, 6:231–245.

Przyrembel, M., Smallwood, J., Pauen, M., & Singer, T. (2012). Illuminating the dark matter of social neuroscience: Considering the problem of social interaction from philosophical, psychological, and neuroscientific perspectives, *Frontiers in Human Neuroscience*, 6(190):1–15.

Ricoeur, P. (1970). *Freud & Philosophy: An Essay on Interpretation*, trans. D. Savage, New Haven, CT: Yale University Press.

Ricoeur, P. (1986). The self in psychoanalysis and in phenomenological philosophy, *Psychoanalytic Inquiry*, 6:437–458.

Ricoeur, P. (2004). *The Course of Recognition*, trans. David Pellauer, Cambridge, MA: Harvard University Press, 2005; orig. *Parcours de la Reconnaissance*, Paris: Éditions Stock, 2004.

Rizzolatti, G., Fogassi, L., & Gallese, V. (2001). Neurophysiological mechanisms underlying the understanding and the imitation of action, *Nature Reviews and Neuroscience*, 2:661–670.

Rizzuto, A. (1993). First person personal pronouns and their psychic referents, *International Journal of Psychoanalysis*, 74:535–546.

Rochat, P. (2009). *Others in Mind: Social Origins of Self-Consciousness*, New York: Cambridge University Press.

Ruti, M. (2012). *The Singularity of Being: Lacan and the Immortal Within*, New York: Fordham University Press.

Ryle, G. (2002). *The Concept of Mind*, Chicago: The University of Chicago Press.

Sartre, J.-P. (1936–1937). *The Transcendance of the Ego*, trans. F. Williams & R. Kirkpatrick. New York: Octagon Books, 1972.

Sartre, J.-P. (1943). *L'Être et le Néant*, Paris: Gallimard.

Searle, J. (2008). The phenomenological illusion, in *Philosophy in a New Century*, pp. 107–136, Cambridge: Cambridge University Press.

Solms, M. (2013). The conscious id, *Neuropsychoanalysis*, 15:5–19.

Solomon, R. (1983). *In the Spirit of Hegel*, New York: Oxford University Press.

Stolorow, R.D., Brandchaft, B., & Atwood, G. (1987). *Psychoanalytic Treatment: An Intersubjective Approach*, Hillsdale, NJ: Analytic Press.

Stolorow, R.D. (2008). Review of Subjectivity and Selfhood: Investigating the First-Person Perspective, By D. Zahavi, *Journal of the American Psychoanalytic Association*, 56:1039–1043.

Sullivan, H.S. (1953). *The Interpersonal Theory of Psychiatry: Beginnings of the Self-system*, New York: W.W. Norton, pp. 158–170.

Taipele, J. (2015). The anachronous other: Empathy and transference in early phenomenology and psychoanalysis, *Studia Phaenomenologica*, vol. XV, pp. 331–348.

Tronick, E. (2007). *The Neurobehavioral and Social-Emotional Development of Infants and Children*, New York: W.W. Norton.

Ver Eecke, W. (1983). Hegel as Lacan's source for necessity in psychoanalytic theory, in *Interpreting Lacan*, Ed. J. Smith & W. Kerrigan. New Haven, CT: Yale University Press.

Wilden, A. (1968). Lacan and the discourse of the other, in *Speech and Language in Psychoanalysis*, Baltimore, MD: Johns Hopkins University Press, pp. 159–311.

Winnicott, D. W. (1956). The mirror role of mother and family in child development, in *Playing and Reality*, pp. 111–118, New York: Basic Books, 1971.

Zahavi, D. (2006). *Subjectivity and Selfhood: Investigating the First-Person Perspective*, Cambridge, MA: MIT Press.

Zahavi, D. (2011). The experiential self: Objections and qualifications, in M. Siderits, E. Thompson, & D. Zahavi, Eds. *Self, No Self? Perspectives from Analytical, Phenomenological, and Indian Traditions*, Oxford: Oxford University Press, 56–78.

Chapter 2

Intersubjectivity in the case of Ms. B.

Having introduced the main themes of my book, I want to present a clinical example of my theoretical perspective on intersubjectivity and how I tried to apply it in practice. Rather than record the complexities of an entire lengthy treatment, I will highlight a few significant themes and moments to bring out my thinking. The patient I discuss was a woman whom I saw many years ago, as I was beginning to orient my work around an intersubjective model.[1] This choice has the advantage of revealing some common ingrained habits I needed to overcome and how I had come to conceive of therapeutic interaction. Already at this time, I had become disillusioned with the traditional method of applying psychoanalytic theory to clinical practice and the accompanying stance that treats the patient as a puzzle to be solved. I knew that the essence of analytic work resides in the process of ongoing interaction, rather than in the interpretations one might make about the content, and I strove to implement this conclusion.

The case concerns a 44-year-old married biologist, Ms. B., who was referred by her physician because of headaches, insomnia, and crying spells. She had been diagnosed as suffering from depression and was medicated, with some symptomatic improvement. Although not psychologically minded, and insistent that "this isn't me," Ms. B. agreed that she needed additional help. Nonetheless, she remained unsure about the use of analytic treatment.

"What is the point of this?" she asked at our first session. "Is it scientific?" As a biologist, Ms. B. may have been skeptical about the value of talk therapy, and she also manifested a kind of wariness on entering treatment that suggested more personal concerns. I made a brief comment acknowledging her doubts and offered a rather general explanation of the benefits of talking through a problem and seeing whether we would discover particular issues she might want to explore. I decided to ask if she could provide me with more details about what was troubling her, hypothesizing that some structure to the session would mitigate her anxiety. She quickly responded to my request by speaking about marital problems, which she attributed to her husband's excessive jealousy and possessiveness. She was depressed about their future and frustrated with a level of tension between them, focusing on how his behavior impacted her. She had married as a graduate student, in part to get away from her conservative and controlling family. This commitment was important to her, however, and she hoped that he might also seek help.

Although composed, Ms. B. appeared in distress, and I listened sympathetically to her portrayal of the situation. I wondered whether she would be motivated to use therapy to explore her own role in these difficulties. We were in a "getting acquainted" phase, and I did not consider myself authorized to go further, but I inquired about her own understanding of the depressed feelings. Fairly soon, I perceived indications of her greater comfort and interest in the sessions, at least in having someone to listen. This increased sense of engagement led me to ask why she thought her problems had come to a head just now. After an interval, Ms. B. admitted hesitantly that she recently spent time away on a professional assignment in another city where she enjoyed recreational and social activities with a much younger male colleague, Bob. They were "pals," she says, and were comfortable with each other "without hassle," unlike the rather strained relationship she described with her husband. She insisted that there was nothing to it, just one night spent together toward the end of their time on the project. Once again, she stressed her husband's irritating nagging, which fatigued her, and reported that she found herself reacting by thinking about the younger man. In fact, she noticed intrusive thoughts about him at times, which she interpreted as "symbolic" of her lack of freedom and acceptance at home. She agreed with my proposal that it could be useful to talk more about this.

As the sessions continued, Ms. B.'s preoccupation with Bob became more striking to me. For example, a poem she wrote for his birthday spoke in blissful terms of their cherished friendship. Finally, after several more weeks, she volunteered that she might briefly have felt she was in love with him during their time in the distant city. Many other indications suggested to me that falling in love with this man (or, rather, her inability to accept this situation) represented the immediate source of her distress. Nonetheless, while her conflicts about falling in love could have led Ms. B. to act in certain ways and even to develop symptoms, to accept her affair as a causal explanation would have left important questions unanswered. Why was this situation so disturbing for her, after all, and what prevented her from resolving it more effectively? Clearly, her account represented a gloss on more complex processes, involving other feelings and beliefs in the context of her life history, and inquiry into these matters was potentially endless.

In my response to this situation, I recognized a familiar desire to work out answers to Ms. B.'s problems, to pose more questions, and to formulate hypotheses. This was the method in which I had been trained, and it has a good pedigree, which we can trace to Freud's pioneering studies of hysteria. Of course, Freud also taught that analytic listening differs from simple fact gathering or a search for measurable variables of dysfunction. The patient herself wanted answers or, at least, something concrete to provide relief, but her demand had more to do with herself and her way of being than her depression. Like many people, Ms. B. looked for patterns in her life and sought to make sense of her recent experiences, perhaps to be provided a more complete explanation of what they meant for her. Despite her initial reservations, she now demonstrated curiosity about herself and even psychological mindedness. For example, she accepted the importance of her thoughts and feelings and their roots in her personal life history. At the same time, she expected me to apply expert knowledge to elucidate her case.

In my reflections, I reviewed a list of ideas that seemed relevant to Ms. B.'s issues. I was influenced by Schafer's (1980, 1992) point that psychoanalysis aims above all to place human action in an intelligible narrative by helping patients make meaningful connections between seemingly disparate phenomena. By intelligible, I assume he intended a thread of emotional significance that leads in an open direction, not a concise formulation. He did not mean a search for objective explanation, which often lurks implicitly in the background of the work. The classic analytic goal of constructing a comprehensive formulation runs up against the problem of competing theories, which are more susceptible than we would like to believe to a variety of hidden prejudices and interests. I entertained several alternative explanations of Ms. B.'s problems that could be put forward by experienced psychoanalysts. A short list included cumulative blows to her narcissism, like major rejections and disappointments in her career; a history of a verbally abusive relationship with her father, whom she had come to hate; and her approaching menopause, underlining her childless status, all of which were very much on her mind. Here, I was confronted with the dilemma with which I had been struggling for some time: How to choose among these directions, as I could not avoid making some selection, or, more importantly, what connections was I predisposed to find in her narrative, while other important associations might go completely unheard?

While psychoanalytic work in some respects resembles the construction of a new story, the final version never includes all the possible life events and psychic realities in play. Rather, the conclusions of an analysis highlight the ambiguous and indeterminate nature of subjective experience. Although new connections are frequently made between the way a patient speaks about different memories and people, and although enduring life patterns can often be identified, the process usually fails to arrive at an end point that can be spelled out like the conclusions of a case report. More typically, the picture becomes increasingly variegated and complex as a therapy proceeds.

Experience with patients has taught me that psychoanalytic treatment does not involve pursuing a coherent narrative, even through collaboration. Life is not necessarily coherent, and an analyst's wishes to make it so can lead him to impose his own ideas on a patient. Nor should the work resemble a search for etiology, as though, in my example, I could put Ms. B. into the appropriate diagnostic category or define her as a type of personality, as if the right label would tell me something important about her emotional pain or personal dilemmas. Rather than trying to translate her distress into a nosologic or theoretic framework, something novel should be created in the course of the analysis. My training had taught me to think along the former lines—for instance, about Ms. B.'s unconscious guilt and the collapse of her long-term denial of marital unhappiness with its inevitable consequences for her life. I noticed, in fact, that I was still largely collecting information to confirm or disconfirm these likely ideas, while also entertaining other hypotheses that fit books and papers I had recently read. Many models of practice were competing in my awareness, which mostly told me how I was seeing Ms. B. at the time. However, our apparently shared desire for understanding and a sense of confusion about what was going on suggested to me that the transference and countertransference were effectively engaged. A therapeutic process was evolving rapidly between us.

This retrospective account of my thought processes allows me to outline what I have come to identify as a common impasse in practicing psychoanalysis. Our theory-saturated field with its emphasis on formulations and interpretations does not provide very clear guidelines for what to do in the consulting room. We can try things on for size and attempt to shift flexibly across models as they seem relevant to a patient's material, but the result can convey a stilted quality to the sessions or an overly detached tone. Although I personally enjoy working out different theories and thinking about what might go on in the minds of patients, I am troubled by the lack of consensual basis for these ideas and, more significantly, see an artificiality in applying them to specific people. A productive alternative to this type of approach, which I call "translational" (Kirshner, 2015) consists mainly in listening to what Ms. B. has to say, paying close attention to her words and affects, while bracketing off my own tendency to speculate or figure out what might be going on. Reflections about the process might alert me to some element of her associations I have neglected, but, more importantly, inform me about how I am hearing her. Reflecting, I look for implicit interpretations revealed by my private associations. Our mutual reactions and responses continuously inflect the dialogic process and determine what unfolds over time.

I am in agreement with the considerable literature on countertransference teaching that the analyst's participation in the dialogue is pervasive and largely unconscious. Remaining in touch with one's own feelings and thought processes and their effects on patients enables us to monitor the intersubjective exchange, although usually in a deferred manner. Attending closely to the specific transactions as they unfold constitutes the key to a productive analysis. Along the same lines, I do not believe that my private experience provides a reliable guide to a patient's unconscious, which remains largely unknown. Instead of attempting to read its contents through my thoughts and fantasies, which mix intuition with imagination, I prioritize the patient's words and associations, as it is there that the unconscious manifests itself.

With Ms. B., our ongoing transactions shaped the content of each session, crystallizing at moments around a set of transference fantasies or a mutual enactment in which I take part, processes which are often indistinguishable. In one session, she comments explicitly about her sense of my disapproval and hidden judgment of her affair with Bob, which she has resumed. She knows this involvement is the wrong thing to do, but maybe it is good for her. Although I asked her to tell me more about her perception, I gradually realize that our relationship seems to be settling into a symmetric configuration. By this I mean a reciprocal role relationship in which our positions remain fixed around identifications. No doubt the presence of a critical transference figure (an image of a harsh judgmental authority) repeats in many of her relationships, but I also observe myself participating in this dyad, even as I think I am taking a "neutral" role. For example, I remarked on her avoiding responsibility for her feelings and, instead, redirecting the conversation onto my supposed judgments, as if she were misperceiving me, perhaps as a resistance. In making this interpretation, I participate unwittingly in a complementary relationship of paternal authority and vulnerable child. Defining her as engaged in a defensive maneuver, I felt slightly annoyed, until I realized that I was taking a critical posture toward her. I thereby assumed a symmetric position to hers. I then thought to ask how my reaction to the relationship had come across. She wasn't sure; she sensed I had concluded that she should end this extramarital affair. I then quickly (without reflection) responded that I wondered why she hadn't left the old one, and she unexpectedly laughed. "Me, too," she smiled, and the tone abruptly shifted, leaving me to ask myself what has just happened.

I view the above example of dyadic symmetry as virtually unavoidable in therapeutic relationships. In this case, I slipped into the part of a judging parent or authority, while Ms. B. assumed the child or inferior role. Infrequently, these roles were reversed, with Ms. B. criticizing the therapy, while I wondered whether I had been doing something wrong. This dyad had taken form over weeks, persisting in various guises until culminating in our exchange about leaving her husband. Perhaps my comment expressed a dialectic alternative to the guilt and blame narrative about her affair that seemed so unavoidable—that is, I spoke as though I were not only *not* opposing it, but favored her leaving. My ironic comment was spontaneous and may have felt like a form of recognition of her dilemma—a moment of sympathetic contact or sharing. Her explicit burst of humor also appeared spontaneous, and the exchange gave me the impression that we had moved to a new place. Humor can easily backfire, of course, but in this instance it helped us connect. We seemed for a moment to share a space. Had I already sensed some shift of tone in her discourse that invited my admission of a judgment about her marriage? Or could it have been that her question about my disapproval put the situation into words in a way that expanded awareness in each of us of what was happening. If Ms. B. had commented further, I might have learned more about the sequence, but she quickly moved into new associations, going on to speak about relationships with men. That, after all, was the implicit, but not explicitly acknowledged content of our exchange. In expressing these ideas and memories, Ms. B. articulated a different, livelier version of herself in which she took a more active part. One could not say that the content of her statements had been unconscious in the classic sense, yet there was a shift away from her repetitive manner of speaking about Bob and her husband.

In the ensuing phase, Ms. B. recounted important events in past relationships and what they meant to her at various periods, as though she stood atop an accretion of historic strata, like Freud's archeological metaphor. I gained the impression of an unspooling thread and intervened very little. Our connection was feeling more secure now. Probably no one had ever listened to her and respected her subjective facts for such an extended period, and she indicated that she appreciated my attentiveness, although with some misgivings about trusting me and therapy. Nonetheless, I continued to be tempted to entertain various formulations and sometimes made inquiries as though looking for confirmation.

When I decentered from my receptive analytic position in this familiar way, I began to recognize Ms. B. reacting to this very process. Why was I interested; what did I expect from her? Did I have some theory about her? I acknowledged that I entertained different explanations and admitted I was curious about her past relationships. Unexpectedly, she joined me by saying that she also was curious; maybe I had some good ideas. Things seemed to be going along okay in the therapy, she confided. Then she ventured a new thought: should she permit herself to have good feelings about me as a man, or was I but a disinterested doctor, trying to be useful but fundamentally estranged? She suddenly asked if I disrespected her for deciding to stay with her husband (my earlier comment returned). My opinions about her began to assume paramount importance, and I developed an unusually clear sense of how I could cause her injury. My old question recurred: which of the many possible perspectives on her problem should I take—her unfulfilled longings, her common sense, her guilt, her vindictiveness toward her father? At each moment I perceived a different gestalt in our exchanges, only to dissolve again in the flux of the telling.

I have come to believe that the analyst's main job is to sustain this fragile intersubjective structure in which the patient, at first tentatively and then with increasing assurance, moves about, trying out various positions as she speaks. The notion of movement seems central. This is perhaps what Lacan meant to convey by his schema L, in which he diagrammed the patient as a subject spread out over the four corners of a rectangle (1955, 1967–68, pp. 106–107). These anchor points of a subject's experience include: (1) a repressed unconscious full of alienated desires; (2) an imaginary self-representation or ego system that provides a coherent identity; (3) a set of internal fantasy objects that support (or attack) this self-conception and can be transferred onto the analyst (and others); and (4) the Other, the symbolic field of language and culture that provides a substrate or ground from which figurations of the individual ego arise. These very dissimilar positions cannot be integrated, but only used to generate a set of evolving possibilities. Of course, they are metaphors for ways of processing the complexity of life experience, not substantive states that can be measured. Probably, one could add other geometric vertices touching on human possibility. The point I take from Lacan is that subjectivity does best in flux, moving among different configurations, while fixed positions are traps, bad solutions to neurotic problems.

If persistence in using frozen metaphors about the self (Modell, 1990) confines and constricts the subject, a semantic openness of the analyst to generating new meanings can expand possibilities. The pursuit of openness, however, continues to be entwined with imaginary representations (what the analyst and patient imagine are going on). The reciprocal back and forth fosters an unending dialectic of possible identities and purposes that characterizes freely moving subjective speech. "I am like a woman who," Ms. B. began to describe herself, soon to branch onto "not quite" or "with the exception of" as she questioned her own conclusions. Closure becomes the enemy here, excluding what may turn out in the course of time to be the most subjectively important discoveries. Therapeutic abstinence, however, does not prevent a stagnation in the flow of discourse (as Lacan, typical of his period, seems to have believed). To the contrary, my experience has been that responsiveness of the analyst/Other to the words and gestures of the analysand usually promotes the flow of speech in a spontaneous way. We know that "abstinence" or silence is not empty, but often speaks quite loudly.

The notion of an intersubjective receptivity of the analyst as Other has affinity to Tronick et al.'s (1998) concept of dyadic expansion of consciousness,[2] in which one partner's openness can enlarge the dialogic field to foster figuration of previously unrepresented experiences (the unconscious) by the other. Associative links constantly appear and fade in a patient's discourse, which is more likely to take new directions if the analyst refrains from settling for a third person, subject to object interpretation. Interpreting meaning by statements such as "you must have felt that x . . ." or "it sounds like you wanted to y. . ." ask the patient to take a position of self-observation or to see herself through the eyes of the analyst. This risks an objectification in both positions. Of course, the affectively engaged analyst cannot avoid slipping into these complementary roles. In Ms. B.'s case, my default position consisted of taking the stance of a paternal authority or the scientific expert she consciously sought.

As an example of a more familiar type of interpretation, I commented at one point, as Ms. B pursued her complaints against her dictatorial husband, "You escaped your father to marry someone like him." This observation interested her and produced a lengthy reflection on how they were and were not similar people. At the time, she believed that her husband was a loving man with unfortunate personality traits. Moreover, she heard my statement as a verdict on her decision to marry, thereby, I realized, placing me again in the ranks of opinionated authority figures. I thanked her for clarifying my misunderstanding and confessed (truthfully) that I didn't really know much about the marriage. Our positions were then reversed, putting her in the stronger authoritative role, and I noticed a shift in affect, with Ms. B. sounding warmer in her tone and conveying a kind of solicitude for me to learn the reality. Meanwhile, I reminded myself of a resistance to hearing her speak as a victim of her husband (the victim role). My formulation about her repetition, as roughly accurate as it may have been (she herself came to the idea of repetition later) distracted me from listening and expressed my countertransference quite effectively.

The analyst's countertransference (along with interactions with other subjects in real life) continually stimulates and disrupts a patient's imaginary ego organization. We want the other to affirm us in our self-image and choose close friends who share many assumptions and beliefs with us, yet the desire for mirroring usually fails at some point, leading to disappointment, hurt, anger, or, under optimal circumstances, growth and insight. An open exchange between two sub-jects affects the internal psychic organization of each through processes that analysts label as introjection and projection. The subject takes in the other's perceptions and suggestions of himself, and expels unwanted thoughts and images. This means that the inside and outside are not always clearly separated. The subject in a formal sense cannot be located entirely inside the head of the speaking person, but exists within a broader intersubjective network of shared language use, pervasive symbols, and unconscious desires, as Lacan's schema L suggests. The analyst participates in this schema at every turn, by evoking and responding to unconscious signals, mirroring or interpreting the self/ego, playing or refusing to play various object roles, and, equally important, by sharing in and submitting to many of the same cultural representations.[3]

On one hand, the record of our field leads me to the chastening conclusion that there are no firm limits to the range of possible interpretations a serious analyst might make from a third person, subject to object approach. This in itself should be sufficient reason to avoid making "expert" interventions. On the other hand, it would seem hard to disagree with the notion that the analyst does have access to historical facts about a person's life, including important affective memories and behaviors of significant others, which provide a set of parameters orienting him to the patient's position. I take a middle-of-the-road position on this. A contemporary clinician should operate with full awareness of the fundamental ambiguity in the use of his "analytic instrument." Analysts have knowledge and experience that can be put into words and contribute to a patient's ability to represent his internal world, but we can easily go astray in the direction of subtle suggestion and private fantasy. The help of an actual third person—a supervisor or peer—may be required to resolve such missteps, especially when the sense of something going wrong becomes palpable. Sometimes our internal monitor-ing "third," although unreliable, may be sufficient for the task (the concept of "the third" is discussed in Chapter 3). Within these limits, analytic interventions have the potential to enhance the dialogue and expand the creative possibilities open to the patient by enunciating a word or noting a connection that has been ignored.

Even though the historical reality of the past can seldom be authenticated or accurately reconstructed, patients do have privileged access to their own histories. Subjects who claim their growing up was dominated by feeling persecuted by their fathers, as Ms. B. did, can adduce lots of support for this belief, even if they have never felt comfortable speaking openly about it. In the course of a successful analysis, patients are also likely to question their prior attitudes and to seek further evidence. Sometimes, surprising memories of affection toward a hated parent surge up and suddenly reconfigure the subject's history in the *après-coup*. A different father or mother emerges from the mists of memory. For this reason, while I did not doubt that Ms. B.'s reports were "true" and "factual" accounts of her life, renderings of what she profoundly felt and experienced, I could not help wonder-ing what might be left out of her story. I was also aware of my countertransferential oscillation in assessing her history. The indeterminacy and slipperiness of language (what exactly did she mean?), my shifting transference position (who I am as an object for her), and the flow of unconscious process on both sides make this fluctuation unavoidable. Above all, I sought to avoid certainty or reductive explanations. I reminded myself to pay more attention to the specific elements of her speech than to the mental picture I was constructing. Thus, I noticed words she used to describe her father's moods that brought in the parental relationship, as when he would complain that Ms. B. monopolized mother's time or asked her to tell his wife to join them for a dinner he brought home. It sounds as if he needed his daughter's help to deal with his wife. I had imagined an oppressed, passive woman, but now began to get hints of a brittle, rejecting person who could withdraw into angry silences. While she felt loyal to her mother, she saw how this behavior provoked her father. I repeated aloud the way Ms. B. characterized her father's tone, and further metaphors and images appeared. "I feel badly for hating him," she announced, "but I had to get out of there." We then looked more at her "feeling badly."

Even though we may try to suppress memory and desire, and erase or suspend our subjective responses, our relationship to a patient cannot be without observation and interpretive interventions on the flow of the material. In the first place, this is what intersubjectivity means; in any relationship, we are entangled to a greater or lesser degree with the other person. Professionally, we carry the record of learning from our teachers and peers, and we use this knowledge to process what we hear. But the inevitable use of theories, published cases, and even research should in the end be subsumed under the major task of enriching a dialogue. If we focus excessively on drawing accurate conclusions about a patient's psychic life, we can miss a lot going on in the room. In analysis, a patient is engaged in a delicate and complex operation to support her own complex subjectivity—support for what it means to be a speaking person—and the analyst becomes part of this operation, opening or shutting down the process. Yet, he is not engaged in the same way as the patient. Although their relationship moves at times toward taking dyadic roles, the therapeutic interaction remains fundamentally asymmetric and unequal. Psychoanalysis can be defined as a unique method of object use that permits a certain kind of decentered conversation to occur in which a patient is free not to speak as a unified subject, not to present a coherent identity, and reciprocally, need not be labeled for every utterance about herself.

Working again around images of her father and her memories of his rejection and cruelty, I commented that she might remember having an idea about why he treated her in this manner. She denied having such thoughts as a child, except for deciding when she left home for college that he was ill. Only later did I suggest, for the reasons noted above, that she might have believed it was because she had come in some way between him and her mother. Both mother and father had allegedly wished for a boy when she was born, and having a daughter stirred up their own painful histories. Her father often expressed indications of negative attitudes toward women and their sexuality, and seemed to get along with Ms. B. best when sharing stereotypic male activities. On outings, he often expressed resentment toward his wife, who was frequently unwell (in fact, she died of a chronic ailment when Ms. B. was in high school). Maybe he would have loved her more as his son–perhaps (I wondered to myself), as she loved the new boy in her life, Bob, whom she was now arranging to meet secretly. Was she gaining vitality and hope from a narcissistic love for an object of desire she wished she had been as a child? I don't know whether my hypothesis about the meaning of gender in the family was accurate, but raising it elicited associations that seemed productive. I thought that looking for a childhood interpretation of her father's motives might be extremely important, but my construction was never "confirmed" in a truly convincing way. Meanwhile, she enjoyed her rendezvous with Bob, who sounded playful and fun to be with, although now she was finding him too unavailable. "What could I expect from any man?" she noted with an edge.

By this point, Ms. B. displayed a new freedom to joke about my own maternal and paternal qualities at certain moments, and I felt empowered to be less circumspect in expressing my thoughts openly. I associate this atmosphere of greater ease in the sessions with movement and spontaneity, away from fixed, complementary roles in the transference. For example, she indicated awareness of placing me in a critical position like other male authorities, but also of devaluing my usefulness to her like her ill or withdrawn mother (the mixture was never clarified for me). The pair (or versions of the two parents) were invisible presences in the room most of the time. Throughout, she struggled with her ongoing ambivalence toward men, which was obviously re-created in the transference. I thought again that she was dealing with a compulsion to repeat, which I strove to avoid joining, yet her greater freedom of thought suggested an attempt to establish a new position as an active, desiring subject, rather than remaining confined to feeling herself the mistreated offspring of a pathological family. Mostly, I tried to attend to the intersubjective level of her affects and associations and my reactions to them, listening closely to the play of variations in our exchanges. By now (almost four years), Ms. B.'s complaints of symptomatic pain and depression had subsided, and we better understood some of their sources. The scientific search for causes had dropped out of her discourse, replaced by the satisfaction she experienced speaking freely in the safer space of my office. Now, she enjoyed coming, but reminded us that this was a transient part of her life, albeit one she hoped would lead to unspecified future changes.

In a series of sessions closer to her termination, Ms. B. summarized these ideas, speaking about herself in a way that challenged many of her former attitudes. I found her comments pointed and engaging, with an enlivening spontaneity. Still, there were moments when she returned to presenting her dilemma as absolutely hopeless and tragic. She reminded me that the past held a tenacious grip on her. She was once again living out a subordinate relationship with a man to whom she was giving herself mostly on his terms (when they could meet), and for which she could not imagine a future. "Maybe I like feeling this way with you, too," she admitted. "It isn't serious like with Bob—the consequences, I mean, if I give in and live with him." For my part, I see how I have become engaged in the drama of this relationship, in which I notice feeling a rather futile bystander who could be potentially damaging to her if I should take a side, as she supposed I would. I shake off the old professional worry about what would be best for her, which I do not know. I am not going to be the brilliant analyst I once wanted to become who could show her the way out of her impasse. Meanwhile, an even, calmer tone came into her voice. "I know that you don't really use me," she continued. "I'm the one who takes it all out on you, which feels kind of good. I don't give in to false situations like at home. My husband sees I am different, and I feel strong." Ms. B. left the session sounding hopeful, with an almost triumphant determination to resist the control of others. "I know you think I get myself into these situations," she declared. "OK. Fair enough. This is why I get so depressed. But you can't really do anything for me. It's all about my own life."

What strikes me most in writing about Ms. B. is the way in which her analysis moved from a focus on childhood anamnesis and developmental trauma to her shifting position in relation to desire. The ways in which her way of speaking displayed a playful and imaginative style suggest her growing comfort in assuming a complex subjectivity. I experienced the ongoing pull in myself between formulating and making sense of her feelings and following the semiotics of our exchange, especially our choices of words and their tonality. Such shifts in attention are probably familiar to most analysts, yet I believe that they are often neglected and deserve explicit attention in training. Ms. B.'s relationships with Bob and her husband (or, rather, how she spoke about them to me) brought an interplay of voices into the therapeutic situation—her world of objects and how she saw herself in relation to them. She cared both for her part-time lover, who benefited from the supposedly easier place in her life accorded to him, and her reliable but insensitive patriarchal husband, with whom she had always felt trapped but who had begun to respond to her new assertiveness. Now, in these relationships and in her work with me, she expressed feeling more in charge of her life. Out of the peculiar entanglement that I consider fundamental to the intersubjective matrix of psychoanalysis, Ms. B. recast her former subjective position in a positive way, rife with future potential, but without certainty or a guaranteed destination.

Notes

1. Parts of this case were previously published (Kirshner, 1999).
2. I prefer the designation "triadic expansion of consciousness" following Lacan's emphasis on the third, developed in the United States by Benjamin (2004). The field is triadic because both participants are subjects, subjected to language and the Other.
3. Kaës has written extensively about the shared unconscious of members of a group or family. He refers to charged signifiers that condense important anxieties and desires as they circulate in the group (Kirshner, 2006).

References

Benjamin, J. (2004). Beyond doer and done to: An intersubjective view of thirdness, *Psychoanalytic Quarterly*, 73:5–46.

Kirshner, L. (1999). Toward a postmodern realism for psychoanalysis, *Journal of the American Psychoanalytic Association,* 47:447–461.

Kirshner, L. (2006). Intersubjective transmission: Families, groups, and culture. The work of René Kaës, *Journal of the American Psychoanalytic Association*, 54: 1005–1012.

Kirshner, L. (2015). The translational metaphor in psychoanalysis, *International Journal of Psychoanalysis*, 96:65–81.

Lacan, J. (1955). "The Purloined Letter" in *Écrits*, trans. B. Fink, New York: W.W. Norton, 2006, pp. 6–48.

Lacan, J. (1967–68). *The Psychoanalytic Act*, trans. C. Gallagher, online at: www.tau.ac.il/~cohenron/ScanSeminar.pdf

Modell, A.H. (1990). *Other Times/Other Realities*, Cambridge, MA: Harvard University Press.

Schafer, R. (1980). Narration in the psychoanalytic dialogue, *Critical Inquiry*, 7:29–53.

Schafer, R. (1992). *Retelling a Life: Narration and Dialogue in Psychoanalysis*, New York: Basic Books.

Tronick, E., Buschweiler-Stern, N., Harrison, A., Lyons-Ruth, K., Morgan, A., Nahum, J., Sander, L., & Stern, D., (1998). Dyadically expanded states of consciousness and therapeutic change, *Infant Mental Health Journal*, 19:290–299.

Chapter 3

The turn to intersubjectivity in American psychoanalysis

The intersubjective paradigm shift

The concept of intersubjectivity has experienced a remarkable growth in psycho-analysis worldwide but especially in North America, touching almost every school and grouping. In this chapter I focus on the history of this development and some of the ways it has been understood by different authors. I began by searching the PEP archive for examples of the term "intersubjectivity" in psychoanalytic journals and was surprised to find how much its use has boomed. Between 1940 to 1960, I could find the term only in two citations; over the next twenty years to 1980, it occurred 17 times; but from 1980 to 2000 there were 974 references; then 1,915 times between 2000 and 2014. Of course, the word gets applied in many ways with multiple interpretations of its meaning. Despite this confusion of tongues, however, "intersubjectivity" has become a kind of shibboleth for contemporary psychoanalysis. Why did this term become so central for different analytic schools and what conclusions might we draw from its prevalence?

I suggest that the current popularity of intersubjectivity indicates a convergence in the development of different theoretical schools that have moved toward the so-called two-person model of mental functioning and clinical process, of which it represents a further step. Looking at the mutuality of the two-person interaction constitutes a paradigm change for psychoanalysis, building on the contributions of many previously ignored or rejected authors, from Ferenczi to Sullivan to Lacan. This shift may only be in its early phases. Important differences among two-person psychologies remain, and the basic assumptions continue to be contested by many analysts who defend Freudian metapsychology. Researchers continue to focus their efforts on the functioning of the isolated mind or brain, and the dynamics of individual mental processes remain relevant to clinical practice. But psycho-analysis itself can no longer be viewed as a scientific discipline that takes patients as its objects to be studied, formulated, and interpreted. As discussed in Chapter 1, the traditional concept of the human subject as an isolated entity possessing thing-like properties has given way in neuroscience, philosophy, and psycho-analysis to a dynamic process of interactions embedded in a symbolic, culturally organized, and linguistic world shared with others.

Psychoanalytic treatment necessarily consists of two subjects in interaction, and its therapeutic results depend on the quality of their work together. Although their metaphors differ, major analytic schools are moving toward a growth and expansion model of clinical process, rather than a medical model of seeking etiologies or pursuing resolution of neurotic conflict by identifying causal factors. A major point of disagreement turns around the place accorded to interpretation, as a hallowed and important aspect of analytic technique. Although an analytic clinician can make useful interpretations about what he understands and experiences with his patients, an emphasis on formulating and interpreting as his major activity misconceives the nature of the work and places the clinician in an expert's position of knowledge. This approach supports a third-person approach toward treating an objectified patient that persists in modified forms.

Many clinicians recognize the necessity of devoting greater attention to the countertransference, but often with the aim of using their own thoughts and feelings to interpret what a patient desires of them or of what is taking place in his mind. While the analyst can sometimes pick up intentions or affects coming from the patient by reflection and reverie, there are significant problems with over-use of this technique, as will be elaborated in this chapter. Some practitioners also highlight an educational aspect of treatment in which the analyst shares with his patient something about himself. An intersubjective perspective takes the position that rather than attempting to identify what is happening in the mind of a patient, analytic process should focus on movement in the dialogue and the emergence of new ways of thinking and speaking. Analytic schools also vary to the extent that a here-and-now, present-tense interaction takes precedence over exploration of history or reconstruction of the past. How to incorporate the past into the current process without distorting it remains a challenge.

The interpersonal turn and intersubjectivity

At first, almost the only way to think about the dual aspect of psychoanalysis was through the concepts of transference and countertransference, with the exceptions, always interesting to Freud, of the possibility of telepathic communication, and his more cryptic and perhaps equally mystical notion that one unconscious can communicate directly with another.[1] In the classic model, the transference arises from the patient's unconscious, from inside out, as it were, not from an external situation like the intersubjective encounter. By the 1930s, however, innovators like Sandor Ferenczi began to write about the influence of the person of the analyst on the analytic process, and, in the United States, Harry Stack Sullivan went further in reinterpreting the phenomenon of transference. He explained the common observation of patients revealing distortions in their perceptions of relationships by referring to their interpersonal histories, thereby replacing the Freudian unconscious, driven by wishes and impulses, with a socially constructed set of learned expectations and fears. Anxiety, for Sullivan, reflected a concern about the response of an important other person, rather than an emerging drive threatening to overwhelm the ego or a signal of instinctual danger. Following splits in the 1940s in the New York Psychoanalytic Society, which rejected these ideas (along with many of Ferenczi's insights), Sullivan's followers, along with so-called neo-Freudians like Karen Horney, Erich Fromm, and Emma Thompson, founded new training institutes like the William Alanson White and, later, Karen Horney Institutes, where the importance of relationships was emphasized, very much in contrast to prevailing currents in ego psychology. The New York University Post-doctoral Program in Psychotherapy and Psychoanalysis set up a relational track in 1972 that produced many influential analysts. Benjamin Wolstein was an important figure in this reorientation (Bonovitz, 2009), by his emphasis on the effect of the analyst's personal psychology, mutuality in the relationship, and inter-subjectivity. His concept of the interlock between analyst and patient, and its relation to the countertransference anticipated much subsequent work on reci-procity of influence.

The decline of the hegemony of ego psychology in the United States opened the door for theories recognizing the two-person shift and the limitations of the drive-defense model. Progress in infant research became a principal justifi-cation for the growing interest in intersubjectivity, influencing almost all schools of analysis, especially self-psychological, relational, and Bionian theories. The mother–infant relational model strongly colors current conceptions of the clinical situation, highlighting its interactive nature and pointing to implicit, non-verbal processes. The prevalent concept of the analytic field, originally advanced by Baranger and Baranger (2008) and widely cited in English language publications, likewise supports an intersubjective model. On a wider cultural level, the post-modern criticism of metatheories and the linguistic turn in philosophy impacted psychoanalytic thinking. The paradigm changing question these sources raise might be summarized as: "What happens in the relationship between two subjects above and beyond the psychic apparatus as Freud elaborated it, notably in the famous Chapter VII of *The Interpretation of Dreams*?"

The personal subject in intersubjectivity

Growing out of its Sullivanian roots, one very common connotation of the word "intersubjective" presents it as a contemporary version of the interpersonal *tout court*, in which case it can support a therapeutic approach almost emptied of Freudian sources. The intrapsychic concept of the unconscious, the importance of psychological defenses, and the infantile transference, for example, play a less central role for interpersonal therapists than patterns of relationships. In return, Freudian analysts criticize what they view as a naive or oversimplistic view of the two-person relationship. Intersubjective theories go beyond the interpersonal to emphasize the contextual shaping of the subject as the effect of an interactive field, unlike the Freudian notion of ego-to-ego relations between sharply defined and distinct agents. Baranger and Baranger (2008) point to a "dynamic range" of subjectivity that depends on the bipersonal field established between analyst and patient in each treatment. From this perspective, the traditional (Cartesian) subject of philosophy escapes from its inner enclosure and isolation to establish itself as necessarily and inherently constructed intersubjectively. The dependency of the subject on contextual interactions, however, does not eliminate a distinct intrapsychic domain. The cumulative effects of having a personal history with its private meanings (and bodily experiences) constitute an independent level of conceptualizing the individual subject. How these separate levels of the private mind and the protean subject of interaction articulate in clinical practice (and conceptually) presents a challenge to psychoanalysis.

Several authors have attempted to preserve our intuition of a personal self, despite its links to the Cartesian split between mind and world that almost every discipline condemns. Modell's private self, Stolorow's version of Zahavi's minimal (non-reified) self, Winnicott's difficult notion of the true self, and Stern's core (infantile) self are prominent examples. Scholars debate whether these concepts successfully bypass Descartes's ontological dualism—his separation of a reflective subject from the outside world—and perhaps in practical terms we are unable to think otherwise than dualistically. Clinical practice cannot very well avoid taking the personal self or the individual subject, with its motives, beliefs, and desires, as the focus of therapeutic work, and this may account in part for the wide range of theories of intersubjectivity in our current literature. Intersubjectivity as relations between discrete nuclear selves with a tendency toward reification (as perhaps in self psychology) defines one pole. At the other, Sullivan might have been satisfied to accept the alternative of eliminating the concept of self altogether (as referring only to a specular image of the appraisals of others). The Lacanian move of separating self (or ego) as imaginary constructions from the subject of a transpersonal unconscious solves the problem in a different way, but in doing so has little to say about the phenomenological experiences of personal identity, continuity of a narrative self, and stability of object relations (I discuss these issues further in Chapters 6 and 8). Within the gamut of contemporary conceptions of intersubjectivity, some seek to preserve features of a traditional Freudian model within the overarching framework of an interactive field. Others would leave traditional psychoanalysis behind to focus exclusively on the interaction between the two subjects. In what follows, I take an historical approach to discussing some major exemplars of these positions.

Intersubjectivity in the psychoanalytic literature

Of historical interest, I found the first appearance of the word "intersubjectivity" in the PEP Archives occurring in an article by Heinz Hartmann, "Notes on the Reality Principle" (Hartmann, 1956). In this text, he referred to the importance of "intersubjective validation" in science, in contrast to the intersubjective acceptance of a shared reality between two persons who are very close—specifically, a mother and her infant. His objective appears to have been to separate the natural sciences from the human reality of the socialization of knowledge. Curiously,

Hartmann chose to situate psychoanalysis as a method of scientific research possessing objectivity capable of validation, based on the capacity for rationality he saw as intrinsic to the ego. He repeated this contrast between two forms of knowledge in a second text from 1958. In this formulation, the analyst functions as an instrument of truth, "reality testing" being the privileged function of the analyst during this period. The attempt by Hartmann and ego psychology to naturalize the psychic apparatus as a legitimate object of science was a forerunner of the subsequent endeavor in the neurosciences to define the subject in terms of homeostatic systems of control and balance in the brain (Feinberg, 2011). Obviously, his definition of intersubjectivity has very little to do with its use in contemporary psychoanalysis, which, to the contrary, resists a naturalization or reduction of psychology to biology (exceptions to be explored below). Hartmann's alignment of psychoanalytic intersubjectivity with objective science was a principle fiercely defended by ego psychology from the post-war period until the 1980s, in part to combat the interpersonalist heresy. Mixed up with the theoretical disputes were political battles within the psychoanalytic movement.

The first appearance in the archives of the term "intersubjectivity" in a form similar to its current usage occurs in the writing of Stanley Leavy, a psychoanalyst influenced by his reading of Lacan. To illustrate the concept, he (1973) referred to Lacan's paper on Poe's tale of the Purloined Letter, scarcely known to American psychoanalysts at the time. In opposition to ego psychology, Leavy asserted that the analyst lacks scientific credentials to interpret the psychic reality of his patient "objectively." The work of analysis, he asserted, differs radically from an observer who confronts dead tissues or even living animals but involves an encounter between persons; instead, the transactions between analyst and patient derive from the fundamental "intersubjectivity" of the situation. He cited Ricoeur's book, *De l'interprétation* ("On Interpretation," retitled by Yale University Press, 1970, as *Freud and Philosophy*), which supported a hermeneutic dimension in psychoanalysis of finding reasons and meanings alongside the domain of impersonal forces like the drives. Leavy makes a complex argument, grounded in the joint immersion of analyst and patient in language and the unfolding, changing meanings growing out of exchanges of words. He portrays the analyst and patient primarily as speaking, interacting beings, linked through an open, polysemic network that carries a plurality of meanings. Here, as elsewhere, he anticipated current formulations of the analytical relationship as primarily an interactive process of mutual influence, rather than applied science.

The important book by the Frankfurt philosopher Jürgen Habermas (1968), *Knowledge and Human Interests*, famously characterized the error of Freudian psychoanalysis as its self-misinterpretation of belonging to the natural sciences. In advocating a hermeneutic approach, Habermas also highlighted the symbolic speaking relationship as intersubjective. In psychoanalysis, Modell advanced a similar position. His important book, *Psychoanalysis in a New Context* (1984), set the tone for this conceptual change at a high level of theory construction, recognizing the developments in philosophical linguistics. In the new context he advocated, separate selves intertwine in ways we are still struggling to understand. "The self experience of both patient and analyst," he wrote (1984, p. 251), "is affected in the transference countertransference process."

Later, Modell (2002) elaborated an interpretation of psychic life based on the linguistic process of metaphorisation. The mind creates shared meaning through translation of bodily experiences into metaphors—i.e. the symbolic function at the base of all subjectivity. Influenced by the linguists Johnson and Lakoff and his collaborations with neuroscientists, Modell sees metaphorization as not only applying to language, but also describing a mode of functioning of the brain and a form of translation between different areas of the brain-psyche. In this respect, he stands out as one of few American analysts who have pursued a link between the two distinct fields of psychoanalysis and neuroscience, rather than reducing one to the other.

Modell's conception of intersubjectivity evokes the ambiguous and paradoxical status of "self" as at once a stable interior structure (as the nucleus of a personal psyche) and an ephemeral and changing entity depending on the other for its existence. Almost by definition, the subject must possess an abiding inner sameness, a coherence or consistency that is needed for its relations with others, while being characterized by a protean fluidity and responsiveness that responds to interactions. This is the paradox that the most serious psychopathologies illustrate by clinical phenomena involving a non-consensual imposition of the self and its subjective reality upon others (delusions, certainty of judgment, rigidity of thinking), typically accompanied by fluid and unstable ego boundaries and lack of subjective identity. Such patients may seem impervious to intersubjective influence, while lacking a coherent self-concept.

Rereading these texts by Modell and Leavy, I am most impressed by the influence of "the linguistic turn" in philosophy on their approaches to psychoanalysis. Modell highlights concepts of translation and metaphor; Leavy the ambiguity of the signifier. Language (or better, speech) opens the way to the subjective and unknown universe of the other. Yet, the return to the sources of psychoanalysis they proposed—the central importance of language and the abandonment of Hartmann's science of adaptation—and their advocacy of intersubjectivity as the new axis of clinical practice seemed doomed to failure. First, their important philosophical and linguistic references were probably foreign to most American analysts. Moreover, the concepts of Winnicott and others in the school of object relations (and, it goes without saying, those of Lacan) remained mostly outside the standard analytic curriculum in IPA institutes until the 1980s. The principal themes dear to Leavy and Modell involving entanglement of self with other from birth onwards had to await the growing popularity of self psychology and the relational movement to gain wider acceptance in American psychoanalysis.

Although not strictly speaking an intersubjective analyst, Heinz Kohut brought about important revisions of theory that supported the new paradigm. By centering therapeutic work on empathy and the important concept of mirroring (developed previously by Winnicott and Lacan), he highlighted the analyst's participation in the therapeutic process. The psychology of the self corrected the mechanistic language of ego psychology by bringing forward the neglected phenomenology of agency, intention, and states of self. Moreover, his concept of the self (which featured an inner kernel of self as the "center of initiative" for the person) was in tune with the individualistic (and narcissistic) culture of the United States. Kohut (1971) portrayed the self as a superordinate structure, rather than an ephemeral effect of ego function, and redefined the position of the analyst as a matter of self with self, although mainly in a one-way direction—that is, the analyst seeks to attune his involvement as much as possible with the subjective experience of the patient, without necessarily being implicated in his own state of being, as Modell argued. For this reason, Ghent (1989), a relational analyst, contested the inter-subjectivity of Kohut's theory, and Morrison (1994) coined the phrase "a one and a half person psychology" to describe it. Despite these conceptual limitations, Kohut largely succeeded in replacing the former technique of close attention to the ego and its defense mechanisms with a focus on the self and its dependency on selfobjects (a function of the other on which the self depends). As a conse-quence, the treatment focused on a patient's need for a reparative relationship in the here and now, where lived experience prevails over the specific choices of language to express it and the presence of the self over structures extrinsic to individual consciousness. Many analysts influenced by Kohut hold to a search for an authentic or core self to be affirmed or restored in treatment.

Stolorow's "intersubjective psychoanalysis"

A student of Kohut, Robert Stolorow, took a further step with his reformulation of psychoanalysis, explicitly organized around the concept of intersubjectivity. If not the father of the use of the term, as claimed by H. Tessier (2004) in her discussion of the intricate themes of empathy and intersubjectivity in American psychoanalysis, he may have been unique in building his theory on phenom-enology. In an inaugural text, Stolorow (1984) accentuated the "experience-near" dimension of psychoanalysis, to which Kohut (1959) had drawn attention in his early writings on empathy, the very opposite of classical metapsychology. His paper argued that self psychology had liberated psychoanalysis from its Procrustean bed—a bed of materialism, determinism, and mechanism—which Stolorow criticized as a residue of nineteenth-century biology that Freud bequeathed to psychoanalysis.

Stolorow gradually moved beyond or away from Kohut by prioritizing the intersubjective situation over developmental formulations or models of internal object relations that the analyst might diagnose and interpret. He presented the core of intersubjectivity as the conjunction or the disjunction of psychic repre-sentations between analyst and patient (Stolorow, 1986). According to him, two types of "inevitable" clinical situations represent the dynamic poles of the relation-ship. In the former, the analyst identifies with the representations and affects of his patient, usually when the "central configurations" of each are sufficiently similar. In the latter, a basic misunderstanding alters the subjective meaning of the material expressed by the patient and prevents the analyst's use of his empathic function. These situations describe the back-and-forth flux of the therapeutic process.

In their book, *Structures of Subjectivity*, Stolorow and Atwood (1984) lay out their basic thesis, which they derived from the phenomenologists, notably the work of Husserl. They write:

> The psychoanalytic treatment seeks to illuminate phenomena that emerge in a specific psychological field, created by a dialogue between two subjectivities – that of the patient and of the analyst. In this conceptualization, psychoanalysis is no longer regarded as a science of the intrapsychic, concentrated on isolated events in a 'mental apparatus'. Nor is it designed as a social science, which would study 'behavioral facts' of the therapeutic interaction seen from a vantage point outside the field studied. Psychoanalysis is rather described by us as the science of the intersubjective, centered on the interplay between the differently organized subjective worlds of observer and the observed.

This work was followed by *Psychoanalytic Treatment: An Intersubjective Approach* (Stolorow, Atwood, & Brandchaft, 1987) in which the authors advocated positions going further than the most radical proposals of Kohut, arguing that psychoanalysis should exclude any and all metapsychology or importations into psychoanalysis from other disciplines. Henceforth, they insisted, the analyst's task would remain confined to the intersubjective field. For example, he should resist the temptation to adopt a supposedly "objective" position as expert or even any pretense to knowledge superior to that of the patient (echoing Lacan's rejection of the *sujet supposé savoir*—the presumed subject of knowledge). Instead, psychoanalysis would define itself affirmatively as "the science of the intersubjective," based on the two subjective worlds of observer and the observed (Stolorow, 1988). The analyst's place is always already in the intersubjective field, and introspection and empathy alone represent his preferred methods (ibid., p. 41). "Clinical phenomena can not be understood outside their intersubjective context," wrote Stolorow. "The analyst and the patient together form an indissoluble psychological system, and this system constitutes the empirical field of analytical praxis" (ibid., p. 64).

In a 1986 article, "Critical reflections on the theory of Self Psychology: An inside view," Stolorow restated his differences with Kohut. He took a categorical position: no link between psychoanalysis and the natural sciences and no support from extrinsic knowledge acquired by practitioners or researchers. Remnants of metapsychological formulations like supposed drives at work in the mind have nothing to do, he asserted, with the actual intersubjective relationship or, importantly, the primacy of affect in this relation. The self, insisted Stolorow, is not a structure (as Kohut claimed), but rather an experience. The notion of a relationship between an entity named the "self" and another called the "other," as presented by object relations theories, promote a "reification" or "mechanization" of the intersubjective field. Likewise, the method of reconstruction of a developmental history and the corollary positing of structural deficits in the personality belong to the old model of an expert analyst imposing his authority. Anything that is not capable of being grasped in the direct experience of the cure, Stolorow concludes, belongs to an imaginary domain outside the legitimate field of psychoanalysis.

Stolorow's radical effort to reorient the practice of those analysts influenced by the psychology of the self toward his version of intersubjectivity had significant impact, while remaining a minority position on the American scene. Renik (1993), for example, spoke for many analysts in endorsing Stolorow's proposal of an "irreducible subjectivity" in the analyst that precludes any claim to Hartmann's scientific objectivity or to the unbiased application of metapsychology to an individual patient. Certainly, Stolorow was correct that the early objective of discerning fundamental structures of the psyche and interpreting implicit and unconscious motives of patients has proven chimerical, and this means that the analyst must forego reliance on a theory of the mind to ground his work.[2] For Renik (1998), theory serves only the interests of the particular analyst—again, to preserve his authority and power. Given that the possibility of analytic neutrality is illusory, the most ethical position for the clinician would be, he said, "to show his cards"—i.e. to disclose his prejudices and personal preferences. The antitheoretical position of Renik, which might look like a *reductio ad absurdum*, expanded a self-evident, partial truth into a universal reality. His papers stirred discussion, perhaps more than Stolorow's theoretically more complex proposals at the time. Ultimately, they pose the challenge to traditional psychoanalysis of whether clinical practice amounts to more than the compassionate and empathic participation of a reasonably stable, authentic, and educated clinician. What more can the analyst provide?

Although unfair to the sophistication of Stolorow's intersubjective psychoanalysis, Renik's ideas exposed the limits of a phenomenologic approach. The issue involves phenomenology's rejection of the Cartesian conception of the subject as an internal observer trying to make sense of representations of the outer world in favor of the immediacy of subjective knowledge posited by Husserl and Heidegger. Do we need to analyze and interpret subjective experience to understand its sources or can we rely on our empathic capacities to enter into it? The phenomenologists' perspective on empathy as inherent in intersubjective experience flows from their observation that from birth we are immersed in the world of others. The palpable truth of this assertion must be balanced against our equally valid experience of otherness and the effort required to understand another person. The pertinent question concerns the nature of the perceiving consciousness, already raised by many philosophers. Does not the unconditioned conscious "for-itself" proposed by Sartre (the *pour-soi*) filter its experience through categories, motives, and desires that are opaque to perception and thereby call for a hermeneutic of interpretation, a deconstruction of the frames used by the subject to organize his experience? The importance of language as a mediating perception (by providing the terms that define experiences) suggests that analysts need to explore the connections of a patient's words to his personal history. Hoy and Durt (2011), for example, critique Husserl's "foundationalist" concept of the perceived "life-world" in which we are embedded, as assuming a presuppositional bottom stratum that grounds us in reality. "Even our most basic experiences," they comment, "are structured by language and therefore open to interpretation" (ibid., p. 24). Can psychoanalysts conceive of a person without an unconscious and unrepresented desires? These contentious points have not been resolved by philosophers, a conclusion that suggests to me the necessity for a dual (or perhaps dialectic) approach between phenomenology and psychology, including but not limited to Stolorow's model.

Relational psychoanalysis

Current psychoanalytic practice has perhaps been influenced most by the contemporary relational movement (with which Renik came to identify), whose roots lie outside the Freudian establishment. The lawsuit which led the American Psychoanalytic Association to abandon its policy of exclusion of non-physicians was a major step in opening its societies to new ideas,[3] recently marked by the inclusion of the William Alanson White Society among member institutes (see Stern, 2015, for a discussion of the rejection of Sullivan and Fromm's concept of an interpersonal field by the American). The broad grouping of relational analysts comprises a number of theoretical subdivisions. For the purposes of this condensed discussion, I divide them into two principal categories: 1) analysts outside the American Psychoanalytic Association, trained primarily in independent institutes growing out of a Sullivanian tradition, and 2) infant researchers working in laboratories of developmental psychology.

Following Sullivan, interpersonal analysts repudiated the drive-defense model dear to classic ego psychology, stigmatizing the classic theory as "a one-person psychology," artificially isolated from the interpersonal and social matrix of subjectivity. The relational shift, as its name indicates, redirected therapeutic attention to the reciprocal relationship between analyst and patient, and especially the influence of the subjectivity of the analyst—a two-person psychology. Relational analysts saw the effectiveness of the treatment and the possibility of beneficial results as growing out of the here and now of personal interactions. Already distanced from the medical identity, models of psychopathology, and the hierarchical style which characterized institutional psychoanalysis of the postwar period, they advocated a more interactive and spontaneous participation by the analyst. On the other hand, while opposing the notion that analysts could function as relatively detached diagnosticians and interpreters of reality, the emerging relational school incorporated many aspects of the Freudian theory of intrapsychic processes, albeit in revised forms.

The appearance of Greenberg and Mitchell's (1983) landmark work on comparative theories of object relations constituted an important moment in the history of psychoanalysis in the United States. The work was original both by its ambition to summarize the major contributions in this area and by the quality of its research and arguments. Widely read and included in many institute curricula, it marked a symbolic end of the era of ego psychology and anticipated the rise of the intersubjective paradigm. In its wake, several alternatives were now open to American psychoanalysis. The school of Kohut retained its adherents, but, in the end, the psychology of the self revealed its limitations—in particular, having evolved without reference to Winnicott, Klein, Fairbairn, Green, Modell, and others who productively explored the territory of narcissism and subjectivity. Mitchell and Greenberg argued for a progression away from Freudian metapsychology toward an emphasis on relationships in psychoanalytic theory. In their view, self psychology lacked the explanatory concepts of object relations models, while the concept of "self" proved insufficient to establish an adequate framework for psychoanalysis. They noted that Kohut's theory of the "selfobject" (an object that performs a function of the self) was already implicit in Winnicottian theory (at the stage of "object relating"). In addition, they supported Stolorow's position that the psychology of the "selfobject" lacks a place for a dynamic relationship between two separate subjects.

Perhaps the growing critique of the drive-defense models of ego psychology and of Kleinian (and other) object relations theories as representing "one-person psychologies" also helps explain the revival of interest in Lacan and Bion by American analysts. Brown's (2011) important book on intersubjectivity presents a Bionian interpretation stressing unconscious communication in therapeutic interaction that must be contained and transformed by the analyst into symbolic elements. This dynamic builds on early exchanges in which the mother takes in unrepresented alpha elements, processes them, and supplies meanings that enable the child to begin to think. Brown integrates the complexities of Bionian field theory with relational concepts. Levine (2012) uses Bion to argue for a revised view of the analytic encounter, emphasizing the interactive process, rather than its specific content. Although his ideas transcend the focus of this chapter, Bion's current interpreters share an interest in infant and neuroscience research with the relational analysts I discuss below (see Civitarese & Ferro, 2013).

Intersubjectivity in relational psychoanalysis: Aron and Benjamin

Many analysts from the relational movement have moved from interpersonal theory to develop models of intersubjective psychoanalysis. The psychologists Aron, Benjamin, Davies, Ehrenberg, Ghent, Hoffman, and Stern are among the most frequently cited. For purposes of this chapter, I focus on two influential authors whose work raises several crucial issues for analytic therapists and which I find most compatible with my own perspective—Jessica Benjamin, Professor at the New School for Social Research in New York and the Postgraduate Program in Psychoanalysis at New York University, and Lewis Aron, Professor of Clinical Psychology and also a teacher at the Postdoctoral Program. As they are collaborators who regularly cite each other's work in numerous publications, I discuss their contributions together, although I refer to individual papers.

In her important book, *The Bonds of Love*, Benjamin (1988) relied heavily on the tradition of European philosophy, including her own elaboration of the parable of the master and slave in Hegel's Philosophy of the Spirit. Her philosophical background and her reading of French feminists reflect a sociological and anthropological inspiration, influenced by her training at the Frankfurt School. In *The Bonds of Love*, she attributes the term intersubjectivity to Habermas, who used the phrase "intersubjectivity of mutual understanding." She notes that this expression was adopted by the pioneering infant researcher, Colin Trevarthen, to describe the baby's communication of its intentions to the mother and their reciprocal protoconversations. For Benjamin (1990, 1995, 1999, 2004, 2010), intersubjectivity refers both to a capacity of the infant that can be directly observed and a theoretical concept that challenges models of mental functioning confined to the intrapsychic. Her debt to the infant developmental research of Trevarthen, Emde, Beebe, and Stern shows clearly throughout her writing (similar to many contributors to the relational movement). Freudian concepts based on analyses of adults involve the substantially different dynamics of intrapsychic processes and constitute a separate field of inquiry for Benjamin. Although she emphasizes the effects of interactions between subjects in preference to intra-psychic conflicts, she admits that this theory "in which the individual subject is no longer supreme must confront the difficulty for each subject in recognizing the other as a center of experience equal to itself"(Benjamin 1995, p. 28).

Benjamin redefines the traditional concept of object relations to describe an ongoing interaction between two subjects, rather than representations of objects within the mind of one person or between a subject and another person taken as object. Like Stolorow, she presents a straightforward definition of psychoanalytic intersubjectivity as "the field where two different subjective worlds intersect" (ibid., p. 29). Of course, this statement can convey a simple tautology without specifying the implications of the terms "field" and "subjective worlds," which cover a set of extremely diverse notions. A field can mean simply an area of study, a locus of social negotiation, or a metaphor from physics or computer science, suggesting well-defined numerical parameters (Civitarese & Ferro, 2013). Benjamin's conception of "the third" (discussed below) reflects her emphasis on the "intersection," the joint construction of an experience by both analyst and patient to which each participant brings a personal history, sometimes involving an intermixing or blurring of psychic boundaries. The sharing aspect seems central to her position.

Aron's articles (1991, 1992, 1997, 1999) present a nuanced conception of analytical work divided between attention paid to the development of a singular subject, in which the analyst's focus remains closer to a traditional intrapsychic model, and that devoted to intersubjectivity, following a relational model. In the latter, the analyst hears every association as a communication, interpretation, or attempt to influence him, rather than simply as evidence of psychic processes. Aron stresses that each analysis is mutual; like the analyst, the patient constantly tries to understand the intentions and desires of his interlocutor and to communicate their effects as he experiences them. Although he acknowledges that there are times when an analyst must be silent to devote his listening to the solitary work of his patient (who seeks to reconstruct, for example, early life experiences), in general the analyst is implicated in these efforts. Moreover, the force of enlightenment and transformation in the cure depends largely on the analyst's ability to put himself in question. He must always consider the possibility that the patient's transference behaviors may be a response to his own unconscious messages (conveyed in words and affects). Here, one can infer the influence of Ferenczi's attention to the effect of the analyst's behavior on patients (he warned how the analyst can unwittingly repeat a trauma) in relational theories. Aron (1992) has developed this connection in several papers, which argue that transference can be addressed within the here and now of clinical interaction, not simply viewed as a repetition of the past.[4] From the principle of transference reciprocity as a mutual entanglement, Aron moves inevitably to consider the advantages and problems arising from the analyst's disclosures of his own thoughts and feelings. He warns that if the analytic situation is indeed mutual, a claim to neutrality by the analyst or a pretense of non-involvement in the transference can have the violent effect of non-recognition and disavowal. But if he intervenes by revealing his thoughts to the analysand ("showing his cards"), what guarantees that he does not inflict as much violence?

In general, relational psychoanalysts appear sympathetic to self-disclosure, but its practice varies widely among practitioners. For Aron (1991), revealing the analyst's subjectivity at a basic level of interaction is an inevitable occurrence in every therapy, if often unwitting and unconscious. Intentional communications, however, must be tempered by an ethic of respect for the otherness of the patient and recognition of the risks of intentional intrusion into his private world. Therapists who employ self-disclosure should be wary of falling into a form of hidden suggestion or authoritarian pressure (because of the transferential asymmetry of the analytic relationship). After all, as Ferenczi learned in his experiments with mutual analysis, the mutuality extends only so far; as much as analysts reject the traditional expert role, they cannot easily avoid being placed in the position of knowledgeable authority in the patient's transference. While analytic therapists themselves may undergo significant psychological changes as a consequence of clinical interactions, the process remains inherently unequal and asymmetrical.

Aron suggests circumstances in which the analyst may usefully express her own ideas or admit some of her feelings, but these are circumstances that do not relate to charged autobiographical material. He proposes self-disclosure of the analyst as a means of opening up a patient's awareness of the intersubjective dimension by permitting him to compare his new experience in analysis with former relationships. At the same time, Aron repeatedly modulates this emphasis on analytical revelation, acknowledging that an analyst cannot claim to know himself well enough to confirm or refute the truth of his self-disclosures nor to validate his understanding of his participation in transference reactions. To deal with this key problem and to prevent an overheating of the dual relationship in the transference, Aron (2006) and Benjamin (2004) find recourse in the concept of "the third" and have collaborated on how varieties of a third position function in clinical practice.

Many theorists from Lacan to Ogden have employed the notion of a third position or a triangulation of the subject-to-subject encounter to avoid a blind entanglement in a transference configuration. Lacan (1953) advanced the concept of the paternal metaphor, the *nom du père* (a pun on the "no" or the name of the father), as introducing a third element into the process of subjectivation. The symbolic name of the father opens a level beyond the mother–infant dyad that inscribes the nascent subject in the family system and culture. Benjamin rejects Lacan's structural conception of the paternal metaphor, which she apparently views as requiring the presence of an actual father (Aron 2006, p. 357). Ogden reformulates the analytic third as an intersubjective creation, noting that "at the same time the analyst and analysand (qua analyst and analysand) are created by the analytic third (there is no analyst, no analysand, and no analysis in the absence of the third)" (1994, p. 16).

The analyst's access to a third position represents a step beyond the interpersonal or relational providing the means to escape from a Hegelian clash of selves over power and dominance or the dead end of rigid complementarity. Benjamin has added different forms of the analytic third (summarized in Aron, 2006). In the type she calls "one in the third," a specific rhythm belonging to each pair represents the third, like a quasi-musical unit composed by the couple over the course of an analysis. This form of third, similar to Ogden's, constitutes a shared construction unique to each therapy that an analyst can turn to as a counterpoint to her individual role responsiveness and private fantasies. In the second type, "the third in the one," Benjamin describes a decentering of the analyst that enables her to gain another perspective on her countertransference, moving away from the lived experience of the therapy to take the independent viewpoint of something learned in training or supervision. One might say that there are many "thirds in the one," many subjectivities in each person. Aron also mentions an "intentional third" to "create a space for differentiation" (2006, p. 356).

According to Aron (2006), access to a third enables an analyst to interpret the transference–countertransference complementarity by directly acknowledging his oscillation between positions. From a third position he can tell the patient how he sees himself responding and link the similarity of this behavior to a former object relationship. The tendency to slip into a dyadic mirroring, usefully redefined as complementarity by Benjamin (1999), becomes a huge problem looming over any relational treatment anchored in the here and now.[5] In the Lacanian model, analytic process should open from a constricted imaginary dyad of projected fantasies onto a symbolic triadic space where the unconscious appears in the spontaneous flow of speech.

Aron (2006) describes several examples of an analyst finding another perspective on his participation in a transference within his own mind—the "third in the one" model. This way of gaining self-awareness is not always made explicit in discussions of technique. To feel trapped or even unable to think clearly in a specific interaction, to search for ways to escape a recurring dynamic configuration during a therapeutic hour, to entertain simultaneously multiple theoretical models, or to be reminded of the words of former supervisors represent familiar aspects of clinical experience. But ultimately, do these concepts of a third represent something other than an attempt to deal with an increasing enmeshment in the intersubjective transference process by attempting to construe what is transpiring? As Jacobs (1993, 1999)[6] writes, unconscious communication largely exceeds the interpersonal and conscious awareness of both participants, rendering the aim of analytic mastery of countertransference unachievable. The use of the concept of a third by relational analysts constitutes a strong attempt to escape entanglement in a complementary dyad, but may itself become a resistance to the therapeutic process (by lending itself to conscious rationalization or to a preferred theoretical formulation). While undoubtedly useful in situations of impasse and paralysis (I employ the concept in Chapters 6 and 8), the phenomenology of an imagined or remembered third does not succeed in resolving the inherent intersubjective problem of sustaining presence without imposition. Access to a concept of the third may help the analyst decenter from a repetitive complementary role response or a prolonged enactment, but calls for further deconstruction. Aron makes the important point: "I do not think of the third as describing a kind of analytic space that exists free of enactment" (2006, p. 362).

Benjamin may be best known for her work on intersubjective recognition. "Intersubjective theory," she writes, "postulates that the other must be recognized as another subject in order for the self to fully experience his or her subjectivity in the other's presence. This means, first, that we have a need for recognition and second, that we have a capacity to recognize others in return—mutual recognition" (Benjamin, 1990, p. 34). Like Stolorow, she builds on concepts from phenomenology, but differs in her dual attention to the intrapsychic and the intersubjective domains. She employs Winnicott's distinction between subjective and objective objects, as well as Mahler's ideas about separation and rapprochement to support her point about the differentiation and separateness of subjects. Her formulation returns us to the Hegelian dilemma of an encounter between two subjects (reminiscent of Modell's earlier analysis) in which the other can affirm but also negate. Recognition of another subject may feel immediate and unmediated in some circumstances, but in adults at least (perhaps even with infants) it vies with private wishes and faces the Sartrean "sting from the encounter with otherness" (ibid., 1990, p. 43). "The reason I brought Hegel into this scenario was certainly not because I wanted to conflate the persons who come to psychotherapy with Hegel's 'self-consciousness,' but because there is an inherent challenge for human beings in depending for love, recognition, and care on others they cannot control" (Benjamin, 2010, p. 251). Benjamin elaborates her position on mutuality and difference in a debate with Orange, who criticizes her for endorsing an unequal power relationship and insisting on the patient's recognition of the analyst. "To see another person as a separate and equivalent center of being can be so relieving," Benjamin responds (2010, p. 249), "I find it hard to identify with Orange's descriptions." Although she denies imposing reciprocity on the patient, Benjamin's commitment to the existential value of recognition seems inherently to involve the goal of mutuality and sharing in the therapeutic relation.

I fully endorse the importance of recognition in intersubjective theory as I develop in Chapter 8. Nonetheless, what we mean by this highly abstract concept remains subject to numerous interpretations. From an ethical, social, philosophical standpoint, acknowledgement of the other as a human being like ourselves ("a separate and equivalent center of being") is a fundamental principle. Recognition like this remains problematic or non-existent in the political or societal sphere, especially in authoritarian countries where relations of power and domination predominate or when racial, ethnic, sexual and other stigmas are highlighted. Benjamin (2011) brings her analytic perspective to these situations in her work on witnessing and collective trauma. In the psychotherapy situation in which many values and assumptions are shared, I suspect that basic existential recognition as indicated by acceptance of personal boundaries, the professional set-up, and common courtesies are more typical (although survivors of personal trauma will often test this frame). Benjamin also refers to "recognition of fundamental needs and feelings" (2005, p. 447) and of "others' intentions" (p. 448), both of which raise problems of objectification of a subject struggling to contain complex and ambivalent attitudes.

However mutual the socially structured therapeutic role may be, the analytic situation encourages a patient to use his analyst for transference and, by implication, to treat him as an object to control or manipulate for defensive or libidinal purposes. The analyst's role requires active management of such tendencies when they emerge and receptivity to their content, especially when repugnant to him. The deepening of psychotherapy typically reveals the otherness of a patient's values, tastes, and choices, which challenge an analyst's non-judgmental acceptance and usually stimulate countertransferential resistances that need to be worked through. Lacan pointed to this impediment to analytic process, designating respect for the alterity of subjects (and their idiosyncratic desires) as a basic ethical objective of training. Bearing a patient's mistaken or accurate perceptions of one's way of life, sexual habits, moral values, and beliefs and eschewing needs for affirmation or affection from him belong to this ethical obligation. But while the end of treatment may bring a decrease in idealization or devaluation and a more "realistic" perception of the therapist as an ordinary human being, should clinicians strive for attaining mutuality? Aron makes it clear that "mutuality does not imply symmetry or equality" (1997, p. 893). Like Benjamin (2010), he may be thinking about the primary intersubjectivity of the parent–child relationship (which is unequal and asymmetric). However, translating from the limited mutuality that characterizes early development to more complex symbolic relationships suggests a category mistake.

The kind of personal recognition that subjects seek in intimate relationships like psychoanalysis operates at a different level from seeing the other as an equal partner. Analytic listening and responsiveness can generate a feeling in some patients of being recognized, as a by-product of a positive interaction and idealization, but the substance of the recognition remains vague. Who or what is recognized and by what figure? Does a reification of the self reappear in this guise? The affective signs of recognition convey sameness and mutual mirroring, which may tilt in the direction of an unproductive narcissistic affirmation of an image (for both analyst and patient), a kind of collusion in an imaginary harmony. Dialogic speech, progressing beyond the equivocal and ambiguous utterances, smiles, and stereotypic hmms and ahs of therapeutic interaction, inevitably disappoints the subject's narcissistic longing for recognition. The analyst says not enough or not quite what a patient expects or too much. At such moments, the framework of responsive listening (and basic recognition of the other) may be temporarily disrupted and in need of repair.

A stress on mutuality may be a differentiating feature of relational theories and a useful counterpoint to the authoritarian position they reject in classical models. When presented as an intention of the therapist, however, significant problems arise. Wilson has explored the neglected issue of the analyst's desire, seldom mentioned in discussions of the mutuality of recognition. He observes, "the analyst cannot help but have desires and want them recognized by the analysand" (2003, p. 71). The problem for Wilson lies in an over-immersion in the dyadic relationship, which stimulates imaginary fantasies and promotes a lack of differentiation. Lacan's (1959–60) seminar on ethics placed the successfully treated analyst beyond the temptation of desiring any gratification from the patient, but spoke of an impossible desire for recognition as a motor for the transference. I find his confidence in the analysed clinician's immunity to imaginary desires unrealistic (and even counter-therapeutic). Lacan himself frequently insisted on the importance of the analyst having, but not acting on, strong feelings about his patient, but this acknowledgement calls for more than restraint. The analyst's wishes, as Wilson argues, may inflect the therapeutic relationship in many ways.

The non-talking cure

In this section, I focus on a tendency in contemporary psychoanalysis to privilege implicit, non-verbal interactions over the traditional speaking relationship. As noted, many authors cite infant research as evidence for a relational approach. Trevarthen's influential concept of primary intersubjectivity drew attention to the intentional interactions of early childhood, which reflect inborn capacities and demonstrate how early exchanges between mother and infant are charged with meaning and operate in reciprocity. Certainly, when we observe a baby playing with its mother, we see all the signs of good attunement or derailing, mutuality or conflict that are aspects of any adult relationship. Moreover, attachment research shows that some relational elements remain consistent from childhood to maturity. From this evidence, it takes only a step to reconceptualize psychoanalysis so that the talking cure with its emphasis on speech and dialogue cedes place to a non-verbal dynamic.

The Boston Change Process Study Group (2007) calls this non-verbal aspect of relationships an "implicit relational knowing," which they applied to therapeutic interactions (a position modified in subsequent papers by an appreciation of the verbal dimension). Yet, as noted above, taking the problematic step of transposing the parent–infant relationship onto the analyst–patient relationship raises serious questions about technique. This analogy has been explicit in the publications of many relational analysts and self psychologists, in whose writings the model of primary intersubjectivity as a pre-symbolic interaction sometimes eclipses subsequent developmental steps toward a complex, triangular intersubjectivity. Moreover, infant–mother interactions are not simply examples of innate biological mechanisms, but involve a semiotic process organized by language. Language itself does not arise spontaneously from an inherited universal grammar, but requires maternal proto-dialogues. The child relies at first on index and iconic signs, which signify the mother's responsive presence, before acquiring the capacity for verbal communication. Concurrently, as Muller (1996) argues in his groundbreaking integration of Trevarthen and Aitken's research (2001) with Lacanian semiotics, the maternal language organizes the entire interactional field, providing an intense training in the use of symbols.[7] Lacan observed that before the learning of language the semiotic field maps the mother's function which represents "the human world" (Muller, 1996, p. 113). In the process of subjectivation, the child learns a code that structures (often retrospectively, as in the *après-coup*) his position as a speaking subject. Meanwhile, the mother's experience is mediated (constructed) by her history, desires, and fears, much as Benjamin suggests, so that preverbal attunement and implicit knowing between her and her child does not by its early appearance in life necessarily bypass cognitive and affective semantic processes.

An additional problem with applying infant studies to intersubjectivity in older subjects concerns the question, "attunement with whom?" Who is the subject of this implicit harmony? Of course, therapists encounter experiences like the "moments of meeting" the Boston Change Process Study Group (2007) evocatively describe, but can that feeling of resonance or sense of recognition be equated with the earliest inscribed, presymbolic patterns of attachment, almost ethologic in quality? The assumption that attunement takes place in the present (rather than evoking a fantasy of a lost object, for example) reinforces this omission of history, as if it describes a kind of mirroring of the phenomenological self (Stern, 2002). The feeling of mutual recognition seems likely to arise from the expression of iconic signs that produce an experience of sameness or oneness, as Muller has proposed.

If the analogy between baby and patient can be traced to roots in the "genetic" metapsychology of Freud (through the concept of early fixation), it remains that Winnicott presented this model directly by treating the clinical set-up as a scene of explicit regression. In clinical cases reported by Winnicott, the sequential modalities of object use (as a subjective object, a part of the self, or as a real objective object) become central to the process of subjectivation. A baby begins to draw the boundary of a self separate from others as he recognizes his mother's survival as an independent subject despite his ruthless, aggressive fantasies (Winnicott, 1969). For Winnicott initially and many writers since, psychopathology grows principally out of early maternal failures like non-responsiveness or impingement that can be identified through the transference. Some patients alert their therapist to the problem by saying that they don't feel seen (perhaps a kind of helpful supervision if accepted). Nonetheless, a formulation of impairment derived from identifying the point of interrupted development appears for better or worse to belong to the classic (reconstructive) model. Formulations from the standpoint of developmental theory, rather than from an intersubjective stance, violate Stolorow's criteria by importing extra-analytic knowledge and can reinforce a complementary dyad in which the analyst takes a third person (subject to object) view that defines the patient. The analyst then becomes an observer, rather than a participant. Can intersubjective theory ever be compatible with the reconstruction of early events and the objectifying position necessary to this task? When the analyst views his patient essentially as a baby, their relationship must be affected, even if he does not attempt directly to repair early deficits in mothering. Such was Green's critique of analysis modeled on the maternal provision.[8] Surely the infantile appears only in its present-day derivatives, highly influenced by later motivations, identifications, and life experiences that are woven into the fabric of the subject.

In attempting to speak to the residues of the transformed infantile, a therapist must navigate between the pitfalls of retraumatization and seduction to avoid imposition of his own psychic reality on his patient. After all, a growing awareness of the unreliability of interpretations and their source in countertransference and theoretical affiliation was what brought about the reorientation toward an intersubjective approach. A combined approach of interpersonal and intersubjective models presents the crucial problem for analysts of how to use the past (as reported, inferred, or reconstructed) intersubjectively. Analysts attempt to solve it in different ways.

The varied applications of the term "intersubjectivity" by different clinicians is the theme of Beebe et al.'s (2005) book *Forms of Intersubjectivity in Infant Research and the Treatment of Adults*. Beebe, an analyst of the Institute for the Psychoanalytic Study of Intersubjectivity, is frequently cited for her studies of face-to-face play between mother and child, where she has used video recordings to perform microanalyses of their interactions. She concludes that each relational partner influences or adapts itself to the other in an implicit and unconscious manner. She comments that those who rely on observations from infant research (like the Boston group) and those whose concept of intersubjectivity derives mainly from psychoanalyses of adults (like analysts influenced by Bion) or the logic of phenomenologic models (Stolorow) take different perspectives (the book describes a few). For this reason, she and her colleagues propose that "intersubjectivity" be replaced by "forms of intersubjectivity," which they categorize according to the theory of dynamic systems.

In all its forms, illustrated in their book through the help of a simple pictoral diagram, the adjective "intersubjective" is applied to a variety of conceptions of what is going on in the interaction of two minds—a dyadic system—throughout life. The particular version Beebe's group favors emphasizes reciprocity and equivalence of influence between the two partners, familiar to studies of infants and mothers. In the psychoanalysis of adults, they acknowledge, each subject brings its prior expectations and its ways of engaging with the other, which inevitably influence the emerging dynamic system of the couple. They hypothesize that the verbal and symbolic relationship rests on a pre-verbal base, the two levels representing a simultaneous adaptation of the system.

Beebe illustrates her model by the case of "Dolores," a patient extremely sensitive to her perception of the facial expressions of the other. To protect herself against a repetition of early relationship trauma, Dolores withdrew as a child from all intimate ties (while her professional life and ability to maintain distant, friendly relations remained more or less intact). The report of her analysis indicates that the corrective experience of treatment enabled her to acquire a new form of relating. According to the neuroscientifically oriented commentator, R. Pally, the psychic change in Dolores was effected at a "procedural" level—i.e. non-representational and implicit. She adds that in psychoanalysis "an emotional and nonverbal exchange can play as important a role as a verbal interpretation" (in Beebe et al., 2005, p. 199).

Pally's position, like the early claims of the Boston Group, is consistent with Trevarthen's original model of primary intersubjectivity, which does not depend on unconscious wishes and fantasies or the symbolic structures of language. Instead, the substance of the intersubjective exchange resides in the music of attunement analogous to an ethological level that can be observed in social animals. Studies of groups of monkeys demonstrate the major effects of the mother–child relationship on the future of the offspring consistent with this viewpoint, which amounts to a naturalized view of human intersubjectivity (as already part of endowment at birth). Clinical case studies like Beebe's that take this standpoint on implicit reciprocity come close to leaving the impression that language and all the baggage of human culture have been grafted onto a set of behaviors genetically programmed to regulate the functioning of primate societies.

In the 1970s, the American anthropologist Birdwhistell (1970) first used video recordings to show that therapists participate in a kind of dance with their patients, seemingly in search of mutually compatible physical positions, although without knowing it. His studies on the science of kinesthetics stressed that the social personality is a space–time system involving movement and rhythm. Roughly only a third of the content of a therapeutic conversation is transmitted through words, he concluded, while the bulk is negotiated through kinesics. Using similar video techniques, infant researchers like Beebe perform microanalyses of interactions between babies and mothers, and the Boston child analyst Alexandra Harrison (2005) studies moments of change in the psychotherapy of her young patients. A video analysis of a session with a 7-year-old boy reveals the onset of very rapid symmetrical movements between Harrison and her patient that preceded and, perhaps, paved the way for her verbal intervention after a long silent period of apparent non-relatedness between them. Their implicit or procedural interaction anticipated a shift toward mutuality before it became part of her conscious awareness.

Pally (Beebe et al., 2005) reminds us that neuroscience confirms the registration of experiences by unconscious pathways that are inaccessible to reflection (recalling the work on mirror neurons). In his research, Stern (2002) found indications that presymbolic systems evolve independently of the psychic organization of the symbolic system. Stern and the Boston Change Process Study Group (2007) argue that the healing process of analysis may be more accurately explained by the effect of non-verbal communications on the implicit (procedural) operations of the patient, rather than by explicit interventions. Like Pally, they conclude that the actions of the analyst can lead to changes in behaviors of patients that rely on procedural memory, without any explicit interpretation being made. Along with this widespread interest in the implicit, one finds a mistrust of metapsychological theories and an attempt to found an intersubjective clinical practice on the basis of scientific data. Here, where neuroscience and infant research join in constructing biological models of intersubjectivity, a hybrid form of naturalisation of the subject appears. The mother–infant dialogue and its physiologic basis in the brain (empathy, mirror neurons, procedural learning) as natural products of evolution then replace the radical psychoanalytic notion of the unique emergence of the subject as an effect of symbolic meanings and transformations.

We might ask whether the notion of independent operations of two brain systems—one non-verbal and in-born, the other a symbolic structure—matches the reality of the organization of the brain/psyche. One might equally assume that reciprocity between levels of processing experience occurs consistently throughout the development of the child, making it impossible to assign a behavior to a particular system. As the neuroscientists Park and Ichinose (2015) observe, "We adapt to our environment through personal, contextualized learning", not through impersonal mechanisms of attunement. The form of attachment, for example, becomes inextricably entangled over time with the sexual, with the child's interpretation of parental messages, with the influence of family structures pervading the culture, and with the internalization of important signifiers that accompany the child's development from before birth. The infant's immersion in semiotic exchanges does not require its linguistic competence to shape the subjectivation process. As Vivona (2006) has observed, noting the tendency to emphasize non-verbal aspects of the therapeutic process, language is not simply a set of abstract symbols, but is deeply rooted in the body (an observation also made by

Lacan). "Understanding that we are born into language," concludes Litowitz (2011), "refocuses our attention on the ways that specific features mediate our relationships with others and with the world, reestablishing an intrapsychic dimension to the concept of relationship." Freud wrote that the human subject was both a function of transmitted culture and language (carrying the history of the chain of generations) and biological imperatives (pursuing survival and reproduction). In a later piece, Vivona (2009) recalls that the frequent reference to the research of Rizzolatti and Gallese on mirror neurons to support the importance of implicit communications (in the countertransference, for example) leaps quickly from empirical results of diverse experiments to applying them to the much different work of psychoanalysis. Psychoanalysis has historically possessed the particularity of highlighting the dimension of meaning, the semiotic network on which all human societies depend. The analyst's evident non-verbal participation in the negotiation of a shared space does not change the fact that the entire treatment exists within a languaged world that makes us speaking subjects, not simply interacting animals.

Conclusions

This condensed summary indicates the complex evolution of the concept of intersubjectivity in American psychoanalysis. The term was adopted and used by psychoanalysts beginning in the 1960s to fill gaps in a theory that did not seem to take full account of the impact of the analyst on the process of treatment and to support relational approaches to patients. The confused and confusing debate between one-person and two-person psychologies derives from this distinction. During this same time period, the search for a scientific support for psychoanalysis turned to infant research and, soon after, to the neurosciences, both of which were used to support an intersubjective perspective.

In terms of its current use, I have tried to trace two major currents in this complex field: one, typified by Stern and Stolorow, has been more antagonistic to traditional psychoanalytic theory, while the other, represented by Aron and Benjamin, attempts to work in continuity with its historical concepts. Across all schools, the intersubjective paradigm has led analysts to recognize the impact of their own activity, including personal style, gestures, language, and affects, in the unfolding of the analytical process. The analyst is engaged in an intersubjective construction of his experience that extends well beyond his conscious control. I have criticized interpretations of this construction that privilege non-symbolic (implicit) interactions or biological mechanisms (like mirror systems). Analysis remains a talking cure, based on semiotic exchanges that carry meaning, shaped by language and culture (discussed in Chapter 8) and involving the individual subjectivities of each participant. How to create a new model of psychoanalysis that encompasses all these elements challenges and enlivens contemporary practice.

Notes

1. Freud's comments about the effects of one unconscious on another, beginning in his 1912 paper, Recommendations to Physicians Practicing Psychoanalysis *SE* XII, 109–120, have been interpreted in different ways. For some, this type of communication is fundamental to intersubjective relations (Brown, 2011), but there are other ways to interpret Freud's observations (see Geerardyn, 2002).
2. Here, the influence of the postmodern is clear. From Lyotard's grand narratives to the principles of Freudian psychanalysis, systems of explanation proved inadequate to address the specificities of human lives.
3. The American Psychoanalytic Association had been granted unique status as a regional intermediary betwen local societies and the International Association in the 1940s, but the growth of independent societies in the United States—many subsequently recognized by the IPA—began to present alternatives to its hegemony. Changes within the societies belonging to the American also forced a reevaluation of standards for analytic practice, leading up to the rewriting of organizational policies and its hierarchical structure.
4. Levenson (1994) has been a strong proponent of the view that the important dynamic issues are always present in the current interaction.
5. Sandler had earlier developed the idea of role responsiveness by the analyst as a part of the analytic relationship.
6. Jacobs was criticized for his presentation at the IPA Congress in Amsterdam in 1997 for building an interpretation from the fantasies and memories that accompanied a session (he gave the erroneous impression of aiming to reduce psychoanalytic formulation to the evidence of his countertransference) (Jacobs, 1993, 1999).
7. Goldberg (2016) has reviewed the experimental evidence for langage acquisition, which in her analysis refutes the Chomskian concept of a universal grammar. When Chomsky's theory was first presented, she writes, "we did not realize how massively repetitive the input was" nor could we "appreciate how closely children's initial productions reflect their input" (p. 8).
8. The fascinating debate between Stern and Green addresses the philosophical, scientific, and clinical issues posed by infant research for psychoanalysis (Green & Stern, 2000). Green takes a polarizing position, rejecting Stern's arguments for the relevance of the data as departing from basic assumptions of analytic theory.

References

Aron, L. (1991). The patient's experience of the analyst's subjectivity, *Psychoanalytic Dialogues*, 1:29–51.

Aron, L. (1992). Interpretation as expression of the analyst's subjectivity, *Psychoanalytic Dialogues*, 2:475–507.

Aron, L. (1997). Are we to have a meeting of minds? A reply to the discussions of A Meeting of Minds, *Psychoanalytic Dialogues*, 7:885–896.

Aron, L. (1999). Clinical choices and the relational matrix, *Psychoanalytic Dialogues*, 9:1–29.

Aron, L. (2006). Analytic impasse and the third, *International Journal of Psychoanalysis*, 87:349–368.

Baranger, M. & Baranger, W. (2008). The analytic situation as a dynamic field, *International Journal of Psychoanalysis*, 89:795–826.

Beebe, B., Rustin, J., Sorter, D., Knoblauch, S. (2005). *Forms of Intersubjectivity in Infant Research and Adult Treatment*, New York: Other Press.

Benjamin, J. (1988). *The Bonds of Love: Psychoanalysis, Feminism, and the Problem of Domination*, New York: Pantheon.

Benjamin, J. (1990). An outline of intersubjectivity: The development of recognition, *Psychoanalytic Psychology*, 7:33–46.

Benjamin, J. (1995). *Like Subjects, Love Objects*, New Haven, CT: Yale University Press.

Benjamin, J. (1999). Afterward, in *Relational Psychoanalysis: The Emergence of a Tradition*, Eds. S. Mitchell & L. Aron, pp. 201–210. Hillsdale, NJ: Analytic Press.

Benjamin, J. (2004). Beyond doer and done to: An intersubjective view of thirdness, *Psychoanalytic Quarterly*, 73:5–46.

Benjamin, J. (2005). Creating an intersubjective reality: Commentary on paper by Arnold Rothstein, *Psychoanalytic Dialogues*, 15:447–457.

Benjamin, J. (2010). Can we recognize each other? Response to Donna Orange, *International Journal of Psychoanalytic Self Psychology*, 5:244–256.

Benjamin, J. (2011). Acknowledgment of collective trauma in light of dissociation and dehumanization. *Psychoanalytic Perspectives*, 8:207–214.

Birdwhistell, R. (1970). *Kinesics and Context*, Philadelphia, PA: University of Pennsylvania Press.

Bonovitz, C. (2009). Looking back, looking forward: A reexamination of Benjamin Wolstein's interlock and the emergence of intersubjectivity, *International Journal of Psychoanalysis*, 90:463–485.

Boston Change Process Study Group (BCPSG) (2007). The foundational level of psychodynamic meaning: Implicit process in relation to conflict, defense, and unconscious conflict, *International Journal of Psychoanalysis*, 88:843–860.

Brown, L. (2011). *Intersubjective Processes and the Unconscious*, New York: Routledge.

Civitarese, G. & Ferro, A. (2013). The meaning and use of metaphor in analytic field theory, *Psychoanalytic Inquiry*, 33:190–209.

Feinberg, T. (2011). The nested neural hierarchy and the self, *Consciousness and Cognition*, 20:4–15.

Geerardyn, F. (2002). Unconscious communication and the resistance of the psychoanalyst, *Psychoanalytische Perspectieven*, 20:591–601.

Ghent, E. (1989). Credo—The dialectics of one-person and two-person psychologies, *Contemporary Psychoanalysis*, 25:169–211.

Goldberg, A. (2016). Subtle implicit language facts emerge from the functions of constructions, *Frontiers in Psychology*, 2016, doi:10.3389/fpsyg.2015.02019

Green, A. & Stern, D. (2000). *Clinical and Observational Psychoanalytic Research: Roots of a Controversy*, Eds. J. Sandler, A.-M. Sandler, & R. Davies, London: Karnac Books.

Greenberg, J. & Mitchell, S. (1983). *Object Relations in Psychoanalytic Theory*, Cambridge, MA: Harvard University Press.

Habermas, J. (1968). *Knowledge and Human Interests*, trans. J. Shapiro, Boston, MA: Beacon Press.

Harrison, A.M. (2005). Herding the animals into the barn: A parent consultation model, *Psychoanalytic Study of the Child*, 60:128–153.

Hartmann, H. (1956). Notes on the reality principle, *Psychoanalytic Study of the Child*, 11:31–53.

Hartmann, H. (1958). Comments on the scientific aspects of psychoanalysis, *Psychoanalytic Study of the Child*, 13:127–146.

Hoy, D. & Durt, C. (2011). What subjectivity isn't, in *Dialogues with Davidson: Acting, Interpreting, Understanding*, Ed. J. Malpas, Cambridge, MA: MIT Press.

Jacobs, T.J. (1993). The inner experiences of the analyst: Their contribution to the analytic process, *International Journal of Psychoanalysis*, 74:7–14.

Jacobs, T.J. (1999). Commentary on paper by Jeanne Wolff Bernstein, *Psychoanalytic Dialogues*, 9:301–306.

Kirshner, L. (2014). Raids on the unsayable: Talk in psychoanalysis, *Journal of American Psychoanalytic Association*, 62:1047–1062.

Kohut, H. (1959). Introspection, empathy and psychoanalysis: An examination of the relationship between modes of observation and theory, *Journal of the American Psychoanalytic Association*, 7:459–483.

Kohut, H. (1971). *The Analysis of the Self*, New York: International Universities Press.

Lacan, J. (1953). The function and field of speech and language in psychoanalysis, in *Écrits*, trans B. Fink, pp. 32–106, New York: W.W. Norton, 2002.

Lacan, J. (1959–60). *Seminar VII, The Ethics of Psychoanalysis*, Ed. J.-A. Miller, trans. D. Porter, New York: W.W. Norton, 1992.

Leavy, S.A. (1973). Psychoanalytic interpretation, *Psychoanalytic Study of the Child*, 28:305–330.

Levenson, E.A. (1994). Beyond countertransference—aspects of the analyst's desire, *Contemporary Psychoanalysis*, 30:691–707.

Levine, H.B. (2012). The analyst's theory in the analyst's mind, *Psychoanalytic Inquiry*, 32:18–32.

Litowitz, B. (2011). From dyad to dialogue: Language and the early relationship in American psychoanalytic theory, *Journal of the American Psychoanalytic Association*, 59:483–507.

Modell, A.H. (1984). *Psychoanalysis in a New Context*, New York: International Universities Press.

Modell, A.H. (1990). *Other Times, Other Realities: Toward a Theory of Psychoanalytic Treatment*, Cambridge, MA: Harvard University Press.

Modell, A.H. (2002). *Imagination and the Meaningful Brain*, Cambridge, MA: MIT Press.

Morrison, A. (1994). The breadth and boundaries of a self psychological immersion in shame: A one-and-a-half person perspective, *Psychoanalytic Dialogues*, 4:19–35.

Muller, J. (1996). *Beyond the Psychoanalytic Dyad: Developmental Semiotics in Freud, Pearce, and Lacan*, New York: Routledge.

Ogden, T.H. (1994). The analytic third: Working with intersubjective clinical facts, *International Journal of Psychoanalysis*, 75:3–19.

Park, S. & Ichinose, M. (2015). Amygdala on the lookout, *American Journal of Psychiatry*, 172:174–175.

Renik, O. (1993). Analytic interaction: Conceptualizing technique in light of the analyst's irreducible subjectivity, *Psychoanalytic Quarterly*, 62:53–71.

Renik, O. (1998). Getting real in psychoanalysis, *Psychoanalytic Quarterly*, 67:566–593.

Stern, D. (2002). The Self as a relational structure: A dialogue with multiple-self theory, *Psychoanalytic Dialogues*, 12:693–714.

Stern, D. (2015). The interpersonal field: Its place in American psychoanalysis, *Psychoanalytic Dialogues*, 25:388–404.

Stolorow, R.D. (1986). Critical reflections on the theory of Self Psychology: An inside view, *Psychoanalytic Inquiry*, 6:387–402.

Stolorow, R.D. (1988). Intersubjectivity, psychoanalytic knowing, and reality, *Contemporary Psychoanalysis*, 24:331–337.

Stolorow, R. & Atwood, G. (1984). *Structures of Subjectivity: Explorations in Psychoanalytic Phenomenology*, Hillsdale NJ: Analytic Press.

Stolorow, R.D., Brandchaft, B., & Atwood, G. (1987). *Psychoanalytic Treatment: An Intersubjective Approach*, Hillsdale, NJ: Analytic Press.

Tessier, H. (2004). Empathie et intersubjectivité: Quelques positions de l'école intersubjectiviste américaine en psychanalyse, *Revue Française de Psychanalyse*, LXVIII: 831–851.

Trevarthen, C. & Aitken, K. (2001). Infant intersubjectivity: Research, theory, and clinical applications, *Journal of Child Psychology and Psychiatry*, 42:3–48.

Vivona, J. (2006). From developmental metaphor to developmental model: The shrinking role of language in the talking cure, *Journal of the American Psychoanalytic Association*, 54:877–901.

Vivona, J.M. (2009). Leaping from brain to mind: A critique of mirror neuron explanations of countertransference, *Journal of the American Psychoanalytic Association*, 57:525–550.

Wilson, M. (2003). The analyst's desire and the problem of narcissistic resistances, *Journal of the American Psychoanalytic Association*, 51:71–99.

Winnicott, D.W. (1969). The use of an object, *International Journal of Psychoanalysis*, 50:711–716.

Chapter 4

Passions and affects in psychoanalysis
An intersubjective approach

Psychoanalysis deserves its label as the talking cure, but we know that important exchanges of affect, facial expressions, and gestures play a major, if dimly understood, part in the process. Affective communications accompany all human interactions, including psychotherapeutic practice, but their meaning remains debated, both within psychoanalysis and in philosophy and neuroscience. In this chapter, I sort out some of the conflicting claims made by scholars in these disciplines, each of which brings its own terminology, methods, and findings to the complexities of human emotion. I supplement these by arguing for an inter-subjective approach to affect in clinical practice against the prevalent naturalizing or biologic reductionism. The social, interpersonal context evokes and shapes emotional expression like other behaviors. Because the size of the different literatures is too vast to summarize in a single chapter, I focus on a few selected authors who have contributed to developing the major themes in emotion studies.

We may still be struggling with the dichotomy associated with the work of René Descartes (1596–1650) who famously theorized a mind–body dualism based on religious suppositions. Emotions clearly differ from symbolic mental processes of thought and have historically been considered closer to the body, less under the subject's control, and more primitive in content than higher-level cognitive activities. Freud endorsed this position, which has been supported by a large body of contemporary research in neuroscience that attributes emotional states to innate (presubjective) biological mechanisms. At the same time, reciprocal emotional expression is clearly a fundamental part of intersubjective relations from birth onward, which seems to present a fundamental paradox. How is it possible that the most personal aspect of human relationships can be the product of an impersonal set of automatic reactions independent of subjective meaning?

The sharp exchange between philosophers Patricia Churchland, Marcia Cavell, and Colin McGinn in the *New York Review of Books*, June 19, 2014, illustrates the conflict between neuroreductionistic and psychological approaches to under-standing emotional expression. Churchland, who has written extensively about the implications of neuroscience for understanding mental functions, dismisses attempts to support a dualistic position of explaining behavior by considering both personal motives and intentions and the biological pathways associated with it.

She presents what might be called a hard version of the neuroscience of Damasio and Panksepp, treating the humanistic logic of reasons as a residue of prescientific thought. For his part, McGinn categorically rejects Churchland's attempts to translate psychological terms like belief and desire into mechanisms in the brain (persons make choices, not brains). Cavell reminds us of philosopher Donald Davidson's attempt to present a theory of dual monism combining both languages (Davidson, 2005). Unfortunately, these interesting debates have failed to produce an integrated theory applicable to psychoanalytic practice.[1]

With respect to vocabulary, I have opted to use "emotion" as a blanket term to cover the categories of feelings and affects, which some authors (including Freud) differentiate, although it is used this way by many theories. The term "emotion" suggests for some a raw expression of animal behavior, while "affect" often connotes a culturally shaped set of processes and "feeling" refers to their conscious counterpart, but in practice the three concepts are difficult to separate. The three terms convey the mixture of bodily expressive and semantic properties that I will discuss (but see Johnston & Malabou, 2013, p. 165, and Damasio for arguments in favor of keeping them separate). Damasio defines emotions as "complex, largely automated programs of actions, concocted by evolution", while "feelings" are internal perceptions of what is happening in body and mind during the emoting (2012, pp. 116–117).

The Cartesian legacy

Descarte's religious conception of an insubstantial soul linked mysteriously to the physical body has faded, but the almost unavoidable tendency to think either in terms of biophysical causation or of personalistic wishes and desires persists. Descartes's "error" of separating the two domains (Damasio, 1994) remains with us as part of a folk psychology, and their integration, which most researchers and philosophers accept as a rational goal, continues to lack a convincing explanation. Moreover, he raised the problem of how mental or psychological processes can influence the physical causality of illness, which he discussed in his famous exchange of letters with Princess Elisabeth of Bohemia between 1643 until 1649. Her personal interest in dealing with the "passions" made her a valuable inter-locutor for Descartes, whose treatise on the familiar opposition between reason and emotion, *Les Passions de l'Ame* (*The Passions of the Soul*, 1659), grew out of their correspondence. The letters offer a basic reference point for applied theories of the management of emotional states, for which Elisabeth sought his advice. She was a careful reader who repeatedly pressed Descartes to explain and clarify his ideas, especially those relevant to her own personal life, which seems to have been troubled by periods of depression. He interpreted the passions as lower expressions of the body, which the subject should strive to master in favor of spiritual goals, but was far from disparaging of their importance. Indeed, he taught that emotions could become an intrinsic part of life to be valued and enjoyed, if viewed from the proper perspective of faith in God.

Descartes's dialogue with the princess was not only philosophical but included elements of a therapeutic relationship (Sibony-Malpertu, 2012). Elisabeth sought his help for problems with her "humors," diagnosed by Descartes as physical manifestations of sadness and pain. Embracing his theory of the independence of the soul and its link with God, she struggled to make sense of the failure of her conscious efforts to throw off episodes of somatic symptoms. Descartes, sounding consistently caring and patient, offered a cognitive approach of reframing and perspective taking that he believed could absorb her unbearable feelings into a broader context of actions and meanings. He saw that emotional states could have their origins in early childhood, like sadness deriving from a diet of harmful foods or an early lack of nourishment (without ever referring directly to the relationship with the mother). Above all, he counseled management and mastery over emotions, as these physical states were inevitable aspects of human existence, not to be avoided. Psychoanalysts were not the first to struggle with solving this most human problem, whose terms we have inherited from the seventeenth century.

Descartes may have been the first thinker to systematically categorize the basic emotions and to link them with formative life experiences. In *The Passions of the Soul*, he wrote about six "primitive" passions: wonder, which he called "the first of all the passions," love, hatred, desire, joy, and sadness, while also referring to other types and variations. A few years later, Spinoza likewise emphasized the importance of what he called the "affects," including his own version of wonder as a basic human expression. While differentiating his views from Cartesian dualism, Spinoza advocated similar goals of taming or maintaining independence from blind emotion, and, like Descartes, offered a kind of therapeutic for those suffering from the passions. "Emotional distress and unhappiness," he wrote, "have their origin in excessive love towards a thing subject to considerable instability, a thing we can never completely possess" (cited by Nussbaum, 2001, p. 595). The uncontrollability of affects, he observed, brings with it ambivalence and a disposition to painful reactions of anger toward a love object, before whom one is passive. Such an analysis is close to the psychoanalytic conception of unconscious object relations and internal representations that govern affective responses. Yet, if we form "a clear and distinct idea" of our emotion, Spinoza stated, sounding a bit Cartesian, it can come under our control, becoming less an affliction of the mind than an active element. For both authors, however, the experience of contemplation of God (rather than knowledge of passing bodily and mental states) was the superior avenue toward personal enlightenment, echoing a classic Platonic ideal.

The attempts by Descartes and Spinoza to clarify the source, value, and functions of the passions in human life anticipate the modern scientific quest to find answers to similar problems, and contemporary scholars of emotion have returned to their writings. Damasio based two of his books on his reading of their works, *Descartes' Error* (1994) and *Looking for Spinoza* (2003); a recent work by the contemporary philosophers Johnston and Malabou (2013) explores the links between Descartes and Spinoza, as well as Deleuze and Derrida, Damasio's research, and the theories of Freud and Lacan. Nussbaum's comprehensive study of emotions (2001) belongs to an interdisciplinary tradition that is comfortable with a broad range of conceptual, empirical, and clinical theories, which seems to me the approach best suited to a field like psychoanalysis. She notes that Spinoza avoided a simplistic naturalism, emphasizing the enormous variety of human emotions, while Descartes remained sensitive to the importance of unique individual histories in which the emotional expressions were not to be condemned or suppressed. Nussbaum sees both philosophers as inheritors of a stoic tradition of containing affects that remains a strong influence in Western culture.

Perhaps the major practical innovation of the past century has been to assign to medicine the control option for managing emotional states. Pharmacologic suppression of emotions as a solution to the kinds of distress Princess Elisabeth reported may represent the scientific equivalent to the philosopher's faith-based method of dealing with unruly feelings (which, of course, persists). Current psychiatric views of affect imply the possibility and desirability of achieving a natural, normative affective life through medication (as guided by the use of paper and pencil tests to score levels of depression, for example). If emotions are markers of biological homeostatic mechanisms, meant to regulate the appropriate responses of the organism, then test responses indicating significant deviation call for medical interventions to maintain the appropriate balance. The popular belief in a literal chemical imbalance as the cause of depression reflects this naturalizing approach. Controversies about appropriate treatment then follow.

The persistence of the Cartesian separation of mind from body in various forms suggests the dead-end, unresolvable quality to this kind of polarized contestation and tempts me to restate Wittgenstein's position: talking about relationships between mind and brain provides interesting and useful ways to look at human behavior, not statements about truth or reality. This caution applies especially to theories of emotion. In the case of affects that are indisputably aroused by "psychological" and symbolic processes like narcissistic injury or perceived personal failure, it makes sense to speak about painful feelings "causing" physiologic changes like headaches or weariness. Conversely, we can talk rationally about physiologic changes influencing mood, like depression after a stroke or physical illness, without evoking testable laws of nature explaining the mind–body problem. Davidson's (2005) point that the brain forms the unique substrate for mental events (monism), which include both physical and psychological dimensions (dual aspect monism) may be the most that one can reasonably conclude (as dangerously close to Cartesian as this dualism may appear).

Accepting the inevitability of the two languages of meaning and causation can provide a helpful approach to therapeutic practice with patients like Princess Elisabeth and many others for whom body metaphors pervade the discourse and whose depression crosses psyche-soma boundaries. The physical terms that patients often use to describe their emotional states indicate a disrupted psycho-somatic state of being and carry more personal significance than diagnostic labels like mood disorder or somatization. Green's metaphor for depressive life experience was that it no longer "sings." Perhaps his metaphor refers to the embodied sense of wonder in life designated as a primary emotion by Descartes and Spinoza.

Neuroscience research on emotions

While mainstream research in neuroscience continues to target the isolated brain, just as psychoanalysis has done traditionally with the individual, some cognitive neuroscientists have embarked on the new challenge of studying the emotional interaction of two minds (Przyrembel et al., 2012). Affective semiotics (Salvatore & Freda, 2011) and naturalistic studies of language (Garcia & Ibanez, 2014) present recent examples of this research, which holds interdisciplinary interest. For the most part, however, researchers in the new field of social cognitive neuroscience have not taken account of psychoanalytic concepts (see review by Hari & Kujala, 2009), nor, with important exceptions, have psychoanalysts welcomed this discipline into their own theorizing. The important exceptions come from the new discipline of neuropsychoanalysis, which has come to include (at least as participating colleagues) behavioral neurologists like Damasio, Yovell, and Fotopoulou (Yovell et al., 2015).

In every discipline, researchers contest various interpretations of the neuro-scientific research that locates the mechanisms and centers that produce emotions. Although the biology of emotion has been worked out fairly well, at least for a few core emotions, scholars continue to debate the implications of these findings. At one end of the spectrum are neuroscientists who emphasize the innate, evolutionary basis of emotional states in mammalian brain-stem centers. Beginning in the 1960s, the pioneering research of Tomkins (1962–63) built on the affect theory of Charles Darwin, who first identified a universal set of emotional categories. LeDoux has nicely summarized the Darwinian perspective: "basic emotions are expressed the same in people around the world. Neuroscientists have adopted the basic emotions idea, and have proposed specific circuits for different basic emotions" (2012, p. 7). The evidence that these basic states represent a product of evolution, generated by the same centers of the brain in all mammalian (and possibly other) species, is robust. A major contributor to neuropsychoanalysis, Jaak Panksepp, may be the most widely cited proponent of this conclusion. From his extensive research with animals, he hypothesizes that even the higher emotional feelings "may reflect the neurodynamics of brain systems that generate instinctual emotional behaviors" (2005, p. 31).

Panksepp sees core emotions like seeking, fear, rage, lust, care, panic, and play as built-in responses to environmental stimuli. "In coarse form," he writes, "primary process affective consciousness seems to be fundamentally an uncon-ditional 'gift of nature' rather than an acquired skill" (2005, p. 30). This natural legacy appears derived from subcortical regions of the brain and does not involve higher level cognition. Solms and Panksepp (2012) point to evidence from seemingly alert babies who lack a cerebral cortex, yet are able to display affective responses to their environment. Panksepp's work demonstrates convincingly that many human emotions are shared with other animals, using the same midbrain centers and suggesting a common repertoire. He writes:

> My personal view is that the shared subcortical heritage, from which the various id energies emerge across mammalian species, provides an essential and solid foundation for understanding the nature of affective processes as well as higher emotion-regulating functions of the brain.
>
> (1999, p. 19)

Later, Panksepp concluded, "A direct neuroscientific study of primary process emotional/affective states is best achieved through the study of the intrinsic ('instinctual'), albeit experientially refined, emotional action tendencies of other animals" (2005, p. 31).

Although Damasio distinguishes feelings or conscious affective experiences from primitive emotion, like Panksepp he defines emotions as "complex, largely automated programs of actions concocted by evolution" (2012, p. 116). Feelings, he writes, are secondary "perceptions of what our bodies do during the emoting." Also like Panksepp, he refers to the universality of certain emotional expressions as established fact, although presenting a more nuanced view of conscious affect and affective expressions, which leaves plenty of room for higher level shaping by cortical systems. This modification leaves him open to criticism by Panksepp for minimizing the foundational importance of the emotional circuits in the brain stem at the base of all conscious experience. Liotti and Panksepp write, "It is probably the thoughts about our emotions rather than the affects that are cortically produced" (2003, p. 205), and Panksepp and Watt specify that this includes "perhaps some complex socially-constructed emotions such as human spiritual happiness and shame" (2003, p. 205). This "bottom up/top down" debate is not always easy to follow (see the exchange between Damasio and Panksepp in *Neuropsychoanalysis*, 2003, p. 201–231). Although mammalian brain centers respond to situations of threat or pleasure by discharges that manifest themselves directly in the behavior or vocalizations of the animal, human emotions present a different order of complexity. Since higher level cortical processes do not appear necessary for the reactions of other species, experts disagree on whether this research can be generalized to humans.

LeDoux (2012), for one, criticizes attempts to equate feelings in humans with emotion-like behavior in other animals. His own research has contributed to a neurologic understanding of the mechanisms of fear reactions in animals, but, in contrast to Panksepp, he avoids calling them emotional states of mind. Underscoring the differences between animal and human consciousness, he comments:

> Most studies that have explored conscious experience in humans have found that when information (including emotional information) reaches awareness the dorsolateral prefrontal cortex is active, and if information is experimentally

prevented from reaching awareness this area is not active . . . The dorsolateral granular prefrontal cortex is a unique primate specialization and has features in the human brain that are lacking in other primates. If human conscious experience depends on these unique features of brain organization, we should be cautious about attributing the kinds of mental states made possible by these features to animals that lack the feature or the brain region. Second, language is a unique human capacity, and conscious experience, including emotional experience, is influenced by language. The once disputed idea that language, and the cognitive processes required to support language functions, add complexity to human experience, has regained respect.

(2012, pp. 436–437)

Clearly, animals possess some kind of awareness, which seems a form of consciousness. On the other hand, we need access to first-person knowledge to find out what personal experience feels like to a subject, and this route is barred for other species. Nagel's oft-cited essay "What is it like to be a bat?" (1974) asserts the phenomenological privacy of all experiential states. But, as LeDoux reminds us, the possibility of a language-free human consciousness seems questionable, as the philosopher Hilary Putnam (1981) has also cautioned. The argument states basically that we cannot know another person's feelings and thoughts without their speaking about it, which depends on how they select words and images to convey it. Social existence relies on people sharing a language and sets of beliefs that make Putnam's concept of internal realism possible (whether people can agree about whether statements are true or false, for example). Of course, translating private experience into intersubjective communication must cross the gap that Nagel insists upon, even in humans. For psychoanalysis, the issue hinges on the extent to which subjects require access to verbal or other means of symbolic figuration to make meaning from experience or whether immediate moments of meeting—as some phenomenologists and the Boston Change Process Study Group (2007) suggest—or empathic immersion in the other's experience (as in self psychology) can bypass the language barrier. From research on babies, we know that a basic level of communication (probably limited to index and iconic signs of emotion) does not involve higher level cortical operations, but these come on line quickly to construct complex cognitive representations of subjective meaning. LeDoux writes, "In the absence of language, experience cannot be partitioned in the same way– English speakers can partition fear and anxiety into more than 30 categories" (2012, p. 437).

Tomkins (1962) pioneered in pursuing the Darwinian hypothesis that innate forms of emotion manifest themselves in action patterns and in characteristic facial expressions that can be correctly identified. He saw human affect, with all its meaningful subjective qualities, as a secondary elaboration of basic brainstem activation common to other species, which may have evolved for the purposes of accurate communication of specific meanings. Like Panksepp, he suggested a "radical dichotomy between the 'real' causes of affect and the individual's own interpretation of these causes" (cited in Leys, 2011, p. 438). The corollary hypothesis that facial expressions of emotion themselves are hard-wired phenomena, present across cultures, including isolated tribal societies, was further developed by Tompkins's colleague Paul Ekman, author of several influential studies of facial emotion (see www.paulekman.com/journal-articles/ for a comprehensive bibliography). Ekman summarized:

As Darwin suggested, the facial expressions of a number of emotions are universal, not culture-specific. The muscles that contract to produce the facial expressions of anger, fear, sadness, disgust, and enjoyment are the same the world over, regardless of sex or culture.

(2001)

Many textbooks of psychology as well as popular articles repeat his conclusion that a universal set of core emotions and their facial expressions independent of culture has been scientifically validated (Barrett et al., 2007). Nathanson, another exponent of Tompkins's hypothesis, has observed that

affects are . . . completely free of inherent meaning or association to their triggering source. There is nothing about sobbing that tells us anything about the steady-state stimulus that has triggered it; sobbing itself has nothing to do with hunger or cold or loneliness. Only the fact that we grow up with an increasing experience of sobbing lets us form some ideas about its meaning.
(cited in Leys, 2011, p. 438)

Research on facial affect demonstrates a strong in-born tendency of young children and adults across cultures to recognize emotions using the set of facial images developed by Ekman and collaborators (Ekman & Friesen, 1971). Subsequent researchers have qualified these conclusions, pointing out that recognition varies according to the emotion studied and cultural factors. In addition, recent research has addressed developmental variables in children's ability to identify emotions by the picture test (Lawrence, Campbell, & Skuse, 2015). What these findings mean for an intersubjective understanding of affect remains contested.

The Ekman approach offers a counterpoint to Lacan's distrust of affect in that it is automatic and non-intentional, which means that, unlike speech, it cannot lie. This contrast also belongs to the intellectual history of emotion theory:

A long standing debate concerning verbal and nonverbal communication has been whether verbal communication can be trusted at all in terms of its 'truthfulness.' In almost any introductory textbook to nonverbal communication, students learn that words may lie, and nonverbal signals do not.
(Sandlund, 2004, cited in Jensen, 2014, p. 4)

The dichotomy rings a bit hollow on common-sense grounds, however. Human subjects struggle with how much to believe in the sincerity of the other, and analysts know that displays of affect may conceal other, less ego-syntonic feelings and be employed defensively. Between the undeniable existence of virtually unmistakable emotional expressions and cryptic affective messages lies the broad range of human interactions. Cultural knowledge forms an essential ingredient of interpretations of the affective exchanges of everyday life.

The ability of people to alter the expressions of even the primary emotions suggests that the display or expression of emotion may be more aptly termed "emotional communication," in the sense that like other types of information, it is shaped for audiences. Indeed, as Darwin theorized, their social function probably explains why emotions have evolved. Expressed emotions may (or may not) represent unmediated manifestations of internal states, but as social behaviors they are packaged in ways that are consistent with other communication practices (Metts & Planalp, 2003, cited in Jensen, 2014, p. 5). Alan Fridlund (1997), a research associate of Ekman in facial emotion studies, came to designate affect as a social communication, relevant to particular social contexts, citing again the "behavioral ecology" view. "The view that emerges these days among students of the evolution of communication," he writes, "is to see displays of all kinds as social tools that help us creatures navigate our social terrain by giving lead signs to our intentions within the context of our social interactions" (1994, p. 84). In a recent review, van Kleef et al. (2016) comment on the "increasing scholarly awareness that emotions are inherently social—that is, they tend to be elicited by other people, expressed toward other people, and regulated to influence other people or to comply with social norms." Ekman has responded to the criticism that emotional displays are not generic expressions of internal processes so much as specific forms of communication. He observes correctly that perception of intentional actions or inference of meaning by others does not necessarily imply that their perception was correct (Ekman, 1997).

Facial expressions looking like familiar emotions in infancy may not yet express personal meaning or intention in the usual sense of these terms (beyond the level of animal awareness), and can more accurately be characterized as automatic reactions of the organism (what Damasio calls "homeostatic") to stimuli. Retaining this model of implicit meaning and core emotions to explain later behavior in development seems to me an unwarranted jump, however. From a developmental semiotic perspective, the immediate emotional expressions triggered by the infant's perceptions of the world rapidly become a component of the larger class of all-important parental relationships within a short time after birth (if not earlier). A sobbing child may not yet be able to provide an explanation for its feelings, but the interpersonal context of the emotion seems inescapable, and soon words will be found to convey the message. Describing the interchanges between infant and mother, Trevarthen and Aitken conclude: "None of these constellations of emotion are easily described by combining the classical discrete categories of emotion. They are coherent, so-called non-basic emotions with immediate interpersonal value" (2001, p. 12). While the ecology of animal societies relies on immediate understanding of emotional signals, which have an obvious evolutionary purpose, human societies require more detail that can express individual subjectivity.

Despite giving a first impression of reductionism, cognitive neuroscience postulates the biology of emotion as the basic source, but not sole determinant of human meaning and value. Solms (2013), reformulating and reversing Freud's theory of affect, argues for the compatibility of current neurobiology of emotion with a drive-oriented Freudian perspective on ego development and sublimation. He hypothesizes that emotional activation of deep structures (the Id) creates the content of consciousness, at least of conscious awareness, while the cognitive operations that process the personal and social significance of this activation (the Ego) are unconscious. Damasio's somatic marker hypothesis (2012) similarly proposes that signals from the emotional brain are sent to higher centers that unconsciously use them to select choices for actions. The force of innate animating emotions drives the cognitive cortical mind (mostly unconscious) to make "decisions" in conjunction with culturally internalized rules for behavior. Secondary or tertiary cortical processing by human beings adds specificity and nuance to subjective emotional experience, enabling it to be communicated in much more detail than basic facial or bodily expressions activated by a hard-wired brain stem circuit could possibly convey. Moreover, the perceptions that ostensibly trigger core emotions are themselves active products of the subject's expectations and history of social learning. The confirmation of Darwin's hypotheses that our emotional lives are shared with other mammals as inherited dispositions and that their overt manifestation follows a common biological program does not negate the crucial role of higher level cultural and personal experiences in shaping subjective feeling and expression of affects.

Social theories of emotion

Some social theorists strongly contest the over-generalization of neuroscience research findings about the core emotions and their universal facial expressions to other disciplines. What concerns these critics is a tendency on the part of scholars in the humanities and social sciences to embrace a bio-reductionist explanation of human emotional responses independent of meaning and intentionality. The recent attribution of violent behaviors to the switching on of primitive rage circuits studied by Panksepp to explain police killings of civilians (Schermer, 2015), for example, suggests a preference for biological explanations over psychological–anthropological ones.[2] The revisionist critique contains two major elements: first, a challenge to the experimental evidence for a set of universally recognized and facially identifiable core emotions, and, second, an argument that the socio-symbolic organization of meaning interacts reciprocally with mid-brain processes to produce expressed affects. I will first review differing interpretations of the research studies, then summarize alternative ways to understand emotional behavior.

A key problem identified by several commentators concerns the methodology by which recognition of emotions in the faces of babies and adults in both Western and non-Western cultures has been studied. This research has relied in most instances on two components: photographs of posed faces expressing the core emotions and forced-choice matching of emotion words to these images. In a few studies, subjects are shown films in which cognitive or emotional features of situations depicted are modified, while undergoing evaluation by physiologic and behavioral tests. Barrett (2006), Leys (2011), and Russell (1994) have published detailed reviews of this research. Russell, who seems exceptionally even-handed in weighing the evidence, endorses the quasi-universal association between some emotions, like happiness, and their facial expression. Yet many studies of this relationship fail to show impressive agreement in their results for other emotions (Kendler et al., 2008; Russell, 1994). The ability of subjects to agree in identifying the emotions in pictures of faces appears to be greater in some populations for some emotions, and varies according to the methodology employed. Russell concludes that much room for interpretation of the research data bearing on the universality of emotions remains.

Other scholars have questioned the significant limitations of using posed photographs of faces in emotion research. Barrett (2006) notes the significant neurologic and social differences between posed caricatures and spontaneous emotion. She cites studies that show that: 1) subjects report having minimal experience of the facial caricatures of fear, disgust and surprise (and to a lesser extent anger) in their actual lives; 2) movie actors noted for their realism do not use similar facial configurations to portray emotion; and 3) people fail to produce these expressions when asked to portray emotion on their faces. As Russell also comments, posed faces do not express the emotion of the poser, but what the poser chooses to pretend in a manner deemed most likely to be understood by an observer. According to the sociologic notion of display rules, voluntarily posed expressions are culturally influenced according to prevailing models. In addition, they may originate in a different region of the brain than do spontaneous facial expressions (Russell, 1994, p. 114; Ammaniti & Gallese, 2014).[3]

Russell's review found that the reliability of recognition of facial emotions varies by culture, exposure to Western influences, and the educational background and training of subjects. Age and gender also have significant effects on the ability to identify emotion (Lawrence, Campbell, & Skuse, 2015). In addition, the manner and context of the presentation of the experimental pictures and word lists of emotions, as well as the research design itself (whether within or between subjects) are important variables in outcomes. Russell concludes: "We have no cross-cultural studies of recognition of emotion from spontaneous facial expressions. Even in Western cultures, too few studies exist to draw firm conclusions" (p. 115). More recently, Naab and Russell (2007) found that endorsement of the predicted emotional labels developed by Ekman occurred significantly less frequently for spontaneous expressions in Papua New Guinea natives than for posed expressions. When subjects were not provided explicit choices of words, but asked instead to describe a picture they were shown, emotion names were much less often used. This finding is a general problem of forced choice techniques in psychological research. A quantitative analysis of ratings of responses by Naab and Russell revealed that the subjects did not score a facial emotion dichotomously as present or absent, but chose several emotion words in varying degrees (for example, on an 8-point scale). Above all, Russell raises the problem of ecological validity— that is, what facial expressions occur under natural conditions, with what frequency, and in what contexts (1994, p. 130). He concludes by outlining a set of alternative interpretations of available data and urges future researchers to take more seriously theories of emotion of other cultures on their own terms.

Ekman's former collaborator Fridlund came to share the critique of posed photographs for studying affects, modifying his earlier views of their relevance to the function of affects in actual life. If affect represents a social communication, he concluded, static pictures without context cannot tell us much. Facial emotions, instead, "represent the manner in which the individual at that particular moment relates or does not relate to the environment" (1994, p. 87). Emotional displays reflect the subject's "positionality," "relational activity," and states of action readiness. Recently, Crivelli, Jarillo, and Fridlund have criticized the lack of an anthropological perspective in cognitive research. They advocate a methodological shift in studying emotion:

> First, studies conducted in indigenous societies can benefit by relying on multidisciplinary research groups to diminish ethnocentrism and enhance the quality of the data. Second, studies devised for Western societies can readily be adapted to the changing settings encountered in the field.
>
> (2016, p. 1)

Many anthropologists have documented important variations in affect words and their meanings across cultures. Independently of the common biological mechanisms in the brain that are associated with basic emotions in mammals, cultures shape the affective experience of their members. They make rules for emotional expression and construct variations in subtypes of emotion that are not always evident to outsiders. The cultural anthropologist Shweder (1991) has commented that children have to learn, not the basic vocabulary of emotion, which may be innate, but its syntax. The rugged hills and valleys of a four-year-old's emotional landscape, to which he refers, are smoothed out in the course of development, and individuals learn to speak about them in appropriate ways. Even a young child has already received considerable training in labeling and managing emotional states, as different societies impose different rules for their expression. Lutz (1988) reported from her fieldwork in a Polynesian culture that unique affect terms characterized the Ifaluk people she studied. For example, passive expressions of pain or unhappiness that might be considered shameful in American society were regarded as admirable among this group. Another anthropologist, Rosaldo, concluded similarly that affect is about social engagement. "Emotions," she wrote, "are about ways the social world is one in which we are involved" (1984, p. 143). She, too, observed constellations of affect quite unfamiliar to most Westerners.

Crivelli, Jarillo, and Fridlund (2016, p. 8) raise a number of issues about the cross-cultural field research on facial recognition of Ekman, Friesen, and Sorenson in Papua New Guinea. They cite the anthropologist Sorenson's later published evaluation of their work showing how "method artifacts" could have led to overestimates of the agreement of emotional judgments between Western and indigenous subjects. "The omission of an exploratory phase (i.e. participant observation, speaking the vernacular, rapport-building) can provide misleading results and show the ethnocentric nature of the stimuli being used," they conclude (p. 9). Shweder makes the balanced observation, "It is ludicrous to imagine that the emotional functioning of people in different cultures is basically the same. It is just as ludicrous to imagine that each culture's emotional life is unique" (1991, p. 252). In her review of the literature, the economist Shuman (2013) observes that emotional regulation itself is a social phenomenon. Social contexts stir and steer emotions, she comments, and the purpose of reciprocal affective exchanges is to influence behavior and regulate emotions in others. In a similar vein, Salvatore and Freda, from a semiotic perspective, criticize basic emotion theorists for not considering "the role played by affect as semiotic regulator of the relationship between persons and their social context" (2011, p. 122).

In his study of the philosophy and neuroscience of psychoanalysis, Johnston argues for a dialectical approach that takes into account the effects of linguistic mediation on "subjects emerging out of plastic neural systems" (2013, p. 101). He writes: "One can and should strive to develop a scientifically shaped account . . . of how humans defying and escaping explanatory encapsulation by the sciences become what they are" (p. 104). This seems to be a more desirable goal than an oppositional debate between the influences of the symbolic structures of culture and language and the biological underpinnings of behavior. As Damasio has wisely stated, "human emotion is not just about sexual pleasures or fear of snakes, but has to do with meaningful moral, and aesthetic experiences" (1999, p. 35).

In an article assessing the role of the amygdala in fear and paranoia, the neuroscience researchers Park and Ichinose conclude their discussion by reminding their readers of the personal dimension of affect. "Detecting change and salience depends on context, memory and personal history," they point out. "Salience may be driven by bottom-up fight-or-flight response (e.g. detecting a snake), but we adapt to our environment through personal, contextualized learning (e.g. becoming a snake charmer), such that salience becomes tailored to the individual and situation" (2015, p. 705).

Damasio and neuroscience

Damasio (1994, 1999, 2003) occupies a unique position in current neuroscience. On one hand, he writes as a classical neurologist, fascinated by the revelations of unusual lesions and pathologies that produce bizarre mental and emotional effects.

For instance, he describes rare cases of brain injury in which the mental outcome consists of an ability to consciously understand a given situation without manifesting any observable affective response (in contrast to the pre-injury personality). These brain-damaged patients apparently demonstrate in vivo the separation of centers of emotion and cognition. On the other hand, he has published a series of broader reflections on notions of self, emotion, and consciousness in light of other disciplinary approaches, making him a bridging figure in the debates discussed above. In this aspect of his work, he pursues an active dialogue with neuropsychoanalysts like Solms and with Lacanian-oriented philosophers like Žižek, and Johnston and Malabou.

Somewhat paradoxically, Damasio also strives unabashedly for a unitary neuroscientific explanation of the seemingly irreducible subjective phenomena he explores in his practice. While his fellow neurologist Oliver Sacks accepts and even embraces the gap between a sophisticated neuroanatomical understanding of lesions in the brain and the complexity of patients' subjective experiences, Damasio pursues the underlying neurophysiology of the phenomena of personal experience. Sacks reports that the neuroscientist Gerald Edelman once told him, "You are no theoretician," to which Sacks replied that he was "a field-worker" who could provide the observational material theorists like Edelman need to construct their models (2015, p. 366). The same might be said of the potential contributions of psychoanalysts to neuroscientific research. As "field workers" they are close observers of the important mental phenomena of which scientists like Damasio attempt to identify the mechanisms, but which, to date, cannot dispense with a psychological level of explanation.

The universality of emotion across species represents the common object for psychoanalysis and neuroscience for Damasio. Emotions provide a substrate for the development of the human mind and the self, as well as for a reinterpretation of basic psychoanalytic concepts. His discussion of the temporal and fragile nature of selfhood, which depends ultimately on primitive emotional sources and time-dependent processes in the brain, on first reading seems to support classical Freudian positions against any notion of an implicit or transcendent "self." He does offer a series of hypotheses about an unconscious "protoself," which appears to be mostly a way of speaking about the organization of the developing brain. The protoself, he suggests, produces an "elementary feeling" unrelated to external objects or events (2012, pp. 341–342) and leads toward the development of a pathway constituting a "core self," whose basis is action, similar to Georgieff's (2011) proposal. This level of subjectivity may be related to, but is not the same as, Daniel Stern's core self (1985), a more psychological concept. Damasio's description of the development of a subsequent autobiographical self (perhaps corresponding roughly to Stern's reflective self) involves "pulses of a core self," again putting the accent on the neural activation that produces the conscious feeling of selfhood (pp. 24–25). Mental processes are like a symphony composed of many voices, he continues, but a conductor is absent, or comes into being "only through the underlying neural processes he is experienced as directing" (p. 25). As in the neuroscience model of Jeannerod, there is no entity here we can identify as the subject or agent, except in retrospect. Damasio's conception of a "headless" agent also holds parallels to Lacan's conception of how the unconscious works, but in terms of biological processes.[4] His approach contrasts with Stern's conception of the developing self and takes us to the heart of the problem of the relationship between mind and brain that many scientists hope to solve by a unitary model of brain function. Can we dispense with psychological vocabularies and ways of thinking about mental processes in terms of personal intentions and wishes? Perhaps researchers will eventually work out the specific pathways and networks producing self-consciousness, but would knowing these details bring us closer to understanding subjective motives and experiences? Žižek asks whether a credible physiologic model can include the existential process of developing a private self and the disturbing awareness of bearing a subjectivity without an intrinsic meaning. He argues that there is no place in Damasio's theory "for what we speaking beings experience (or, rather, presuppose) as the empty core of our subjectivity. Who am I?" (2006, pp. 226–227).

Psychoanalytic theories of emotion

Psychoanalysis shares the Cartesian tendency to separate emotion from higher level psychic processes. Freud followed Darwin in deriving emotions from basic biologic mechanisms of arousal and discharge as a product of evolution. In his early writings, he interpreted the cause of trauma in quantitative terms as a matter of excess emotional stimulation (extreme fright), a breaching of a stimulus barrier he hypothesized that protects the bio-psychic organization. As Green (1992) showed in his ground-breaking study of emotion in psychoanalysis, Freud's first theory of affect conceptualized emotional expression as a derivative of the drives, erupting from a primitive unconscious and the real of the body (the Id). As such, affects express something more fundamental to the psyche than the symbolic superstructures added in the course of development, and the discharge of their energies by abreaction emerged as basic to therapeutic action.

Freud's famous observation in his essay "The unconscious" that affects, almost by definition, could not be unconscious weaves through much of the early psychoanalytic literature. Affects, by definition, describe something one feels and, as such, belong to conscious experience, while the nature of the drives from which they derive remains inaccessible to conscious thought. Freud wrote:

> Strictly speaking, there are no unconscious affects as there are unconscious ideas. . . . The whole difference arises from the fact that ideas are cathexes—basically of memory-traces—whilst affects and feelings correspond to processes of discharge, the final manifestations of which are perceived as sensations.

(1915, p. 178)

In the case of neurosis, words and memories are repressed, and the remaining affective components displaced onto some other set of signifiers where they may appear incongruous, like an irrational phobia or obsession, or transformed, like desire into a feeling of sexual disgust. The drive-based feeling simply attaches itself to a different mental representation. The important thing for Freud was to uncover the true source of the affect beneath its distortion by defenses—for example, in a forbidden sexual impulse.

Lacan adopted Freud's position that affects were not "protopathic," not fundamental or given in an unmediated form to the subject (1962–63, p. 10), but effects of structure.[5] He went even further to assert somewhat dogmatically that pursuit of affects in psychoanalysis leads nowhere. He saw affects as deceptive, since they lack connection to the repressed word associations that anchor them and that remain the key to resolving symptoms. Affects express only a kind of floating experience attached to wishful images or fantasies, which divert the subject from the nature of his desires. The crux of therapeutic action instead involves exploring a patient's specific use of words and the web of hidden associations underlying them. "The confused nature of the recourse to affectivity" in analytic treatment, he wrote, "always leads us toward an impasse" (p. 102).

For classic psychoanalysis as well, a focus on conscious affect without reestablishing its links to repressed wishes and fantasies was not likely to arrive at the true causes of neurotic conflict. The goal of treatment was to free the original complex of memories, drive derivatives, and word representations from repression and enable its management by the conscious ego. Tradition holds that the early technique of abreaction was soon replaced by an emphasis on the ego and its defenses, but the basic notion of achieving the cathartic expression of repressed affects has persisted and in modified form remains common in therapeutic practice.[6] Its advocates hold that a patient should be helped to express fully and freely the desires and thoughts that he (his ego) previously defended against. Published cases often recount the recovery of previously unavailable painful experiences as a crucial moment in analysis, when, to the surprise of the patient, "forgotten" childhood feelings reappear. In many cases, historic facts like the history of a cold parent or a traumatic loss have been remembered or even incorporated into a personal narrative, but their full emotional importance remains minimized or denied. The latter phenomenon seems hard to explain without admitting the reality of unconscious affects, not simply "a potential beginning which is prevented from developing" (Freud 1915, p. 178) but a state kept actively out of awareness.

Certainly, the pendulum of clinical methods has now swung away from the impersonality and abstinence of an earlier era toward a responsiveness to affect and the pursuit of emotion-laden memories. Fosha's work provides a radical example of the reorientation of clinical technique around affect permeating many contemporary dynamic therapies. She writes of moving the clinical focus

> away from in-the-head cognition and toward moment-to-moment in-the-body sensing and feeling ('lose your head and come to your senses'), a process

that restores access to the wisdom of the body and releases natural healing processes

(2005, p. 517)

The descriptions Fosha provides resemble cathartic theories of therapeutic action by discharge of unconscious emotions. Examples of the work of Davanloo and Perls, to whom she refers, illustrate the power of the therapist to evoke immediate and surprising emotional outbursts in ways that standard methods of allowing the analytic relationship to unfold gradually over time rarely can bring about.

Green (1992) argues that Freud's distinction between memories and affects broke down with his recognition of the role of the ego, a point addressed earlier by Pulver (1971), who differentiated merely potential from actually repressed affects. Stein (1991) similarly underlined the central role of affect as an unconscious motivator of action. Loewald comments that

> a careful study of Freud's discussion of the cathartic method and of the normal mechanisms of dealing with affective experiences can show, however, that abreaction and associative absorption are essential elements of the analytic process. They are supplemented and often made possible, but by no means superseded, by the interpretation of defenses and instinctual derivatives.
>
> (1955, pp. 207–208)

He points out that Freud's early term "associative absorption" referred to his idea that abreaction could also occur through using a surrogate for action—namely, speech—which had initially been unavailable to the immature ego. The action in question, however, pertains to relational fears and wishes about interactions with other people, not Id-driven impulses. In Lacanian terms, unconscious desire can only be represented by "surrogates" that consist of fantasies stimulated by intersubjective contact. Its effective expression through speech in therapeutic practice, I contend, depends principally on the properties of the intersubjective field constructed by each clinical couple on a continuum from expansion and growth of consciousness to constriction and repetition.

Green emphasizes the shift in the evolution of psychoanalytic technique from interpretation of derivatives of unconscious drives to an analysis of the ego and superego as the sources of repressive processes. He noted that this change in focus inevitably implicates ego-generated affects like shame and guilt, which can remain unconscious. Clinical attention to putting these affective experiences into words differs from Fosha's techniques of pursuing abreaction of strangulated emotions and Green's own interpretation of drive derivatives. The analysis of states of shame and guilt necessarily involves relationships and social meanings, not an abreactive discharge of pent-up arousal. Green saw a danger in this turn of therapeutic attention toward affect because of its one-sided emphasis on conscious feelings (and, as a corollary, working from a position of empathy), a return to a phenomenologic approach that neglects the dynamic unconscious.

He mistrusted the contemporary focus on empathy and jointly shared states of affect as avoiding the importance of sexual wishes and promoting a self-enclosed, mirroring dyad of analyst and patient. This concern perpetuates a false distinction between a responsive focus on a subject's conscious affective experience and an exploration of his unconscious conflicts and inner world. It speaks to the extreme situation of the analyst's affective participation in a self-enclosed, mirroring dyad. An equally one-sided avoidance of responding to feeling states, as Lacan appeared (inconsistently) to advocate, would make for a very artificial analytic experience.

The crux of the theoretical problem identified by André Green remains the Cartesian separation of emotion from ideational representation in mental life. Modell addresses this dualism explicitly. "It is clear," he concludes, "that the ancient separation of mental faculties of cognition and feeling is false" (1973, p. 120). Representation, in whatever manner defined, falls under the traditional rubric of cognitive operations, generated in different centers of the brain from emotion, but this physiologic/anatomic separation does not translate into clinical practice without ignoring the ways in which symbolic structures and social meanings shape human emotional response and expression from birth. Psychoanalysis takes wishes and desires as fundamental to the subject, irreducible to Darwinian instinct or biological impulse. Personal and social meanings of actions, goals for relationships, and reactions to messages from others intertwine with emotion, and these generators of psychic life depend on intersubjective communication.

By treating affect clinically as a means of communication and influence, not simply abreaction, the intersubjective perspective on emotion resolves the artificial separation between direct bodily presence and the analysis of language suggested by Fosha. The presence (or absence) of emotional expression forms an inescapable part of the semiotic exchanges between patient and analyst. Modell (1978) first drew attention to the importance of non-communication of affects as a stimulus for reactions in the analyst (of discouragement, boredom, or rejection, for example); these negative responses often repeat symbolic failures of early relationships to respond, express, and share emotional states in an affectively present way.[7] Conversely, affect endows words and other symbolic communications with significance, although they form ambiguous and complex mixtures. Modell proposes the analyst's perception of communicated affects as the basis of empathy (1978, p. 168), but the perception can be partial and even promote dyadic complementarity as Green warned (by neglecting repressed affects and responding to role reciprocity). Just as in any human interaction, the analyst usually feels something before being entirely sure what is happening. Affect is rarely unmistakable, and, even when relatively transparent, may conceal other feelings. The empathic efforts of the analyst are bound to fall short of knowing the private experiences of the patient and make the analogous goal of intersubjective recognition equally problematic. I return to these issues in Chapter 8.

Conclusions: intersubjectivity and affect

An intersubjective model of affect takes as its starting point the ongoing trans-formation of embodied emotion into symbolic codes from birth onwards. Affective states emerge as interactive constructions within family and social contexts that provide their meaning. "Humans are indeed social animals," the neuroscientists Decety and Jackson conclude, "and virtually all of their actions (including their thoughts and desires) are directed toward or are produced in response to others" (2004, p. 71). Manifestations of emotion cannot be separated from the activation of intentions and desires directed toward another subject whose responses have been crucial in shaping them. Affect appears in the voice, facial expressions, and bodily gestures of both analyst and patient, along a spectrum ranging from highly organized symbols with private associations to memories and fantasies to reflexive physical expressions apparently lacking mental representation (perhaps like a sudden fright or rage). In semiotic terms (as I will elaborate in Chapter 6), the first level of response to any sign consists of a biopsychic state that often passes outside conscious awareness. The back and forth of communication of affect takes a direction determined by the state of the bipersonal field, which fluctuates according to the transference and countertransference, the history of the therapeutic relationship, and the subject's default relational positions. The nuanced succession of affects in analytic process evolves intersubjectively over time.

In clinical practice, intersubjective transactions tend to fall into recurrent patterns. Without the daily constraints of real tasks to accomplish and social codes structuring meaning, subjects unconsciously repeat variations of internal models as a kind of implicit negotiation between the partners. The work of psychoanalysis enables the affective component of the exchange to become gradually represented symbolically and able to be spoken about. By helping to put the patterns into words, the analyst expands the range of possible commu-nication within the bipersonal field, promoting a greater degree of subjective ownership. Lacan retranslates Freud's aphorism, "Where Id was, there shall ego be" in terms of the process of subjectivation: "Where it was, there shall I become" (1955, p. 121). Similarly, for Bion (1962), analysis should foster the production of thoughts and expansion of conscious possibility. The two share the analytic goal of enabling more of the unconscious to become available to the thinking subject, and thereby open to greater freedom and choice. When a patient's expres-sion of signs comes mainly from the real of the body, as occurs in some emotions and gestures, thinking (symbolic mental representation) may be lacking, and the responses of the analyst may be correspondingly physical. Interactive movements between subjects accompany all exchanges, however, and are usually unconscious, as was first demonstrated by the anthropologist R. Birdwhistell, founder of the field of kinesthetics in 1970. He drew attention to the intricate dance of recipro-cal bodily postures between therapist and patient revealed by slow-motion films. Bodily movements can be viewed as physical manifestations of emotion (de Gelder, 2006), but can also carry learned symbolic (culturally specific) meanings.

Affectively charged expressions form the substance of transference and counter-transference interactions, but they do not express "inside to outside" intrapsychic wishes only. Affects cross the gap that separates an impersonal physiology (Lacan's "interiorised bodily emotion," 1961–62, p. 192) from meaningful human communication. They have the properties of signs or signifiers addressed by one subject to another subject. Everything experienced cannot be expressed in words, of course, but everything arising in awareness carries symbolic resonance and its manifestation becomes a message to the other. The range of communication through all channels varies as a function of the state of the relationship, which facilitates or forecloses the exchange. Reactions and counterreactions in the interactive dialogue reverberate rapidly, expanding or shutting down the expression of affects. Eventually, a successful therapeutic process enables words to be attached to these "unthought" experiences. The liveliness, freedom, and creative possibilities available for emotional expression depend on the quality of the inter-subjective dimension.

Notes

1. The recent volume by Johnston and Malabou (2013) pursues this objective through a comparative study of affect in philosophy, neuroscience, and psychoanalysis. They argue for a dialectical, rather than unified approach to integration. Žižek (2006) includes recent cognitive psychology research in his searching discussion of the symbol-brain interaction.
2. "A charitable explanation for why cops kill is that certain actions by suspects (running away, or resisting arrest, or reaching into the squad car to grab a gun) may trigger the rage circuit to fire with such intensity as to override all cortical self-control" (Schermer, 2015).
3. Some recent researchers have used more elaborate methodology to score posed children's faces, but the influence of stereotypes in media to which even diverse young subjects are exposed remains an issue.
4. The "headless" description of the unconscious occurs in Lacan's interpretation of Freud's inaugural dream of Irma's injection. In this dream, he comments, "there's the recognition of the fundamentally acephalic character of the subject" (1954–55, p. 170).
5. The separation between representation and affect was addressed importantly by Laplanche. "In Lacanianism, unfortunately, this dissociation [between representation and affect] leads to the rejection of one of the two terms, and to an absolute priority being accorded to representation, to the primacy of the 'signifier', adopting the term used by Lacan. You do not need to read many Lacanian texts to be convinced that the Freudian distinction between affect and representation has become – in Lacanianism – a real rejection, sometimes scornful, of the affective and of lived experience, which moreover, are usually *affected* by signs of irony or inverted commas" (Laplanche, *The Unconscious and the Id*, Rebus, 1999, p. 18).
6. Citing many authors including both analytic and others in the experiential therapy tradition, Fosha (2005) emphasizes "processes by which intense, sudden, undefended, and surprising emotional experiences can lead to lasting, even lifelong, transformations" (p. 516). She states that "Accelerated Experiential Dynamic Psychotherapy (AEDP) places the somatic experience of affect in relationship and

its dyadic regulation at the center of how it clinically aims to bring about change" (p. 516). Fosha's methods can be regarded as a sophisticated descendant of Freud's early cathartic approach, as well as suggesting the influences of Gestalt therapy and the short-term model of Davenloo (which she mentions).

7. Ferro (2007) also emphasized the importance of a lack of expressed affects in his book on emotions in psychoanalysis.

References

Ammaniti, M. & Gallese, V. (2014). *The Birth of Intersubjectivity: Psychodynamics, Neurobiology, and the Self*, New York: W.W. Norton.

Barrett, L., Lindquist, K., & Gendron, M. (2007). Language as context for the perception of emotion, *Trends in Cognitive Sciences*, 11:327–332.

Barrett, L.F. (2006). Solving the emotion paradox: Categorization and the experience of emotion, *Personality and Social Psychology Review*, 10:20–46.

Bion, W. (1962). *Learning from Experience*, London: Karnac Books.

Birdwhistell, R. (1970). *Top of Form, Bottom of Form: Kinesics and Context: Essays on Body Motion Communication*, Philadelphia, PA: University of Pennsylvania Press.

Boston Change Process Study Group (BCPSG) (2007). The foundational level of psychodynamic meaning: Implicit process in relation to conflict, defense, and unconscious conflict, *International Journal of Psychoanalysis*, 88: 843–860.

Brown, L. (2011). *Intersubjective Processes and the Unconscious*, New York: Routledge.

Crivelli, C., Jarillo, S., & Fridlund, A. (2016). A multidisciplinary approach to research in small-scale societies: Studying emotions and facial expressions in the field, *Frontiers in Psychology: Hypothesis and Theory*, 7: article 1073.

Damasio, A.R. (1994). *Descartes' Error: Emotion, Reason and the Human Brain*, New York: Putnam.

Damasio, A.R. (1999). *The Feeling of What Happens: Body and Emotion in the Making of Consciousness*, New York: Harcourt Brace.

Damasio, A.R. (2003). *Looking for Spinoza: Joy, Sorrow, and the Feeling Brain*, New York: Harvest Books/Harcourt.

Damasio, A.R. (2012). *Self Comes to Mind: Constructing the Conscious Brain*, New York: Vintage Books.

Davidson, D. (2005). *Truth, Language, and History*, Oxford: Clarendon Press/Oxford University Press.

Decety, J. & Jackson, P. (2004). *Behavioral and Cognitive Neuroscience Reviews*, 3:71–100.

de Gelder, B. (2006). Opinion: Towards the neurobiology of emotional body language, *Nature Reviews & Neuroscience*, 7:242–249.

Descartes, R. (1989). *The Passions of the Soul*, trans. S. Voss, Indianapolis, IN/Cambridge: Hackett Publishing Company.

Ekman, P. (1997). Should we call it expression or communication? *Innovations in Social Science Research*, 10:333–344.

Ekman, P. (2001). Facial expression, in *Oxford Companion to the Body*, Eds. C. Blakemore & S. Jennett, London: Oxford University Press. Online citation Encyclopedia.com., December 29, 2014.

Ekman, P. & Friesen, W.V. (1971). Constants across cultures in the face and emotion, *Journal of Personality and Social Psychology*, 17:124–129.

Ferro, A. (2007). *Avoiding Emotions, Living Emotions*, trans. I. Harvey, New York: Routledge, the New Library of Psychoanalysis.

Fosha, D. (2005). Emotion, true self, true other, core state: Toward a clinical theory of affective change process, *Psychoanalytic Review*, 92:513–551.

Freud, S. (1915). *The Unconscious: The Standard Edition of the Complete Psychological Works of Sigmund Freud, Vol. XIV (1914–16)*, pp. 159–215.

Fridlund, A. (1994). *Human Facial Expression: An Evolutionary View*, Cambridge, MA: Academic Press.

Fridlund, A. (1997). The new psychology of facial expressions, Ch. 5 in *The Psychology of Facial Expression*, Ed. J. Russell and J. Fernández-Dols, Cambridge University Press.

Garcia, A. & Ibanez, A. (2014). Two-person neuroscience and naturalistic social communication: The role of language and linguistic variables in brain-coupling research, *Frontiers in Psychiatry, Systems Biology*, v5: article 124.

Georgieff, N. (2011). Psychoanalysis and social cognitive neuroscience: A new framework for a dialogue, *Journal of Physiology*, Paris: Elsevier, online at: www.elsevier.com/locate/jphysparis

Green, A. (1992). *Le discours vivant*, Paris: Presses Universitaires de France (*The Fabric of Affect in the Psychoanalytic Discourse*, The New Library of Psychoanalysis, London and New York, 1999).

Hari, R. & Kujala, M. (2009). Brain basis of human social interaction: From concepts to brain imaging, *Physiological Reviews*, 89:453–479.

Jensen, T. (2014). Emotion in languaging: languaging as affective, adaptive, and flexible behavior in social interaction, *Frontiers in Psychology, Cognitive Science*, doi: 10.3389/fpsyg.2014.00720

Johnston, A. & Malabou, C. (2013). *Self and Emotional Life: Philosophy, Psychoanalysis, and Neuroscience*, New York: Columbia University Press.

Kendler, K.S., Halberstadt, L.J., Butera, F., Myers, J., Bouchard, T., Ekman P. (2008). The similiarity of facial expressions in response to emotion-inducing films in reared-apart twins, *Psychological Medicine*, 38:1475–1483.

Lacan, J. (1954–55). *The Seminar of Jacques Lacan, Book II: The Ego in Freud's Theory and in the Technique of Psychoanalysis*, Ed. J.-A. Miller, trans. S. Tomaselli, Cambridge: Cambridge University Press, 1988.

Lacan, J. (1955). The Freudian thing, in *Écrits*, trans. B. Fink, pp. 107–137, New York: W.W. Norton, 2002.

Lacan, J. (1961–62). *Seminar IX: L'Identification*, unpublished, trans. C. Gallagher, available online.

Lacan, J. (1962–63). *Anxiety: The Seminar of Jacques Lacan, Book X*, trans. A.R. Price, 2014, London: Polity.

Laplanche, J. (1981). *The Unconscious and the Id*, trans. L. Watson, London: Rebus Press, 1999.

Lawrence, K., Campbell, R., & Skuse, D. (2015). Age gender and puberty influence the development of facial emotion recognition, *Frontiers in Psychology, Perception Science*, article 761.

LeDoux, J. (2012). Evolution of human emotion: A view through fear programs, *Brain Research*, 195:431–442.

Leys, R. (2011). The turn to affect: A critique, *Critical Inquiry*, 37:434–472.

Liotti, M. & Panksepp, J. (2004). On the neural nature of human emotions and implications for biological psychiatry, in Panksepp, J. Ed., *Textbook of Biological Psychiatry*, pp. 33–74, New York: Wiley.

Loewald, H.W. (1955). Hypnoid state, repression, abreaction and recollection, *Journal of the American Psychoanalytic Association*, 3:201–210.

Lutz, C. (1988). *Unnatural Emotions: Everyday Sentiments on a Micronesian Atoll and Their Challenge to Western Theory*, Chicago: University of Chicago Press.

Modell, A.H. (1973). Affects and psychoanalytic knowledge, *Annals of Psycho-analysis*, 1:117–124.

Modell, A.H. (1978). Affects and the complementarity of biologic and historical meaning. *Annals of Psychoanalysis*, 6:167–180.

Naab, P.J. & Russell, J.A. (2007). Judgments of emotion from spontaneous facial expressions of New Guineans, *Emotion*, 7:736–744.

Nagel, T. (1974). What is it like to be a bat? *The Philosophical Review*, 83:435–450.

Nussbaum, M. (2001). *Upheavals of Thought: The Intelligence of Emotions*, Cambridge: Cambridge University Press.

Panksepp, J. (1999). Emotions as viewed by psychoanalysis and neuroscience, *Neuro-Psychoanalysis*, 1:15–38.

Panksepp, J. (2005). Affective consciousness: Core emotional feelings in animals and humans, *Consciousness and Cognition*, 14:30–80.

Panksepp, J. & Watt, D.F. (2003). "The ego is first and foremost a body ego": A critical review of Antonio Damasio's Looking for Spinoza. Critical issues in the conceptualization of emotion and feeling, *Neuropsychoanalysis*, 5:201–231.

Park, S. & Ichinose, M. (2015). Amygdala on the lookout, *American Journal of Psychiatry*, 172:704–705.

Przyrembel, M., Smallwood, J., Pauen, M., & Singer, T. (2012). Illuminating the dark matter of social neuroscience: Considering the problem of social interaction from philosophical, psychological, and neuroscientific perspectives, *Frontiers in Human Neuroscience*, 6: article 190.

Pulver, S. (1971). Can affects be unconscious? *International Journal of Psycho-analysis*, 52:347–355.

Putnam, H. (1981). *Reason, Truth, and History*, Cambridge: Cambridge University Press.

Rosaldo, M.Z. (1984). Toward an anthropology of self and feeling, in *Culture Theory: Essays on Mind, Self, and Emotion*, R. Shweder and R. LeVine Eds., pp. 137–157, Cambridge: Cambridge University Press.

Russell, J.A. (1994). Is there universal recognition of emotion from facial expression? A review of the cross-cultural studies, *Psychological Bulletin*, 115:102–141.

Sacks, O. (2015). *On the Move: A Life*, London: Picador.

Salvatore, S. & Freda, M.F. (2011). Affect, unconscious, and sensemaking: A psycho-dynamic semiotic and dialogic model, *New Ideas in Psychology*, 29:119–135.

Schermer, M. (2015). Why do cops kill? *Scientific American*, July 1, 2015.

Shuman, V. (2013). Studying the social dimension of emotion regulation, *Frontiers in Psychology, Emotion Science*, v4: article 922.

Shweder, R. (1991). *Thinking through Cultures: Expeditions in Cultural Psychology*, Cambridge, MA: Harvard University Press.

Sibony-Malpertu, Y. (2012). *Une liaison philosophique*, Paris: Stock.

Solms, M. (2013). The conscious Id, *Neuropsychoanalysis*, 15:5–13.

Solms, M. & Panksepp, J. (2012). The "Id" knows more than the "Ego" admits: Neuro-psychoanalytic and primal consciousness perspectives on the interface between affective and cognitive neuroscience, *Brain Sciences*, 2:147–175.

Stanford Encyclopedia of Philosophy (2013). Elisabeth, Princess of Bohemia, online at: https://app.gonightshift.com/user/get-started/step2/

Stein, R. (1991). *Psychoanalytic Theories of Affect*, London: Karnac.

Stern, D.N. (1985). *The Interpersonal World of the Infant*, New York: Basic Books.

Tomkins, S. (1962–63). *Affect, Imagery, Consciousness*, 2 vols. New York: Springer.

van Kleef, G., Chesin, A., Fischer, A., & Schneider, I. (2016). Editorial: The social nature of emotion, *Frontiers in Psychology*, v7: article 896.

Yovell, Y., Solms, M., & Fotopoulou, A. (2015). The case for neuropsychoanalysis: Why a dialogue with neuroscience is necessary but not sufficient for psychoanalysis, *The International Journal of Psychoanalysis*, 96:1515–1553.

Žižek, S. (2006). *The Parallax View*, Cambridge, MA: MIT Press.

Chapter 5

Affect in clinical work

In this chapter I discuss clinical presentations of affect and their management, and present case vignettes to illustrate three different forms of emotional expression. I emphasize their intersubjective aspect—how expressions of emotion (or their non-communication) lead to varied responses by the therapist. As we saw in Chapter 4, many authors privilege intense emotional expressions as carrying an element of authenticity and truth coming from the core of a subject's existence and actively seek to elicit them. Others observe that affects can be misleading, self-serving, or perpetuate a static relational pattern. Lacan argued that a focus on feelings stimulates imaginary fantasies, images of self and other that can function like a hall of mirrors between two partners. Yet a lack of affect can serve as a sign of avoidance of contact or of severe psychopathology. An intersubjective perspective on emotion enables a therapist to put these variations in context. The important clinical issue in managing affect turns on the movement of the dialogue, which may be expanded, deepened, frozen, or dampened, to a large extent depending on a therapist's responses.

Lacan's criticism of the recourse to affect in treatment echoes familiar therapeutic clichés about "getting the feelings out" or "saying what you feel" as descriptions of dynamic treatment. Anyone who has watched the HBO television series *In Treatment* can recognize the pitfalls of this kind of monothematic approach. Determining which feelings need to be gotten out depends on the theoretical preferences of the therapist, and the pursuit of "true" feelings can be an endless quest. Moreover, the venting model of powerful emotion, like Freud's concept of abreaction, implies the discharge of a pent-up reservoir, as though it consists of a fixed quantity from a single source. Yet in clinical practice, repetitious displays of strong feelings can persist over long periods of time without leading to growth or change. A familiar example of stasis around an affective exchange is the so-called borderline patient, who may continuously express intense feelings like rejection or victimization, which typically appear in the transference. Encouraging such expressions as a purging or confessional release can obscure the function of the repetition and perpetuate a stereotyped relationship, a dyad defining both participants. On the other hand, interpreting an emotionally charged transference as a set of projections (or the classic judgment of "distortions") usually elicits negative reactions, as it is heard as a criticism from a powerful imaginary figure blaming the patient for what he experiences as mistreatment. The therapist can sidestep participation in this pattern of enactment by mirroring a patient's feelings in a more empathic mode, which can quiet down a volatile situation (in a way, joining with the patient). Still, it may be difficult to move beyond this stance to accomplish more exploratory work.

A technique centered on affect can lead to the error of reducing the position of a patient to a defined role or single emotional state. The analyst responds to what he believes the patient is feeling, while ignoring messages and meanings that express other aspects of his subjectivity. Encouragement, support, or interpretation of affects, which may be useful at the right times, become counterproductive when applied as an ongoing way of relating to a patient, who remains confined by the complementary role situation they induce, enacting a form of transference. When the intersubjective dynamic of mutual influence and interpretation is not taken into account, the therapist tends to join a mirroring dyad. He may then fail to notice the symbols and signs of unconscious affects he himself communicates and how they shape the ongoing interaction.

The pursuit of feelings as an enactment: the case of Adriana

Treating the expression of affect as a goal in itself risks perpetuating a fruitless search for "true feelings" in analytic therapy, as illustrated by a case presented by a senior candidate, Dr. Bates, to a supervision seminar. His patient, Adriana, a successful manager with some conflicts at work, sought psychotherapy at the suggestion of a sibling, who believed that their family upbringing had adversely affected their ability to get along with other people. Adriana herself seemed remarkably unreflective about her feelings and patterns of behavior, which she described concretely. She was functioning well; she had a family, and there were no real symptoms. She told Dr. Bates about growing up in another country in a family atmosphere that featured a lot of action. She recounted parental affairs, abrupt moves, and separations, along with a lack of attention to the children's daily lives. The parents seemed materially care taking, affectionate on occasion, and even encouraging in terms of school and recreation but with little close interaction. The patient was accustomed to this pattern and did not express anger or sadness about it, although her story suggested a sense of emotional isolation, which may have spurred efforts to win the parents' approval. Dr. Bates described Adriana as a good enough mother in a conventional-sounding marriage. She had strong ideas of the right things to do in her job and at home. At the same time, she was often perplexed about the behavior of people at her office, and, despite her affability and cooperativeness, felt disregarded by them. She also commented that her husband, while caring, did not seem aware of her burdens of work and family. She initially posed her therapeutic goal as getting help to solve professional problems at work, which she saw as largely cultural, but the content of her sessions quickly turned to her interpersonal difficulties.

Dr. Bates told us that he had become frustrated with his client after four years of treatment. She seemed invested in her frequent sessions, but what she was looking for and how she felt about her therapy eluded him. She talked about her interactions with colleagues and family and sought his advice about what she might do to improve relationships, but lacked curiosity about her own behavior. She responded to queries by saying that maybe she just wasn't trying hard enough, while expressing uncertainty about what, if anything, could make a difference. When Dr. Bates inquired about her feelings during the episodes she described, Adriana tended to provide detailed descriptions. He wondered why she was holding back and how he might get beneath her façade of resigned reasonableness and good humor. Frequently, he stopped her narrative to ask what she was feeling while speaking, suggested she pause and attend to her feelings in the moment, and made interpretations about the difficulty of expressing emotions in her family and perhaps even with him. She seemed a compliant patient and reported that these interventions were very interesting and helpful; yet not much change in the process occurred.

Listening to the accounts of these sessions, members of the supervision group commented on the obvious attachment of the patient to her therapist and her tenacious commitment to the treatment, which no doubt offered her something worthwhile and unfamiliar. The process notes did not sound entirely flat to us, but full of associations and a persistent sense of her struggle to do or say the right thing, especially around men she worked with at her job. She saw Dr. Bates as helping her get along better with people, although she admitted this was hard for her, and she looked to him for approval of her efforts. There may have been something bland or childish about her way of expressing herself, but members of the seminar disagreed about this. Some of us responded sympathetically to her wistful and earnest affect, while others admitted impatience with her immaturity and naivety. For his part, Dr. Bates worked with a model of treatment in which he would help his patient uncover and express blocked feelings from the past that were preventing her fullest development and a capacity for deeper relationships. In this effort, he was becoming frustrated, and Adriana may have picked up on his dissatisfaction, as indicated by her comments about not trying hard enough and relationships being difficult for her. In one way, she had found a good parent who supported her values and ambitions, but a less positive aspect of her early relationships may also have been repeated. Namely, it struck the group that often the therapist took for granted the meaning of what she was saying and did not inquire further about her statements. He interpreted her associations as an avoidance of the deeper emotional expressions he sensed under the surface. Although he commented about her parents' hurtful behavior, for example, what seemed most important to him was the absence of intense feelings in her descriptions, not the actual language and affect she employed. His interventions sounded concerned and caring, but detached from her actual words, as though he already knew what she was feeling. A safe, but static, situation had been established.

Some features of this case are relevant to thinking about the therapeutic use of affect from an intersubjective perspective. First, like most people's, Adriana's affects were not straightforward, but presented amalgams of feeling tones that evoked different reactions in the listeners. Members of the seminar responded with affect to her story, but they were also able to step back and reflect on what was happening in the room. Dr. Bates's presentation suggested that he and Adriana were caught in a repetitive dialogue, even if its meaning was hard to determine exactly. She stuck to stories from work and home where she wondered if she was doing the right things. Dr. Bates expressed an empathic concern about Adriana's uncertainty about people; he was kind and made supportive comments about what she told him. At the same time, he held up a goal of freely expressing emotions that she was manifestly not meeting. In a reversal of positions, he admitted to us that he wasn't sure if he were handling the case properly, and felt that Adriana expected something more form him.

Members commented that Adriana repeated a configuration in her life in which she felt left on her own, with no one paying much attention to what she was going through. Both roles in this relationship pattern seemed replicated in the therapy, with Dr. Bates attributing her difficulties to her own behavior with people, but also feeling somewhat alone and not listened to by his patient. Adriana presented herself as assuming the positions of dutiful child, spouse, and colleague, always awaiting understanding or appreciation from unresponsive partners, and now again in her therapy was seeking love and approval from someone she looked up to but who didn't seem to hear her. She had increased the frequency of her sessions as a way to work harder at making progress, but felt unable to supply what Dr. Bates was asking of her. When questioned about her feelings, she tried to come up with something, but her answers sounded strained and artificial. The supervision group used words like resistance and lip service, and the therapeutic dialogue appeared in danger of getting stuck in a silent struggle that wasn't recognized. We sensed other possibilities, however, like an occasional tone of irony in Adriana's reports—for instance, when she wondered what she needed to do to be appreciated by people. We felt that Dr. Bates may have been influenced by her matter-of-fact style of delivery to disregard the actual phrases and expressions she used and to see her as telling only one story. His approach of pulling for intense feelings appeared to have interfered with his ability to explore the variations in her experiences in relationships. In this respect, he was reacting to what Adriana wasn't expressing, rather than to what she actually said.

Lacan considered this type of impasse as a clinical problem in which attention is paid to what is imagined to be the difficulty (in this case not expressing true emotions), rather than to a patient's actual words. We should add that the words, affective tone, and bodily movements are intertwined as part of a complex communication and inevitably influence the position of the therapist, but without reflective processing of his own reactions and their effects on his patient, the exchange can take on the quality of a continuous enactment of reciprocal roles. Dr. Bates's impatience with Adriana was a sign of a negative view of her that mirrored her own self-evaluation (not trying sufficiently). Lacan describes this configuration as the imaginary transference, consisting of a dyadic relationship in which the analyst identifies with one or both partners in a relational pair. Identifying with or assuming a complementary role to a perceived message from the other leads to a static and symmetric relationship. Aron (2006) evocatively portrays this as a seesaw-like series of exchanges of roles that doesn't go anywhere. In Lacanian terms, this set-up defines the patient univocally in an ego-to-ego dialogue, rather than as a polyphonic subject moving freely across different representations of self. As discussed in Chapter 3, recourse to a third person to discuss a therapy in progress can help an analyst avoid or become more aware of his participation in this situation. Speaking with colleagues or supervisors, learning from teachers or professional publications, and the habit of perspective taking on one's interactions may suggest other options. Our supervision group functioned in this way, pointing out Dr. Bates's participation in a dyadic pattern with Adriana. Fortunately, he was receptive to this input and could see how he had become implicated in a repetition, especially his underlying critical opinion of her as a patient. This insight seemed to help and we heard a different tone of interaction in the next sessions. Although he may have been correct that Adriana was warding off powerful emotion, his technique supported an enactment.

A countertransference response to powerful emotions: the case of Nancy

What follows is a much different situation taken from my own practice in which strong affects were central. A 17-year-old young woman, Nancy, was referred for therapy after bursting into the home of a female classmate who had just broken off their amorous relationship, making a violent scene to which police were finally summoned. Nancy was likable and engaging, but enraged and very sad. The rejection by her friend was on top of learning that her divorced mother had developed metastatic cancer with a poor prognosis. I want to focus this discussion on a period near the beginning of treatment, after she was discharged from an adolescent in-patient unit. During this time, Nancy increased her frequency of sessions to five days a week, sometimes with an added Saturday morning. Typically, she arrived early, and, when I opened the door, rushed into my office where she threw herself sobbing onto the floor. Often she remained like that, saying a few sentences, but mostly wailing and pounding the carpet. I made efforts to encourage her to speak more about what she was feeling, but without much success. She was a bright young woman and aware that I was a bit nonplussed by this scenario. This was all she could do, she explained. "I don't know what to do."

I thought about notions of regression, especially Winnicott's ideas of returning to the point of environmental failure, and felt the emotional pressure of Nancy's desperate sense of abandonment. I knew she was buffeted by suicidal thoughts and wondered about rehospitalizing her, a step she strongly opposed. Finally, I told her that I gathered from what she said that she felt totally alone in the world without a mother or her girlfriend to take care of her. I said that if she felt safe coming to my office I would accept that role while she needed it. This seemed to relieve her, but for a few weeks the situation remained the same. I found little more to say except that her pain must be unbearable, that it was hard for her to go on, that she needed to let these feelings out before she could get beyond these losses, and so forth. One day, she sat up and asked gravely, "What am I supposed to do?" I looked at her for a moment and then replied, "Get up in the morning and go back to school. Rejoin the chorus and your music classes. Come here if you can't bear it." She nodded wryly, as if to say, "What else did I expect you to tell me?" Then she looked up and said, "OK," and left the session. We then entered a mostly talking phase.

Nancy's case illustrates some of the previous points about intersubjectivity in treatment. Her emotional display was not simply a release, but a communication. As a sign (or set of signs), it signified to me the profound losses of her emotionally unavailable mother and her girlfriend, who may have served as a replacement. This reading strongly shaped my response to Nancy. Her affects, like Adriana's, although more dramatic, consisted of a mixture involving rage and hurt, as well as love for her objects. For a time, I responded to only one aspect of these messages —her sense of abandonment—with an offer of nurture or protection. I felt in the beginning as if I were dealing with a mewling infant, which might have perpetuated one of those rigid dyadic pairs that freezes the therapeutic process. Instead, Nancy herself helped break the cycle, which immediately resulted in a different type of response from me. Her question about what to do seemed addressed to someone in a different position from the one I occupied when experiencing her as a child needing to be taken care of.

As noted above, powerful emotional outbursts do not in themselves necessarily produce therapeutic progress, especially when they provide unprocessed sources of satisfaction. Perhaps more importantly, communications dominated by intense affects tend to evoke complementary intersubjective responses in the analyst, depending on how he experiences the patient. Sometimes, by recognizing our oscillation between impatient, rejecting, indifferent, caretaking, or other positions we can contextualize the therapeutic interaction as taking place in a shifting dialogic field. Stepping outside the immediacy of the here and now to reflect on the process that structures it requires training and practice (it doesn't come easily), but constitutes an essential skill, which enables the analyst to observe his movement across varied ways of constituting the other (again, the metaphor of a third can be useful). Rather than classifying a patient as a provocative, demanding, vengeful, lovable, or some other type of person (and rationalizing our response by this assessment), we can step back and observe ourselves caught up in a complex interaction. From this vantage point, we regain our capacity to think about what is going on.

For a time, Nancy and I did seem stuck in a complementary scenario in which I experienced her as a young child calling for a nurturing response to her distress. Perhaps this dyad (we could call it a child–parent dyad) stabilized the situation and created a relatively safe situation for Nancy. Not much work was accomplished during this period, although her comfort and security were probably improved. However, something changed that enabled her to speak more. What may have helped was that although I did not set very high expectations for her, I did not see or treat her only as a helpless child. My trusting her to manage outside the hospital came from a different vantage point. Later on, I came to appreciate other components of her emotional state that were drowned out for me at the time by her powerful outbursts. Our dialogue then expanded to include associations to her father, her sexuality, and her aggressiveness with people.

A colleague once told a somewhat similar crying patient, "After all, psycho-analysis is not the wailing wall." He insisted she speak to him, and it seemed to work out. But I did not agree with his metaphor, meant to engage his client by a humorous confrontation. The image of the wailing wall suggests the early Freudian–Lacanian view of affect summarized in Chapter 3: split off from words, emotions consist of primitive arousal discharged without personal meaning being elaborated. An alternative view is that emotions always carry signification; they are not (or not solely) some kind of automatic discharge of primitive energies disrupting the cohesion of the subject but an intersubjective communication, if one quite difficult to read. Emotions always produce responses in the listener—not necessarily correct or accurate responses, as theorists who rely on what appears in their minds as a guide to their patient's unconscious sometimes seem to advo-cate, but a sign of engagement. The flow of the process matters more than the interpretation of its unconscious meaning. I emphasize that affective signs typically elicit a spectrum of responses in the listener, as occurred in our super-vision group listening to Adriana's case or perhaps simply in reading these examples.

An accidental eruption of affect: the case of Ramon

My third vignette describes a case in which a strong emotional outburst did lead to productive work. My patient, a Spanish man, Ramon, was referred by his former analyst because of severe and persistent obsessive-compulsive behaviors, which consisted in part of spending hours researching cell-phone options and dating sites without taking any action. He explained these symptoms as self-destructive, but nonetheless successful attempts to avoid overwhelming anxiety. For this reason, he was dubious about giving them up, and frequently expressed misgivings whether analysis could really help him. At the same time, he criticized himself for being unproductive and risking getting into trouble in his work. This became a recurrent and circular story that always returned to what he called square one, his impossible, self-defeating dilemma.

When I inquired about Ramon's interest in the dating sites, since he did not use them, he explained about his repetitive difficulties with demanding women, mostly on the job but also with some family members, for whom he felt responsible but inadequate. He described interactions in which he felt used and humiliated, feeling manipulated into a charged encounter. While trying to placate a woman, he experienced a vague sexual arousal, along with feelings of helplessness, anger, and inadequacy. These associations seemed promising and pointed us in a new direction, but we were not able to make much progress beyond the concrete details of these scenes, nor did we link them to his massive anxiety. Ramon's affective expression was quite muted, and I wondered about his motivation for actual relationships and, specifically, his ability to make use of analysis. Listening, I sometimes found myself feeling critical of his jumping around from topic to topic without conveying a clear emotional reaction. At other moments I thought about how he wasted his life on empty activities and wondered why he would do this to himself. Was he transferring his self-criticism onto me in the transference and was I compliant with a fantasy that he be punished or berated? More than usual, I tried to let him know the kinds of thoughts I was having—"things going through my mind while listening." Unfortunately, these efforts at sharing my experiences of the sessions fell flat, and I soon realized that he took them mainly as requests for reassurance about my behavior, which he gave without considering the content. Experiencing a sense of non-communication in our relationship, I puzzled about the nature of his problems and began privately to share his doubts about the value of the analysis.

One day, while discussing another incident, Ramon suddenly asked me if there were an English word "rancorous." He thought it might mean a vindictive desire to hurt someone, which is not the precise dictionary definition (we looked it up), but certainly approximates the more accurate notion of a persistent enmity. He then told me he had thought of the Spanish term "*rancoroso*," whose meaning is similar. The word had come to his mind before, but he hadn't been certain of its English equivalent. His question to me immediately aroused my interest, first, because of his curiosity about the translation of a word, which I took as an inquiry about the possibility of sharing a signifier with me; second, because of the form of his direct question. I then asked him to tell me more about *rancoroso*, making an awkward effort to use an approximate Spanish pronunciation, with an affective emphasis on the syllables.

After a long silence, he reported suddenly and vividly picturing a scene between his father and grandmother that had recurred many times during his growing up. His grandmother would belittle and disparage people who had shown concern for his father during an impoverished and isolated childhood, stemming from his illegitimate birth. Father attempted to defend these relationships, but ineffectively. In the end, he was left to take his son and leave, seemingly helpless to deal with his implacable and bitter mother. Ramon then reported a painful sensation in his chest and began to sob freely. This was a decidedly new development. "What if she had been correct about these people's hypocrisy?" he cried. "If they didn't really care, then my father would have had nothing at all to hold on to!"

I recognized aspects of this situation from other contexts, but it seemed to have been the word, perhaps the vibrations of the letter "r" in his chest in pronouncing it, which opened onto the remembered scene of humiliation and the "nothingness" it covered. He had told me before that his grandmother was mean-spirited and critical of his father, but the emotion, the somatic accompaniment, and the vivid memory achieved a new figuration by his evocation of the Spanish word, which linked to his symptomatic interactions with women. One might say he derived a dangerous secret pleasure or *jouissance* from his feelings of humiliation during these encounters, which helped to cover a void in himself. The frightening abyss of anxiety and "nothingness" seemed to call to him, necessitating a massive escape through his compulsions or enactments with women. Finding the word *rancoroso*, on the other hand, permitted something significant to shift in his subjective posture, enabling him to sob and express intense affect while speaking about what he experienced.

What might we conclude from Ramon's sobbing? First, his crying occurred within an intersubjective relationship in which a transference was active. He had brought me into a remembered scene in a more personal and intimate way than he had been capable of before. Yet his sobbing was similar in form to other cases I have encountered of people facing a threatening and overwhelming situation (like Nancy). The manifest emotional expression in his face and posture and the wordless tears were organized in roughly the same ways as core emotion theories might postulate—that is, revival of a painful childhood memory set off a built-in bodily response system of distress. But in addition, a personal meaning was conveyed through the affective outburst, implying a dynamic unconscious dimension. One might reasonably infer that Ramon had been defending himself all along from experiencing an unbearable existential situation involving elements of his relationship to his father, with whom he seems to have identified in the triangle with his grandmother, repeated in his own relationships with women. The meaning of his crying was not obvious but opened into the family history in a new way, which his symptoms had diverted him from facing, perhaps by sexualizing them. Only his repeated descriptions of compulsive behaviors permitted an indirect or displaced expression of an unconscious affective state, whose charge, as Freud hypothesized, could not be abreacted. The affect–memory–ideation complex in his unconscious, like another voice within him, remained active and needed to be warded off. The word opened the way for a surrogate expression of this unrepresented material.

Affect in the clinic: some conclusions

Following Freud, could we find indications of a quantitative factor of discharge of pent-up emotion in the outburst of sobbing in these vignettes? In the example of Nancy, the unbearable intensity of her grief and anger seemed to point in this direction. Yet she did not cry all the time, apparently reserving it, for the most part, for our hours. With Ramon, who suffered the dread of anxiety, I had the sense of an uncontrollable "Real" threatening to tear him apart into nothingness, but that is a theoretical predilection. All the same, the menace of the void he conveyed had a more profound and ominous quality than the understandable pain of Nancy's losses. In Adriana's case, we might expect tears and anger to emerge later in her therapy, but, even in that event, would strangulated emotion be the explanation for her difficulties or, rather, her inability to express (or to use a dialogue to verbalize) the implications of her childhood experiences for her current relationships? Emotion indicates a position in relation to unconscious desire, but does not discharge a quantity.

However we choose to interpret their unconscious meanings, the linkage of affects to words was important for all three patients. For Ramon and Adriana, the interlinguistic situation was quite significant. The two might have felt freer to express themselves in their native tongues than in the cooler Anglo medium. The therapeutic situation itself is always culturally inflected, so that cross-cultural aspects of the transference may have served as an obstacle to more open affective communication. Homayounpour and Movehedi (2012) summarize the literature to support this hypothesis, following Barthe's stress on the connection of the maternal language to the mother's body. In the intersubjective relation, words, gestures, voice, and affect are distinct signs, although they present as a unity that is like a personal signature in their relative emphases and intensity. The listener responds differentially to this complexity, resulting in a level of uncertainty that precludes interpretation. Clarification by questions cannot resolve the problem. The sender lacks full awareness of what he is expressing in the several channels available, so that his answers only resolve ambiguity up to a point. In everyday life, the context of an event often explains the general meaning of our messages, at least enough for practical purposes, but psychoanalysis is inherently lacking in this kind of situational information. The only way to achieve understanding involves pursuing a dialogue that moves the subject toward a more inclusive and plural self-expression of the signifying networks within him.

References

Aron, L. (2006). Analytic impasse and the third: Clinical implications of inter-subjectivity theory, *International Journal of Psychoanalysis*, 87:349–368.

Homayounpour, G. & Movahedi, S. (2012). Transferential discourse in the language of the (M)other, *Canadian Journal of Psychoanalysis*, 20:114–143.

Chapter 6

A semiotic approach to intersubjectivity

Introduction

In this chapter, I present a semiotic interpretation of intersubjectivity in psychotherapeutic practice. Since semiotics is a complicated matter, here I only discuss the basic elements relevant to therapeutic action in psychoanalysis. The field of semiotics involves the study of signs, and its founders are usually considered to be Charles Peirce and Ferdinand de Saussure. Lacan spoke about both authors in his seminars and, in many ways, can be credited with innovating a semiotic approach to psychoanalysis. Some excellent introductions to this topic can be found in Barclay and Kee (2001), Eco (1984), Muller (1996), Chandler (2013), and Litowitz (2014). A recent work by Salvatore (2015) presents a comprehensive theoretical model of the details of semiotics in human relations and psychoanalysis.

I begin by reviewing some fundamentals of semiotic theory, before describing how we can apply the concepts to ordinary human interactions, including early parent–child communications and psychoanalysis. I argue that attention to semiotics enables an analyst to sharpen his awareness of an unfolding intersubjective process with his patient. Moreover, listening to the words themselves rather than imagining their meaning can help the couple avoid reenactment of a fantasy. I use clinical vignettes to illustrate this point. Next, I unpack Lacan's early paper on the "Function and Field of Speech" (1953), which makes the argument for a speech-based theory of psychoanalysis. In this work, he set forth basic principles of an ethical intersubjective practice that remain relevant today. Unfortunately, Lacan later repudiated intersubjectivity and a phenomenological approach to recognition in favor of an abstract formulation of the analyst's structural role as Other. I support the early Lacan of the 1953 paper by maintaining that the analyst assumes culturally symbolic roles defined not only structurally but also in an active, engaged way. I spell out this approach in Chapter 8, where I advocate a mode of participation that integrates empathy, recognition, and responsiveness—intersubjective stances that begin in infancy.

What is semiotics?

Semiotics studies the use of signs in living beings. Peirce defined a sign as "something which stands to somebody for something in some respect or capacity" (1932, p. 228), demonstrating that the technical definition of a sign is not simple. Peirce presented numerous varieties of signs in his many papers. Symbols, like words, seem the clearest type, as they can only be understood as intending to convey a message from one subject to another, who interprets its meaning. More accurately, the recipient subject responds, often unconsciously, with an interpretation (Peirce called the reaction to a sign its interpretant), which then becomes another sign. This response evokes another reciprocal interpretation. Almost anything can function as a sign as long as someone interprets it as signifying something—that is, referring to or standing for something other than itself. Chandler writes, "We interpret things as signs largely unconsciously by relating them to familiar systems of conventions. It is this meaningful use of signs which is at the heart of the concerns of semiotics" (2013, 2014, p. 16). Psychoanalysis adds to Chandler that conventional attributions of meaning alone fail in most personal encounters and require more word signs to explain private intentions and meanings, a process which is never fully complete.

Visual symbols, images, and gestures are also signs, according to Peirce's definition. He distinguishes iconic, indexical, and symbolic signs, all of which can be either present in awareness or registered unconsciously. An icon resembles what it signifies, like a fearful scream or a picture of mushroom cloud. It has a limited meaning that does not require interpretation; only a learned or, in some instances, innate knowledge of the code is necessary. A mother's smiling face might be considered an iconic sign of her loving presence for her baby. An index carries a direct link to the signified—usually sensory, like an odor or lock of hair. Perhaps the mother's voice functions this way. Icons and indices share in possessing a specific referential function and serve as important vehicles of communication. They have been described as analogic signs, as opposed to digital symbols. Analogic systems present information using a continuous range of intensities (like emotion) or of a variable (like proximity), while digital codes are either yes or no and discontinuous. The analogue/digital distinction is frequently presented as differentiating natural from artificial codes. Chandler cites Wilden's observation that a deliberate intention to communicate tends to be present in digital codes, while in analogue codes it is almost impossible not to communicate. Beyond conscious intention, we communicate through gesture, posture, facial expression, intonation, and so on. While speaking to another person usually involves a conscious intention, there are obvious exceptions, as in sleep or inebriation. This suggests that access to speech may be a major reason for the evolution of reflective self-awareness. For psychoanalysts, however, much of the meaning expressed (or its interpretation) remains unconscious, precisely because of the combinatory, metaphoric, and metonymic character of symbols. Word symbols lack the specificity of reference of icons or index signs, and require additional symbols to clarify their meaning. For the recipient of the message, conscious understanding does not capture the many unconscious links that influenced the sender, although they may be registered and incorporated into the interpretant response. The subject's capacity to respond to analogic signs or unconscious word associations may be one explanation for the phenomenon of so-called unconscious to unconscious communication, with the important qualification that, although the recipient picks up many messages, the interpretant remains subjective, reflecting the receiver's way of organizing experience. The mind is always reading—assimilating, matching, and seeking familiar patterns, being reminded of something.

Analogical signs (such as emotions, images, bodily gestures, textures, tastes, and odors) involve a range of possible signifieds on a continuum from concrete to vague. Some convey only a hazy sense of what they signify, like a piece of music. Others instantly express nuances of meaning that would be cumbersome and slow to put into words. Think of a romantic situation where small changes in facial expression and movement can have powerful effects on the partner; or, of subtle changes of tone in a conversation that immediately inform the listener of an altered relationship. Humans share many of these analogic signs with other species (as in the case of emotional expressions like extreme fear). But human communication is distinguished by the co-presence of the "digital" signs—symbols that can be combined in endless and complex ways for the abstract categories and concepts that structure all social life. Romantic looks and intonations eventually have to be put into words or the nascent love affair will wither.

The combinatory possibilities of word signs, which can be rearranged almost infinitely, make human thought distinct. We can look back as far as Plato (in the *Sophist*) to link thinking to language. C.S. Peirce may have been the first modern philosopher to propose that thinking itself consists of an internal dialogue of signs, writing in the 1890s that "We think only in signs" (Peirce, 1932, p. 302). Recently, the cognitive theorist Clark summarized the case for the elaboration of word symbols as the crucial evolutionary step enabling internal and social dialogue. He writes: "Language is . . . a form of mind-transforming cognitive scaffolding: a culturally heritable, persisting, though never stationary, symbolic edifice that plays a critical role in allowing minds like ours to exist in the natural order" (2012, p. 198). From a semiotic perspective, words linking spontaneously with other words to construct chains of meaning more or less govern our experience of the world. We could not think in the human sense without language, nor could we communicate the specifics of our felt needs and wishes. "A sign," Peirce notes, "stands to somebody for something" (1932, p. 228)—that is, the sign exists only within a social network of other subjects. Words are the substance of intersubjective life.

Psychoanalytic semiotics

In psychoanalytic practice, we can easily forget when sitting with patients that we are engaged in exchanges of words, not just talking about important matters outside the interaction to which our words refer. In ordinary relationships we often assume that we share such common references in our conversations, but psycho-analysts know that this is not necessarily the case. Rather than take the meaning of our dialogue for granted, we learn to pay attention to the style and content of the discourse and to retain an openness about our patients' statements, even apparently straightforward ones. Moreover, although no doubt there is considerable redundancy in human communication that helps resolve ambiguity, we cannot consciously register all the signs we receive. In everyday interactions, for the most part, we disregard the ambiguous aspects of a communication (slips, double-meanings, suggestive associations, and so forth) without much being lost, but when the matter at hand is personally significant, we work hard to gain clarification. The structure of everyday conversations supports a high degree of mutual understanding of their message, by relying on the context of interaction, practical details of items of concern, and redundancy of signs. Psychoanalysis pursues a different strategy that disrupts normal social intercourse and fosters associations ostensibly unrelated to conscious intentions (like recounting recent events or social greetings or farewells). For example, analysts choose to respond or not to res-pond to comments and questions, immediately complicating the meaning of the interaction.

Laplanche taught with justice that children may struggle over a lifetime with making sense of enigmatic messages from parents that they received in childhood. How they have been interpreted (or misinterpreted) at different times can be the source of considerable suffering and confusion. A patient, Ms. J., whose father had frequently spanked her naked buttocks as a young child, wondered about his motivation—whether he found erotic pleasure in the act or the chasing that became a part of the scenario, or if he wanted for some reason to humiliate her. He displayed little affect and always explained calmly why she had been punished, but this behavior only increased the mystery. Her behavior with a sibling and much later with men suggested the repercussions of these early experiences on her later relationships. Many situations revived her perplexity about what was or was not sexual, what was real and what pretend, creating anxiety and leading to various strategies to resolve her doubts. The construction of an imaginary scene (based on the events) became the organizer of an emotionally charged fantasy with set roles in which she felt overwhelmed and trapped. Paying attention to the words that had been spoken and which she used in her reconstruction helped her move away from the images of this familiar scenario and to represent her position in alternative ways that helped her think about herself as other than an erotic and eroticized object. The images repeated like a hall of mirrors; her speech led in many directions.

Mr. Q., who sought analysis for issues of identity and intimacy, repeatedly talked about an event from age 11 in which his usually detached father took him aside in the washroom ostensibly to instruct him how to cleanse his penis. Using the boy's fingers, he demonstrated on his own organ how to roll back and cleanse the prepuce. This situation frightened my patient into a silent paralysis and afterward made him wonder whether his father were homosexual (with a sexual interest in him). Moreover, the disturbing experience made him question his own masculinity. What had his father seen in him and why had he done this to him? These questions and other variations came up repeatedly in relation to his ongoing doubts about himself as a person, problems with self-esteem, and sexual anxieties. He struggled to recall his father's exact words and intonation, straining to understand what might have been in his mind. Attempting to figure out his father's psychology was a consuming interest, but led us in circles. Father seemed attracted to working with adolescent boys and Mr. Q. spoke about his possible pedophilia, which had been discussed in a much earlier psychotherapy. Although I too might have been able to make plausible interpretations of Mr. Q.'s story (my construction of what it may have been about), I focused instead on his attempts to translate the enigmatic aspects of the father's communication. The scene in the washroom produced the effect of a frozen metaphor about being the submissive object of his father's behavior and a recursive narrative of his passivity and lack of masculine identity, which flowed over into his assessment of other situations. I might have assumed the active position of the father, perhaps like the first therapist, by wanting to show Mr. Q. things and to help him. "Figuring out" or imagining his father's motivation and what kind of object my patient represented for this man had reinforced familiar ways Mr. Q. thought about himself. Instead of falling into a parallel structure in the transference/countertransference, I tried to focus on comments about what he had wanted and missed from his father and the language he employed in describing him. Some of the expressions he used turned out to have been spoken by his mother. Being a compliant child to a dominant man he looked up to did not exhaust the subjective positions he occupied at different times, although he reverted often to this image. As we pursued these threads of signifiers, Mr. Q.'s affect and demeanor shifted, and multiple versions of his story emerged. Meanings of events are constructed through an ongoing dialogue, by speaking more freely with another person, rather than from introspection, which tends to produce a recounting of familiar images.

The problem Laplanche posed does not only involve parental sexuality in early life. Analysts themselves inevitably transmit enigmatic signs that become an important part of the therapeutic situation. For instance, the analyst is interested, but indifferent; affectively present, but hard to reach; seductive but off limits. Another patient's first analyst often inquired about details of her family's business, making remarks and suggestions about financial issues that puzzled her. What was she trying to convey by this interest? Was something amiss in the business she was neglecting? The analyst encouraged her to take assertive steps in her life, but was the money she stood to earn her real interest? Perhaps, she surmised, the questions pertained to the analyst's own desires and not to her. Another patient felt troubled when her former therapist began to dress in an open collar shirt for their sessions. He also displayed more enjoyment in sharing the humor of incidents she recounted, on some occasions erupting with a hearty laugh. Were these enigmatic signs indications of a boundary issue or an undue interest on his part? Unfortunately, she felt unable to raise these questions with him directly, and he apparently missed the allusions to these concerns in her associations. Perhaps because they involved behaviors that he did not notice or considered unimportant, he fell into a pattern that suggested a countertransference repetition. As a result, the therapy ended without achieving much.

A patient reacts to and reads the signs received from the analyst, often only indirectly and unconsciously. Even an interpretation of contradictory statements about finances or a warm laugh about an incident may convey a personal motive or judgment to a patient that will strongly impact his relationship to the analyst. Such situations arise all the time, and the analyst should take the opportunity to hear how he has been heard by listening for the ensuing responses of his patient. "Listening to the listening" (Faimberg, 1996) can inform the analyst of the transference position from which the patient sees him,[1] or, more importantly, can indicate something about his own countertransference. In all the vignettes cited above, the patients pursued important existential questions through taking the perspective of another person rather than as subjects of their own intentions and desires. Imaginary identities (images of how others saw them) obscured their own symbolic positions as agents. In the therapeutic situation, the patients' imagining or attempting to find indications of what the analyst wanted took the place of exploring the multiple meanings and implications of their memories and the subjective positions behind them.

Overall, the psychoanalyst as sender deliberately chooses to be relatively ambiguous in his communications, with the goal of encouraging a patient's subjective constructions of the situation. Were he to insist on a meaning of his expressions, initiate topics of conversation, or answer too many questions about treatment, he would establish a position of expertise and a practical format for the interaction. At least for the moment, the therapeutic situation would conform to the clarity of a familiar social process of information gathering or medical history taking. Since patients tend to be anxious at the start of therapy, a more structured approach like this may offer a comfortable starting point by supporting defenses against excessive stimulation of fears and wishes by the unfamiliar situation. All kinds of things get stirred up in the encounter with an unknown other, and a vulnerable patient may not be fully prepared for this confrontation. Questions and explanatory comments, for instance, are probably routine at the beginning, but many patients need help in organizing the content of their hours for a long while. Once a therapy gets under way, however, the goal shifts gradually to destabilizing familiar patterns of professional rituals and practical interactions. Analytic ambiguity, not as a role-playing exercise but arising from a genuine state of not knowing and openness to the other, invites further departures from social reality. The topic at hand becomes less important than small details and the manner in which the material is expressed. Thoughts arise that seem at first glance unrelated to the problem at hand. A memory of a conversation, an image from a book, a word may come to mind, and these associations represent the metonymic production of signs (private and personal links to the received sign), which remain relatively unconstrained by social convention. Freedom to make "looser" associations does not usually result from the impossible instruction "say everything that comes to your mind," but depends primarily on the behavior of the analyst. The analyst's attention to the interaction, attitude of openness, and receptivity sets the tone.

The analysand conveys his interpretation of the therapeutic situation and of the analyst's intentions by the signs he produces. The analyst, likewise, reacts with signs on the plane of the exchange. For example, he may respond to narratives of unhappiness with apparently caretaking verbal or facial expressions or by signifiers of suffering (as in the case of Nancy in the previous chapter) or with implicit rejection or disapproval (as perhaps with Adriana's therapist). "That sounds very painful" suggests empathic concern, while "How did you get into this situation?" is a reaction that puts the onus back onto the patient, refusing consolation. Either statement supports a particular kind of transference, which will in turn promote further associations. No intervention is inherently correct; there are always numerous possibilities, each of which leads in a different direction. Only in retrospect can the direction taken be discerned and brought into a progressive dialogue that can generate new meanings for the subject. This movement depends primarily on the analyst's ability to speak about what happens in the transaction instead of coming up with the right intervention.

The analyst's tendency to slip into symmetric responses, as described in the three case vignettes of the previous chapter, derives directly from the actual verbal content of the dialogue, not from unconscious fantasies projected onto the analyst. Fantasies appear in the patient's speech as gaps, allusive or unusual words, repetitions of phrases, and images that open onto other scenes. Over time, the analyst may grasp their significance, but most signs expressed in the rapidity of moment-to-moment speech are registered (and interpreted) unconsciously, perhaps as fleeting impressions or feeling states. As Salvatore (2015) shows in his analysis of pathways to meaning in human interaction, most of the steps are implicit and unconscious. The influx of signs meets a set of expectations and dispositions in the analyst that produce interpretants which the patient's responses reveal over the sequence of exchanges. The notion of using reverie to capture some of these internal responses (or to suggest meanings about the patient's unconscious messages) offers a heuristic but unreliable method of self-analysis, and seldom addresses the impact of the time of reverie itself. Attention to the spoken and nonverbal signs should be primary.

Reverie and projective identification

The phenomenon of private reverie often comes up in Bionian clinical discussions as a means of accessing projective identifications and the unconscious-to-unconscious communications that appear to be involved (Brown, 2011). One might consider the analyst's use of his own images and daydreams as evidence for such processes, as the Botellas (2004) argue in their illustrations of figurations emerging in the analyst's mind. Typical semiotic exchanges may offer a better explanation of their examples, however. Rather than employing the difficult concept of unconscious communication, we can understand what occurs in such intersubjective sequences in terms of expressions and interpretants of signs. I will describe a few case vignettes to pursue this technical disagreement.

For several sessions, a functioning psychotic patient had been elaborating a series of abstract preoccupations that I found difficult to follow. One day he arrived with a dream described quite vaguely in similar terms to an unusual architectural structure he once told me about. While trying to picture the objects of the dream, I saw a strong image of an old structure I was refurbishing in my country home (an arched brick support for a chimney), and I decided to tell him this. His response was bland and dismissive of the irrelevance of my comment— rather convincingly so, in my opinion. My strange association or figuration seemed to produce no detectable effect as he continued in the same vein with his thoughts. It then occurred to me that I had been feeling quite disconnected from my patient and hoped to find some personal link to his obsessive preoccupations. My attempt involved a kind of mirroring response, as if we shared the same object or could somehow occupy the same mental space. At a subsequent time, I brought up my making this association again, but he indicated no interest, typical of his lack of curiosity for what went on in my mind during this period. I realized then that his message (the series of signifiers in his speech) conveyed a wish *not* to communicate, which might have been the relevant current issue for me to attend to. My impulsive response was wishful and countertransferential.

In a second case, a man recounted his struggle to distance himself from ideas that other people could read his thoughts. I knew already about his trouble with assessing the reality of these referential beliefs and his shame about this difficulty. At one point, I commented that sometimes we reveal things in our actions and gestures of which we are unaware. He picked up on this immediately and opened a rather intellectualized conversation on the same theme, reminding me of a session when we talked about his having a negative effect on co-workers by not responding to them. The interchange, beginning with my educational, cognitive comment about how we can communicate more than we know, seemed useful. Then I suddenly remembered a disturbing feeling from my early childhood that God and probably my father could read my thoughts. This subjective reaction (my interpretant of his message) did not belong with my previous mode of thinking "psychologically" about his story, but emerged from another level of processing. After a pause to weigh my response, I said that children sometimes believed their parents could know what they were thinking. As in the previous vignette, I wanted the exchange to build a meaning between us. "Oh, yes," he replied, he too remembered those feelings. He then told me about a similar period in his life involving secret guilt and anxiety, about which I had not previously known. I felt we were now on the same wavelength.

I could see how the partial repression of my childhood memory had been stirred by the patient's transference, like the examples given by T. Jacobs (Jacobs, 1993, 1999)[2] of his use of countertransference imagery. The production and interpretation of signs underlies these phenomena. In this instance, the communication of my patient (the chain of signs in his message) had met a resistance that first took the form of my taking a teacher-to-student stance, avoiding the mirroring interpretant (my similar ideas as a child) that emerged later. My attempt at producing meaning involved offering a lesson he should learn, in which I thought about him as a clinical object (useful to a degree), rather than an interacting subject. With my childhood memory, I realized we had both been in a similar uncomfortable place, and felt I could put part of that feeling into words. Although the aspect of teaching remained, I was speaking from a different, more engaged position than a psychiatric perspective on paranoia. Something shifted in the comfortable field of our discussion about revealing unconscious intentions to others that enabled me to recognize that his message resonated with my own history.

My third brief example concerns an analysand who recounted fantasies and dreams in which she smashed her head in a bike accident—usually following what often appeared as minor failures or criticisms of her work. After one vivid dream report, I remembered chipping my tooth in a careless minor accident that seemed at the time unconsciously caused. I believe this memory indicated an index response, both of us mirroring an impulse to hurt ourselves as self-punishment. I felt strongly in tune with her powerful image of turning against herself, or perhaps with a need to placate an imaginary bad object (something of the sort). We seemed to occupy symmetrical positions in an intersubjective field of self-blame, which resonated with intensity in me. I said after a time that analysis can be a dangerous situation, bringing my memory (my interpretant) into connection with our current experience in the analysis.

The sense of the rapid semiotic exchange appeared obvious to me, and I did not feel stuck in a dyadic or complementary position. I believe any analyst attuned to important dynamics could have made my interpretation. At our next session, however, the patient reported a dream about coming upon an accident victim with a broken skull, which she carefully pulled apart to examine the living brain underneath. My attention shifted to her words, which immediately reminded me of something she had said the previous week about her attempt to psychoanalyze me, "looking into your head." She acknowledged the repetition of signifiers. Her dream now seemed like a reciprocal interpretant to my interpretation of the previous day, perhaps pointing out the danger to me in her turning the tables (although mitigated by her care-taking posture in the scene). This connection led us away from the self-hating theme toward memories and desires for other kinds of interactions in the transference, and a new meaning took shape. Again, I do not feel that a concept like projective identification (which could be used to describe such interactions) adds to our understanding of these sequences, which involve a basic intersubjective process of semiotic exchanges.

Analytic reverie and reflection have a place in attempting to understand an analysand, but the hypotheses generated must filter through a third position. The analyst's images belong to the intersubjective field that has evoked them, where, if eventually expressed, they will prove fruitful or not. Most often they will be filed away until circumstances suggest an opportunity to say something relevant about them. Once, a supervisee and I worked out a plausible interpretation of a patient's fantasy about her, based on her later thoughts and images that came to mind the evening after the session. We agreed that our construction explained puzzling aspects of the transference and awaited an opportunity for the therapist to express it. We shortly learned, however, of an important historical event that negated our conclusions about the hidden content we had inferred. This new information necessitated a mutual analysis by the supervisee and myself of our investment in the previous formulation and what it might indicate. Our mistake proved harmless, but often enough the analyst's efforts to interpret "the transference" can lead the patient astray.

Transference as a semiotic process

Although every patient inevitably brings long-standing expectations to the treatment situation, the actual transference evolves intersubjectively as a function of a mutual semiotic process. The transference is not a stable set of wishes awaiting interpretation. My patient Mr. Q., for example, assumed for a long time that I would provide answers about what his father intended and advise him how to deal with it. He asked frequently what I thought about his story and related memories. I privately interpreted his expectations of me as a pressure for repetition in the transference, with sexualized undertones. My formulation seemed to fit, but I withheld these ideas as coming from my own construction of his psychic processes. I later learned that he was actually mistrustful I would give bad advice. He had a way of testing business associates to reveal their ideas, which he would then disparage. When I did not validate his expectations, he expressed relief, but then struggled with whether my "hands-off" approach represented indifference toward him. Had I proposed a meaning for his transference wishes, I would have narrowed the field to a familiar psychoanalytic formulation, rather than allowing him to express different kinds of fears and demands. Whether and how I could care about him became a question of his own desire in the evolving transference.

The common misunderstanding of transferential attitudes as a rigid construction the patient imposes upon the analyst often conceals a shared enactment. Stereotyped and repetitive patterns occur most commonly as a defensive byproduct of constricted countertransference listening. That is, if the analyst hears and responds to what may seem like a single message, he creates a complementary dyad, analogous to the Lacanian imaginary transference (often based on index signs of sameness). In such cases, an image of the analyst (for example, as punitive or blameworthy) represents the counterpart to the patient's own ego identifications. Commonly referred to as "role responsiveness," such mirroring reactions by the analyst are typical default modes in many types of interaction. An analyst may attribute the transference to his patient's distortions or projections, but interpreting in this way (explicitly or reflectively) basically reinforces his participation in the dyad and perpetuates the interaction. Thinking this way influences how he hears the material and the position he will speak from. For instance, a reply to a patient who asks for approval about some behavior tends to convey a positive or negative judgment from a position of authority. The important thing becomes the analyst speaking from that place, not the actual content. Likewise, a clumsy response like "you are treating me like your father" verbally enacts the father–son relationship. Of course, the role pressure on the analyst (sometimes labeled as projective identification) can be difficult to manage. The father-deprived Mr. Q. seemed to take the part of a boy needing guidance easily, and I felt a corresponding pressure to respond to his demands for advice. My interpretant/image of his seeking to involve me in a repetition interfered with hearing other aspects of his associations.

Kernberg's transference-focused psychotherapy

Kernberg contributed a useful alternative technique to transference interpretation based on his model of an internalized object relationship in which a patient alternates between reciprocal roles that can be demonstrated to him (Yeomans et al., 2005). When the intervention is successful, the patient sees that he assumes both roles of a given dyad at different times, rather than one side of a unidirectional complementarity,[3] like being stuck in a victim role. The cognitive aspects of this therapeutic approach work well for many patients. Kernberg's theory reminds the clinician to step outside the dyad to look at the structure of the interaction. Showing a patient how he repeatedly falls into an either/or choice of roles (like becoming a persecutor or victim) has been shown empirically to be useful for some patients (the reported studies apply to Borderline cases). I found a similar approach very helpful with Ms. J., the child whose father liked to spank her. She recognized very quickly how she often became either the aggressor or the recipient of punishment in certain interactions. Having these thoughts helped her see other possibilities and to wonder about her failure to consider them.

Kernberg's method applies a Kleinian concept of projective identification to explain the transference, rather than a relational attention to the semiotics of mutual interactions, which I find more helpful. In my experience in dealing with the very common impasses that arise with "borderline" patients, closer scrutiny of one's own messages often proves most valuable, as the patient quickly picks up any hint of a countertransferential response. From an intersubjective vantage point, acknowledgement that both analyst and analysand are caught in an exchange of signs repeating an alternation of static roles can reopen a rigidified field. A woman presenting with a lot of angry affect about authority figures who had mistreated her in the past began to question words I used to describe her current work situation. She complained that I was taking the side of her supervisor. My first thought was that she was playing out a repetitious relationship pattern with me. However, I accepted her point about my language by commenting mainly as a matter of technique that I must have jumped into the role of the supervisor for some reason. She responded quickly that she did not expect to have to supervise me, but maybe she needed to. This rapid alteration of positions opened up a rich discussion of how and why she gets into one side or the other so frequently. Modell named this dyadic situation "the iconic projective transference" (Modell 1990, p. 56), iconic because it evokes sameness (as Muller clearly demonstrates). My patient and I traded the roles of critic and criticized (supervisor and supervisee) in a mirroring fashion; internal structures in both of us were activated by her affective communications. Talking about our shared roles replaced experiencing ourselves in one position.

By definition, symbolic transferences in the Lacanian sense, as opposed to affectively intense iconic transferences, are more bound up with language than images, but I do not find them so easily separable from the other types.[4] Mixtures and variations constitute the usual situation, unlike the naive notion of "the transference." When the analyst finds himself reflecting that his patient is stuck in a repetition of one message and object relationship, it may be a warning of his producing a complementary role response. I believed that my patient wanted to put me in a supervisory role to play out a transference fantasy, but by "owning" my behavior (by assuming that I had unknowingly enacted something), I opened other possibilities for her. We were then able to see the dual interaction from a third perspective. As noted, imaginary, symmetrical, complementary, mirroring, and projective versions of transference (which all refer to a very similar type of interaction) represent the common default position in two-person interactions. Both parties tend to interact on the same plane, communicating iconic and index features of sameness—feeling the same way or affirming complementary roles. Failure to respond to others in this manner in everyday life can even amount to lack of involvement or indifference. Nonetheless, by training, personal analysis, reading, and direct supervision, the analyst has learned to take up a symbolic "third" position and gain a perspective outside the dyad (the symbolic third differs somewhat from the version discussed in Chapter 3). He can move out of a symmetrical role by paying attention to the signs being communicated, rather than simply being captured by them. I believe that this side-stepping of an enactment explains the process described by Kernberg.

Litowitz (2014) reminds us that, for Peirce, thirdness is implicit in semiosis. The field of signs subsumes both parties who operate within it. Similarly, Lacan saw a third position as inherent in intersubjectivity, both parties being subject to the symbolic order. The potential for triangulation exists in every interaction and probably works to prevent constant conflict between fixed roles, although the default tendency to mirror and fantasize about the other can impair any relationship. In practice, the analyst is in and out of a third position (or positions), where he catches glimpses and eventually gains clearer moments of retroactive understanding of what has been communicated. The analysand also comments directly at times on the process, but usually the growth of mutual awareness depends on the analyst's attention to the patient's interpretants and on his openness to hearing his own. His task includes recognizing the transferential positions in play and his own involvement (as confirming, disconfirming, participating, or remaining detached). By listening from an asymmetric (third) position, the analyst steps out of the iconic transference dialogue and becomes capable of moving the process into new territory.

Lacanians emphasize picking up and repeating an ambiguous or surprising word or phrase, or underlining a discordant affect, rather than formulating an interpretation of the discourse, a technique which risks narrowing the field by defining the patient's identity and by enacting a role of knowledgeable authority (Fink, 2007). Playfulness with words can be another useful way to avoid a simple message. The accent is not on translating a patient's signs into their correct meaning, but on expansion of the semiotic field of the analysis. Unlike ordinary speech that typically seeks to limit a personal exchange to shared references and agreement about meaning, analytic dialogue aims to produce new signs that expand subjective space. In a spontaneously flowing exchange, the discourse departs unexpectedly from important words or gestures, which act like Freud's notion of junction points of intersection between multiple chains of reference. A particular symbol may condense a set of diverse personal memories and desires, enabling them to enter into the stream of discourse. Movement of associations and metaphors accompanies creative expansion of subjective possibility: "The object of the analysis is not to be able to say everything but to think everything; it is, finally, the freedom to think and the resistances to it" (Widlöcher, cited by Georgieff, 2016).[5]

Lacanian semiotics

In this section, I review Lacan's important early paper, "The Function and Field of Speech in Psychoanalysis" (1953), which reformulated psychoanalysis around the semiotic nature of intersubjectivity. Lacan referred to Peirce several times in his seminars, and was clearly influenced by his work, although Saussure remained Lacan's major linguistic reference. (I consider Peirce's concept of the interpretant as a constant feature of all communication an advance over Saussure's formalism.) The linguist Benveniste also played a part in Lacan's theoretical development, especially his work on personal pronouns.[6] Finally, the phenomenologic tradition, including readings of Hegel and Heidegger, echoes in the background of Lacan's thinking. These diverse influences moved the Lacan of his early period toward an intersubjective understanding of psychoanalysis that has been neglected in the mainstream literature.

Lacan began by reminding analysts that the entire course of treatment is embedded in speech and that Freud's pioneering discoveries involve the nature of language. As Peirce stressed long before, reflective consciousness and the sharing of thoughts depend on language and speech; yet, already, Lacan observed a "growing aversion" to these functions by psychoanalysts and a "temptation to abandon the foundation of speech" in favor of other disciplines (what he called "established languages"). Vivona and Litowitz recently voiced similar concerns about a temptation to neglect speech in favor of non-verbal mechanisms, especially in applying work from infant research to psychoanalysis (Vivona 2006; Litowitz 2011).

Addressing the growing emphasis on early development in British object relations theories, Lacan was skeptical of an emphasis on stages. He insisted that we need to understand more about the effects of symbolization on development, referring to the fact that language enters a child's world from the beginnings of the "primordial, primitive" relationship with the mother. He points out that the child is surrounded by a symbolic world organizing everything happening within it. He writes: "the symbolic relation is constituted as early as possible, even prior to the fixation of the self-image of the subject [qua ego] introducing the dimension of a subject into the world" (1954–55, p. 254). The conception of an unfolding sequence of stages was anathema to Lacan, who saw it as contrary to the discontinuous and unpredictable analytic experience of time, punctuated retroactively by important moments of new meaning.

Along with Lacan's criticism of replacing attention to language with fantasies about objects came his familiar peroration against American psychoanalysis, which he considered adaptational and behavioristic. He lists the main principles of his position: 1) There is "no speech without a response, even if it meets only with silence, provided it has an auditor"; 2) if the analyst does not understand the function of speech and "if emptiness is the first thing to make itself heard . . . he will feel it in himself and he will seek a reality beyond speech to fill the emptiness"; 3) this search leads the analyst "to analyze the subject's behavior in order to find in it what the subject is not saying" (1953, pp. 40–41). Here, Lacan warns against strategies he saw as replacing Freud's teaching with searches for historical and scientific facts independent of speech or with non-verbal signs. Litowitz (2014) makes a similar criticism from a linguistic perspective. Encouraging introspection about what a subject can remember of his past reinforces defensive, ego-centered constructions in a circularity of self-consciousness, and supports partial or incorrect interpretations.

Lacan contends that the importance of eliciting a history lies not in recovery of factual events or developmental sequences, but in articulation of a past embedded in the ongoing speech relation to the analyst. By speaking freely, rather than responding to questions that might help the analyst imagine what happened, the analysand expresses the important terms received from others, which organized his history and alienated him from the subjective truth of his own experience. The self-images or identifications he presents in analysis reveal themselves as crystallizations of positions he has assumed in the eyes of others at crucial moments (and taken in as the object of their regard). These moments are not strictly linear, chronological events but belong to significant punctuations of psychoanalytic time. From birth, the subject occupies a place designated for him by others; a symptomatic place that alienates him from his own desires and will break down in the context of the experience of interlocution with the analyst. In these passages, I find echoes of Winnicott's notions of the true and false self, which possibly influenced Lacan's formulation. Elsewhere, Lacan makes use of the concept of destiny in discussing the transmission of a position prepared in advance for the subject— for example, in his account of Antigone, which bears resemblance to a fate of neurosis (Lacan, 1959–60).

To illustrate the intersubjective logic of psychoanalysis, Lacan refers to his interpretation of the allegory of the prisoner's dilemma, first published in an art journal (Lacan, 1945). The dilemma concerns a scene in which three prisoners are told that either a black or white sign will be placed behind their heads. The guards show they have two black and three white circles to place. Each prisoner can see the others' signs but not his own. If you, as subject of this situation, determine correctly that your sign is white, you may leave and be freed; if it should be black, however, and you err, you face execution. As prisoner A, you can immediately see white circles behind your two neighbors. Now you must determine whether your own is white or black. The three prisoners take time to look around at each other's circles—a "time for understanding." Finally, at a certain point a decision is reached, and all three prisoners rise to leave together. The logic works as follows: if I (prisoner A) am black, another prisoner (B) would conclude that if he were black as well, (C) would leave, as he could then see two blacks; (C) did not leave. Therefore, I must be white. Each prisoner comes to this realization by seeing no one leave immediately. Lacan adds that the three hesitate in a retrospective moment of shared doubt until observing that all have paused together, before resuming their departures.

Lacan speaks of this allegory to illustrate how the subject is determined by its place in a signifying network. The social structure of racism has also been explored through this black/white circle scenario (Hook, 2013[7]). To escape his confinement, each prisoner must take the point of view of the others, realizing in the first logical moment that no one in the room can possibly see two black patches. Then, each deduces from the actions of his fellow prisoners the correctness of this reasoning, and, at a second moment, rises to leave. In a psychoanalysis, the analogous first period involves an analysand's coming to understand the symbolic determinants of his hitherto implicit, unconscious position in relation to others. Lacan appears (his language is never so clear) to be pointing to the dialectic truth of a speech relationship in which the subject assumes his history through an exchange with an interlocutor, where his spoken words place a particular coloration on the past and on his current situation.

For my patient Ms. J., briefly discussed in the previous section, our interaction evoked the image of a spanking (that she joked about sarcastically), but she surprised me one day by actually slapping my foot. For a moment, I was caught up in the "funny" game of repeating or enacting the past without any conscious processing. Eventually, I was able to ask about "spanking," which, after a pause, led to her reflecting about the nature of caring or love. Our repetition of a dyad devolved to an underlying set of life issues of great concern to her. Major existential questions like a basic right to exist or what being a woman means are often absent from speech, presumably because thinking about them suffers from repression and leads back to traumatic memories. A Lacanian account of J.'s unrepresented unconscious might resemble a Freudian transference model (as a revival of an early Oedipal configuration), but focusing on her words instead of picturing a relational configuration (imaginary) helped me return to a third position (symbolic).

Lacan describes an onion skinning of the imaginary ego that strips away the alienating identifications that comprise it. If it proceeds freely, the analytic dialogue (Lacan does not use this term) creates openings for the unconscious to appear or, rather, enables the unconscious to speak. The unconscious is not like a spatial container with hidden contents to be excavated but consists of the unsymbolized, unknown, and unrepresented real that we want the analysand to recognize and name in his history. Lacan comments: "It is not a question of passing from the unconscious, plunged in obscurity, to consciousness, site of clarity, by some sort of mysterious elevator . . . not a passage into consciousness but of a passage into the Word" (1953, p. 52). The speaker is constituted in the act of addressing the analyst (*allucitaire*), he states, "as intersubjectivity," in "an intersubjective continuity of the discourse" (1953, p. 49). He means that the speaker's own position takes shape because of the language he employs with his analyst.

The function of speech "is not to inform but to evoke," writes Lacan, meaning that it evokes a response from the analyst, either confirmation of an imaginary identity coming from the past or recognition of a new possibility. "What constitutes me as a subject is my question," he continues, adding, "In order to be recognized by the other, I proffer what *was* only in view of what *will be*" (1953, p. 84). The analyst can reinforce a familiar identity by responding from a place of complementarity and symmetry or he can destabilize it by ambiguity or a failure to understand. Lacan underscores the importance of the analyst's response, but doesn't provide guidelines for framing this except to suggest wittily "a neutrality other than that the analyst is simply in a stupor" (1953, p. 79). We gather that the analyst neither affirms nor denies the identity (which in either case would support the transference), but tries to promote the free flow of speech, the production of another question, and a different subjective position. Lacan notes: "The decisive function of my own response . . . is not . . . simply to be received by the subject as approval or rejection of what he is saying, but truly to recognize or abolish him as a subject" (1953, p. 85).

The sequential appearance of formative identifications in the past recreates the important moments of a subject's history, the decisive steps toward what he believes he already "had to become." Lacan was influenced during this period by Heidegger's concept of an already "having been" in the past that emerges retroactively in the *après-coup*, as if it comes from an anticipated future. I understand this logic as the placing of a label or *appellation*, a coercive naming, that the subject accepts and internalizes as defining who he is, a designation that revises the meanings of past events that now emerge as indications of what he was already moving to become. Mr. Q.'s father's lesson about cleaning the prepuce carried a message of something he had not understood about his organ. It organized a series of episodes in which he was uncertain about the meanings of sex and gender. He was and would always remain someone with an unsolved problem about his penis. Like the prisoner, a patient gains his freedom at the moment when he understands and can reinterpret the signs by which he has been determined. Mr. Q. changed by being able to see how he had been trapped by his father's enigmatic message to him and his own interpretations of its meaning. In a sense, he was caught in a web of unspoken signs that constrained the entire family.

Lacan refers to what he calls the transpersonal dimension of the subject, meaning the dependence of the subject on the intersubjective network in which his speaking existence developed. His insistence on the entanglement of subjects recalls Modell's articulation of the narcissistic human dilemma cited previously: "The sense of self needs to be affirmed by the other, and yet a response from the other that is nonconfirming or unempathic can lead at best to a sense of depletion or at worst to the shattering of the self" (1984, p. 131). Yet how is the analyst to affirm this self he does not know? And does not simple affirmation, however relieving it may be for a time, put the analysand in thrall? A concrete response can define the other in the manner of an *appellation*, and, in this sense, the demand for recognition can become a dead end—perhaps gratifying, perhaps alienating, through an illusion of understanding. By contrast, conveying a willingness to listen invites openness to the process. As both Bion and Laplanche taught, the analyst's curiosity about a patient must not lead to objectifying him or reach a final conclusion.[8] Interpreting (even silently) that Mr. Q. suffered from a negative Oedipal conflict, that his father was perverse, or some other possible formulation, as an analytic end-point would likely reinforce his passive position in the family drama.

Lacan defines the goal of analysis as the assumption of desire through speech. Desire, he suggests, individuates the subject and protects him from being totally captive to the web of symbols that envelop him from before birth in a particular destiny. With Freud, he recognized the continuity of the chain of generations at work in his patients, like the uncanny links discovered in the transgenerational transmission of trauma. Whether this kind of fate can ever be entirely overcome can be questioned, but Lacan's point appears to be that the unique desire of the subject opposes this determination, enabling a kind of ontological freedom.[9] I am reminded of Winnicott's ideas about the spontaneous gesture as an in-born manifestation of the true self that resists compliance as a false self. Like Lacan, Winnicott referred not to an "entity" but to an inner source of vitality for the subject. Lacan defines this kernel of our being (a term taken from Freud) as a virtual or implicit fantasy of fulfilled desire, a yearning for completeness. "What is at stake in an analysis," he writes, "is the advent in the subject of the scant reality that this desire sustains in him ... and our path is the intersubjective experience by which this desire gains recognition" (1953, pp. 67–68).

The distinction between affirmation of an ego identity and recognition of desire can be grasped in terms of opposing a static image to the affectively vital state of seeking or wanting, but it can be difficult to make in practice. I have elsewhere discussed Lacan's concept of opening a path toward desire (Kirshner, 2012) as part of the ethics of psychoanalysis.[10] The analyst's task entails supporting the creative path an evolving subject can take, rather than promoting accomplishment of a wished for object-to-object (or ego-to-ego) relationship, which perpetuates a patient's illusion of a complete relationship. Lacan expressed the importance of recognition in his early seminars, with their phenomenological influences, but eventually turned elsewhere. Fink writes that what the analyst recognizes has nothing to do with the patient's "alienated" self-experience but, rather, "the desire that lurks within her discourse of which she herself is unaware" (2007, p. 252). Although I agree with the problems of recognition raised by Fink, I criticize Lacan's abandonment of phenomenology as eliminating an irreplaceable dimension of human experience. The subject in a humanistic sense has dropped out of the picture.

Lacan repudiated intersubjectivity for supporting a pre-psychoanalytic conception of complete subjects and denying the asymmetry of transference. This change accompanied his turn from phenomenology toward the more abstract and formal models of *mathemes* (algebraic formulae) and the theory of knots, which came to occupy his attention. Yet, although some phenomenologists appear to hold conceptions incompatible with a psychoanalytic view of the unconscious (and a divided subject), intersubjectivity does not necessarily imply a complete or coherent subject and can accommodate the inequality of the analytic (and other forms of) relationship. Something was lost in Lacan's response to the riddle of the subject by moving the analyst from the interactive field portrayed in his 1953 paper to the impersonal place of the Other in the transference. Even for the late Lacan, however, the semiotic (symbolic) framework of human interaction does not limit itself to mathematical notation or the pure acoustics of the signifier, although he moves at times in these directions. The more important change in his thinking concerns his growing emphasis on the unsymbolized "real" governing the subject. Already in the "Function and Field of Speech," he speaks of the real body being expressed through the symbol, the ways in which words mysteriously link to and are bound up with bodily functions from birth. "Language is not immaterial," he states, "it is a subtle body, but body it is" (1953, p. 45). The living organization of the body does not exist at a level totally independent of words but depends on the symbols defining it. The concept creates the thing: there is no "prediscursive reality; every reality is founded and defined by a discourse" (Lacan, 1972–73, p. 32). The functions of the body have been shaped by language, and the major signifiers of the subject act like levers attached to physical functions, as we see in conversion symptoms or somatization, but also in everyday affects. Freud was not the first to realize that words have impact on physiologic responses, but dualistic habits of thinking about mind and body can obscure this reality. As Žižek contends in his analysis of the mind–body problem, subjective organization develops in constant interaction with the circuits and structures of the brain (2006, pp. 208–222).

Lacan regards desire as the organizer of the process of becoming a human subject, but not defined as Freudian drive or impulse. He interprets the Hegelian theme that "man's desire is the desire of the other" as referring to the effect of the infant's experience of loss of the mother (the first Other), or, rather, of a fantasy of loss bound to the memory of primary bodily functions (nursing, defecating, the gaze, and the voice) mixed up with the maternal relationship. Love and desire grow out of the pursuit of an impossible (virtual) object that seeks representation

(Lacan, 1972–73, p. 126)[11]. He aphorizes, "Psychoanalysis exploits the poetic function of language to give his desire its symbolic mediation" (1953, p. 103). "Mediation," in my reading, refers to a flow of speech that carries the affective pulse of desire, without reaching a definite endpoint. The question I raise in Chapter 8 pertains to how psychoanalysis can foster this path. After all, it is not "psychoanalysis" that provides the symbolic mediation or the poetry of desire, but an actual analyst who chooses to assume that function. As Muller observes, an over-emphasis on language can obscure a broader understanding of the basic structures of intersubjectivity and the unconscious, which are dialogic intersections of cultural and personal formations (Muller, 1996, pp. 187–189). The challenge for analysts lies in how to balance the impersonality of the semiotic function with assumption of a personalized symbolic role.

Notes

1. Faimberg contributed the concept of an evolving meaning of an analyst's inter-pretations based on a patient's unconscious identifications. From a semiotic standpoint, I propose that the patient's responses depend on numerous additional factors. She states that using her model "it is possible to overcome the dilemma of whether the analyst with his interpretation or the patient with his own reinterpretation of it is right" (1996, p. 667). Although she sees this rectification as a mutual process, rightness of interpretation remains in question.
2. Jacobs was criticized for his presentation at the IPA Congress in Amsterdam in 1997 for building an interpretation from the fantasies and memories that accom-panied a session (he gave the false impression of aiming to reduce psychoanalytic formulation to the evidence of his countertransference [Jacobs, 1993, 1999]).
3. In Kernberg's theory of internal object relations, the subject experiences herself internally as being in relation to a particular object, modeled on a person in the past, but actually identifies with the dyad itself and typically plays out both roles at different times. This pattern repeats in the transference where it can be labeled and interpreted.
4. Fink (2007) comments that Lacan came to see the presence of transference as a refutation of intersubjectivity, abandoning his early use of that term. He critiques a number of authors in this regard from the standpoint of the non-equality of the two subjects and also refers to the fading of the subject in the transference.
5. "L'objet de l'analyse, c'est de pouvoir non tout dire mais tout penser, c'est finalement la liberté de penser, et les résistances à cela." (The object of the analysis is not to be able to say everything but to think everything. In the end it consists of the freedom to think and the resistances to it) (Widlöcher, 2016).
6. Benveniste's contributions are summarized usefully by Muller (1996).
7. Hook (2013) provides an extended analysis of the puzzle and its implications for intersubjectivity from a Lacanian perspective.
8. Bion's axiom to leave behind beyond memory and desire comes from a similar concern. Laplanche (1998) elaborates that the offer of analysis resembles the original "seduction" of childhood through transmission of enigmatic messages, with an implied promise to resolve the enigma. The analyst tends to be seen as "the one supposed to know." In order for an analysis to progress, it is crucial that the analyst remains in touch with his own enigmatic core. By refusing to know—or, more accurately, being aware that he does not know—the analyst provides a "hollow" in which the process can evolve.

9. Žižek (2006) emphasizes this aspect of negation of the other as a necessary accompaniment of becoming a subject.
10. "We might conclude that for an analytic ethics the path of desire should retain to the end its ambiguous, tempting, and unfinished character without a defined or normative stopping point, because that is the essence of having a subjective life, as Lear compellingly reminds us. And this vital movement should be reflected in the patient's affect, sense of well-being, and purpose, not in any conventional accomplishments or standards of health, as Lacan insists" (Kirshner, 2012, p. 1237).
11. The object in question is Lacan's concept of the *objet a*, which became increasingly important in his work. The *objet a* (object a) represents the fantasy of a residue left over from a primal separation.

References

Barclay, M. & Kee, M. (2001). Towards a semiotic psychotherapy: Semiotic objects and semiotic selves, *Theory & Psychology*, 11:671–686.

Botella, C. & Botella, S. (2004). *The Work of Psychic Figurability*, London: The New Library of Psychoanalysis.

Brown, L. (2011). *Intersubjective Processes and the Unconscious*, New York: Routledge.

Chandler, D. (2013). *Semiotics: The Basics*, New York: Routledge.

Chandler, D. 2014. *Semiotics for Beginners*, an ebook, available at: www.aber.ac.uk/media/Documents/S4B/semiotic.html

Clark, A. (2012). How to qualify for a cognitive upgrade: Executive control, glass ceilings, and the limits of simian success, in *The Complex Mind*, ed. McFarland, D, Stenning, K., & McGonigle, M. London: Palgrave Macmillan.

Eco, U. (1984). *Semiotics and the Philosophy of language*, Bloomington, IN: Indiana University Press (paperback version: Midland Book edition, 1986).

Faimberg, H. (1996). "Listening To Listening", *International Journal of Psycho-analysis*, 77:667–677.

Fink, B. (2007). *Fundamentals of Psychoanalytic Technique*, New York: W.W. Norton & Co.

Hook, D. (2013). Towards a Lacanian group psychology: The prisoner's dilemma and the trans-subjective, *Journal for the Theory of Social Behaviour*, 43:115–132.

Jacobs, T.J. (1993). The inner experiences of the analyst: Their contribution to the analytic process, *International Journal of Psychoanalysis*, 74:7–14.

Jacobs, T.J. (1999). Commentary on paper by Jeanne Wolff Bernstein, *Psychoanalytic Dialogues*, 9:301–306.

Kirshner, L. (2012). Towards an ethic of desire for psychoanalysis: A critical reading of Lacan's ethics, *Journal of the American Psychoanalytic Association*, 60:1223–42.

Lacan, J. (1945). Le temps logique et l'assertion de certitude anticipée: Un nouveau sophism, Paris: *Cahiers d'Art*, pp. 32–42.

Lacan, J. (1953). The function and field of speech and language in psychoanalysis, in *Écrits*, trans. B. Fink, pp. 32–106, New York: W.W. Norton, 2002.

Lacan, J. (1954–55). *The Seminar of Jacques Lacan: Book II, The Ego in Freud's Theory and in the Technique of Psychoanalysis*, Ed. J.-A. Miller, trans. S. Tomaselli, Cambridge: Cambridge University Press, 1988.

Lacan, J. (1959–60). *The Seminar of Jacques Lacan: Book VII. The Ethics of Psychoanalysis*, Ed. J.-A. Miller, trans. D. Porter. New York: W.W. Norton, 1992.

Lacan, J. (1972–73). *Encore: The Seminar of Jacques Lacan: Book XX*. Ed. J.-A. Miller, trans. B. Fink as: *On Feminine Sexuality, the Limits of Love and Knowledge, 1972–73*, New York: W.W. Norton, 1998.

Laplanche, J. (1987). *New Foundations for Psychoanalysis*, trans. D. Macey. Oxford: Basil Blackwell, 1989.

Laplanche, J. (1997). The theory of seduction and the problem of the other, *International Journal of Psychoanalysis*, 78:653–666.

Litowitz, B.E. (2011). From dyad to dialogue: Language and the early relationship in American psychoanalytic theory, *Journal of the American Psychoanalytic Association*, 59:483–507.

Litowitz, B.E. (2014). Coming to terms with intersubjectivity: Keeping language in mind, *Journal of the American Psychoanalytic Association*, 62:294–312.

Modell, A.H. (1984). *Psychoanalysis in a New Context*. New York: International Universities Press.

Modell, A.H. (1990). *Other Times/Other Realities*, Cambridge, MA: Harvard University Press.

Muller, J. (1996). *Beyond the Psychoanalytic Dyad: Developmental Semiotics in Freud, Pearce, and Lacan*, New York: Routledge.

Peirce, C.S. (1932). *Collected Papers of Charles Sanders Peirce*, Ed. C. Hartshorne & P. Weiss. Cambridge, MA: Harvard University Press.

Salvatore, S. (2015). *Psychology in Black and White: The Project of a Theory-driven Science*, Charlotte, NC: Information Age Publishers.

Vivona, J. (2006). From developmental metaphor to developmental model: The shrinking role of language, *Journal of the American Psychoanalytic Association*, 54:877–902.

Widlöcher, D. (2016). Entretiens, Paris: unpublished manuscript.

Yeomans, F., Clarkin, J., & Kernberg, O. (2005). *A Primer on Transference-focused Psychotherapy for the Borderline Patient*, New York: Jason Aronson Books/ Rowman & Littlefield.

Žižek, S. (2006). *The Parallax View*, Cambridge, MA: MIT Press.

Chapter 7

The subject as text

The limits of semiotics

The comparison of psychoanalytic practice to the study of a written text takes us to the heart of the problem posed by the impersonality of the semiotic and neurophysiologic subject. Formal linguistic codes and mechanisms in the brain seem to leave little place for an actual person, a living being in the world, and suggest reductionism or schematizing of complex human relationships. Yet the traditional conception of a cohesive subject proves equally untenable, masking an idealization and justification of bourgeois individualism that provoked structuralist philosophers a generation ago. Sartre called the survival of theological assumptions about man in psychology and philosophy *"la grande affaire"* (in Hartman, 1978b, p. 91). The radical analogy treating the subject as a kind of text created a small intellectual scandal in the heyday years of structuralist thought and revealed (or revived) the semiotic underpinning of Freud's discoveries. The textual comparison disturbed scholars, including many psychoanalysts who saw the comparison as a dehumanizing, impersonal move bordering on a kind of nihilism.

One of the principal targets of the structuralist deconstruction of personal identity was psychoanalysis itself. The philosopher Louis Althusser (1996), who showed a remarkable sensitivity to the hazardous emergence of subjectivity in the cauldron of early childhood, also expressed suspicion of the cooptation of psychoanalytic practice by mainstream capitalist culture, with its accent on adaptation. Jacques Derrida, whom Althusser praised as the greatest of his contemporaries in philosophy, remained consistent in his enterprise of ruthlessly deconstructing psychoanalytic language. Hartman says he made Freud's text unreadable as a scientific thesis.[1] Hartman comments, "After reading (unreading) Freud's text in the light of Derrida, we realize that the troubling question of the relation of persona, of author to text, has been exponentially deepened" (1978a, p. xiv). Michel Foucault clearly mistrusted the entire analytic project as part of an institutional apparatus of biopolitical control over individuals disguised as science.

Provocative statements such as Sartre's religious metaphor for psychoanalysis, Foucault's famous announcement of the death of man,[2] and the tone of essays in the volume edited by Hartman (1978a, b) evaluating psychoanalysis from the standpoint of literary studies and Lacanian concepts elicited strong reactions.

Especially in the new light of neurosciences and a revived interest in linguistic approaches to analytic work, the controversial collection merits revisiting. "Ideally," Hartman suggests, "psychoanalysis should provide a closer model of close reading" (1978a, p. xiv). Amati-Mehler et al., for example, in their book *The Babel of the Unconscious*, counter unequivocally that 'analytic material' is not a text. . . . The analytic material is an experience" (1993, p. 234). They argued that the intersubjective dimension of psychoanalysis differentiates it from the translation of text—a position that speaks for many analysts. André Green (2002) based a comparable argument on the analyst's responsibility to care for troubled patients, and Lacan apparently made a similar comment (pertaining to Derrida) during a lecture at Johns Hopkins University. I recall members of the Boston Psychoanalytic Society displaying incredulity and outrage at a presentation on French theory by Harvard University Professor S. Suleiman at an annual meeting in the late 1980s where she advanced the structuralist position that psychoanalytic conceptions of the subject are unwitting byproducts of powerful ideological forces. And their reaction was not difficult to understand.

On its face, the comparison of a living human being to a dry and artificial piece of writing seems outrageous and even offensive. Especially for psychoanalysts who are deeply invested in a therapeutic relationship with roots in medical practice, an abstract reductionist approach to subjectivity seems dehumanizing and threatens the very basis of the work. Yet classical psychoanalysis itself has been charged with these same impersonal tendencies for its theories of psychic determinism and the unconscious, which undermine the notions of free will and conscious responsibility. Freud himself spoke of dethroning the ego as a center of authority. His famous assertion declaring that the ego is not master in its own house, but subservient to powerful outside forces, proffered a revision of traditional humanism no less radical than the theories of Foucault.[3] So it would seem that the immediate rejection by psychoanalysts of a structuralist perspective on subjectivity as the product of various conventions and assumptions deserves closer examination. After all, analysts might regard the motivation for this dismissive response as open to question, particularly when the narcissistic investment in the rejection is so obvious. However unpalatable on its face, pursuing the textual metaphor may have value.

I divide the analogy into two parts: one, the weaker and more obvious version, implies that the presentation of a person can be read similarly to a work of fiction or artistic creation, as carrying meanings not explicitly stated, but which must be interpreted. This process of reading the other person, of discerning signs and symbols, behaviors, and possible meanings of expressions, simply describes what human beings do all the time. Gallese (2001) notes that the capacity for a kind of intraspecies reading does not belong exclusively to *Homo sapiens*, but represents an evolved process that was necessary for other primates, perhaps other species as well, to survive in groups. The complex behavioral hierarchies of primate communities make clear the life or death urgency of accurate communication and reaction to signs of danger. This capacity represents an example of primary intersubjectivity, before the appearance of a symbolic personal identity in a structured society. I have argued in Chapters 4 and 6 that secondary intersubjectivity imposes a level of symbolic interpretation on processing sensory information. Unraveling the content of unconscious interpretations in Laplanche's terms constitutes one definition of analytic practice. As we have seen, however, the widespread adoption of mirror neuron research as an explanation for empathy and immediate understanding of another person veers toward a radical reductionism.

The second, stronger version of the textual analogy, on the other hand, makes the more challenging claim that the human subject as a speaking being amounts in an important sense to a collection of texts that govern his discourse. From a semiotic perspective, it argues that as a language-dependent creature the human subject is composed of discursive figures (signs), which determine its thinking and speech. The subject takes form through the concepts and narratives at its disposal in ways of which the actual person is usually only minimally aware. In short, a subject embodies the stories it tells. Since narrative theory resides at the core of contemporary analytic thought, one might conclude that the textual metaphor would necessarily impose itself. To speak of a subject implies a narrated subject. Schafer summarized the narrative turn in psychoanalysis as radical. He writes:

> Perhaps the most significant and exciting new frontier of psychoanalytic theory, practice, and research is the examination of the construction of meaning within the analytic dialogue, a construction that involves prominent narrative features. On this frontier the concern with traditional metapsychological formulations is relegated to the background, if not discarded altogether.
>
> (1983, p. 403)

From this perspective, a patient presents a narrative to his analyst, only partially conscious of its equivocations and ambiguities, while the psychoanalyst listens carefully with a floating attention to pick up traces of other narratives. These newer or coexisting accounts take shape in the current interactive analytic process, as Schafer emphasizes, and involve important affective elements. He writes: "In the process of trying to explain how the analysand got to be 'that way' in the present, one keeps on finding out what 'that way' is, that is, how to characterize it or what it means" (1979, p. 20). Hopefully, an analyst does not translate what he hears in the form of "x really means y" but maintains an awareness that not only the single story "x" but also other stories y and z are being told—multiple narratives. Schwartz referred to "an endless process of triangulation" in which participants in the analytic dialogue "can contain the ambiguity, ambivalence . . . and reparative symbolization of their language and action" (1978, pp. 10–11).

Schafer's theory of narrativity meets the common objection to the textual analogy that, unlike a work of art, a human subject is a living creature evolving in interaction with its environment, especially its intersubjective one. He observes (with Lacan) that the subject, far from being a self-repetitive entity like a mono-logic story, takes unpredictable and often surprising shapes in different contexts and at different times. More crucial to the matter, each subject can observe the people reading it and actively exchange with them, attempting to influence their understanding—what the philosopher Ian Hacking calls "looping" (1995, 2006, p. 23). Hacking reminds us that human "objects" have a way of responding to their contextual situations that constantly alters their self-perceptions and the manner in which others see them. Because of looping, he argues, human kinds like psychiatric diagnoses or social groups are transient categories, with the label changing its connotations or its usage even being effectively abolished over time. This situation becomes more striking in one-on-one interactions like marriage, in which the famous struggle to define the relationship becomes a troubling or invigorating feature. Intersubjective looping in pairs can function rhythmically like a dance or awkwardly like wrestling. Psychoanalytic couples present a spe-cial situation (not unique, however) in their inequality and asymmetry, yet the negotiation of how partners want to be seen also constitutes a pervasive theme of clinical process. Even when a patient wishes to be taken as an object for purposes of treatment and the analyst chooses to apply his knowledge about a category to which his patient may belong (like post-traumatic stress disorder or major depression), the consequences of expert intervention are unpredictable in a way that makes a post-modern literary creation—the protagonist of a Philip Roth novel, for example—seem lead-footed in its attempts to anticipate and thwart the reader. The living subject emits a stream of nuanced and subtle messages that continuously undermine any determined reading or, at the least, make this exercise futile and quixotic. In the end, psychiatric knowledge and expertise do not take a clinician very far in helping an individual patient make meaning out of his experience. Likewise, attempts to pin down the psychic truth or reality of a subject using psychoanalytic theories evoke the clichés of a bullheaded cinematic character pursuing his certitudes oblivious to the absurdity of his pretension to knowledge. The communications of a patient, unlike a text, include continuous affective expressions, not necessarily verbal, which evoke a succession of counter-affects. This dialogic interplay engages a would-be analytic reader and his object in a progressive tar baby-like mix-up, until their subjective experiences become inseparable from the field of interactions between them. Thoughtful clinical presentations must include the analyst as part of the matter to be discussed; speaking of "the patient" in professional settings amounts to a narrative fiction, constructed for educational or political purposes.

I described in Chapter 2 my efforts to formulate the relevant aspects of Ms. B.'s history according to my developmental and psychoanalytic knowledge, and advanced several hypotheses to this end. Together we embarked on a search for causes of her depression, which I did know something about and which she initially set as her goal for the treatment. Yet over time, her focus turned increasingly toward what I was doing with her, and what interactive patterns in the present exemplified her real-life issues. Perhaps the change represented a form of "looping" in the analytic encounter, in which my challenge became how to alter my understanding in response to Ms. B.'s messages of how she experienced our work. Multiple narratives emerged, of course, but her goal evolved toward constructing a novel way of being herself and determining whether our work could support this change.

The most persuasive distinction between an actual person and a text relies on the therapeutic intention of the analytic "reader." As Green and Lacan remind us, the analyst assumes an explicit healing or transformational role, not a philosopher's project of exploding myths of free will and autonomy. "Texts cannot be cured," Schwartz writes (1978, pp. 11–12). Since Freud, however, we know that admirable wishes to help can block progress, and the professional role of healer incorporates social values that may resist change. Hacking observes that healers (in psychiatry, for example) follow an agenda that consists in returning a patient to a normal range of function (1995, 2006). He describes social science categories as defining exceptional or deviant states that are implicitly undesirable. A label like "teenage pregnancy," for instance, implies that women in this group are too young or immature to have children, that there is a social problem involved, and that some intervention, whether psychological, educational, or political, should be carried out to improve the situation. Although psychoanalytic diagnoses are arguably more individualized, it is difficult to make them exceptions to Hacking's interpretation. Similar to his other examples, psychoanalytic views of sexuality, gender roles, and family relationships have evolved along with the rest of society, partly in response to the looping feedback from patients singly and in groups. While contemporary analysts no longer believe in adapting patients to societal or medical norms, but instead in helping free them from unconscious forces to pursue their own unique paths, they cannot totally escape the assumptions and prejudices of the society in which they work. The ethical obligation to monitor one's countertransferences recognizes this limitation. Both patient and analyst are creations of the world in which they live. Nonetheless, psychoanalysis assumes a capacity in the subject for potential freedom that is absent from what is generally called a text, which Hacking's concept of looping recognizes. The Lacanian aphorism, "Pay attention to the text, not the psychology of the author," means that the analyst should listen to the analysand's words, to the text as it unfolds and is modified continuously by what comes next in a discourse, not that the subject *en toto* is a coherent text. In his work on the signifier, Lacan was objecting to the naive notion of a unified subject (lacking an unconscious), not to the textual metaphor itself.[4]

The textual analogy holds the merit of reminding us that the development of newborn babies into self-conscious, speaking beings involves the internalization and rearrangement of affectively charged messages from others for which the subject becomes the vehicle. Clinicians can listen to speech as a polyphonic self-presentation that carries diverse voices—i.e. as a complicated form of text. This comparison of a speaking person to a collection of texts does not imply that the subject is blindly pushed along by his words (although he may be), or that he consists only of words (he does have a corporeal existence and embodied affects).

It suggests rather that the work of the psychoanalyst focuses on the multiple meanings and affective content of the words and phrases his patient employs. They contain a history that may have imposed a task or fate on the patient, as exemplified by Lacan's riddle of the three prisoners discussed in the previous chapter.

No serious critic of literature would claim that a novel has but one correct interpretation, nor would a philologist assert the univocal meaning of an ancient text. Psychoanalysts have, perhaps reluctantly, come to a similar conclusion. Freud bears responsibility for the classic analytic ambition of finding accurate causal interpretations of a symptom or behavior (despite his many contradictory remarks). Consequently, psychoanalysis became famous for offering keys to unlock the meaning of mysterious aspects of human life. Even near the end of his life, in *Constructions in Analysis*, Freud continued to assert a positivist point of view about coming to the truth of interpretation. It is possible, he suggested, to construct a correct view of the unconscious factors determining a neurotic illness (1937). Of course, unconscious factors of the psychoanalytic type have become well known in our culture, and on first pass our clinical attention is drawn to them. I have argued instead that a search for causes and explanations can lead us quickly astray. A plurality of contemporary therapeutic approaches has supplanted Freud's aim of reconstructing the infantile sources of neuroses, but the scientific goal of seeking to get to the sources of a problem remains strong in the profession. In addition to sexual conflicts, some current analysts look for early deficits in mothering or problems in attachment to understand a patient's current difficulty. Reconstructing early history in these or similar terms creates a portrait that can reduce the person to an illustration of a theory, which has been a hazard of case discussions. Psychoanalysis itself courts the danger subsuming a dynamic, interactive process of subjectivity under a unified "text" of formulation and interpretation that is generally absent from literary studies.

I began this discussion by reviewing the innovations of structuralist thought that posit the subject as an effect of specific conditions, rather than as an intrinsic property of the biological individual. The notion that subjectivity can be understood in some sense as a written text followed—a text composed of the assumptions and values of dominant discourses within which the subject has been formed. In my view, the analogy remains useful if it refers to an open text that keeps being written and unwritten: not a document to decipher, but a text that never "stops not being written," as Lacan proposed.[5] The living embodied subject, as a creative locus of speech, always escapes its determining narratives. It is a moving point of metaphoric expression and synthesis of experiential states that is not disparaged by comparison to a work of art—like a Shakespeare play in which the many characters and storylines are part of one entity. The danger of the textual analogy lies in its impersonal connotations and a tendency to overemphasize the function of the reader, which can slight the actual author's part of the equation. Like the vocabulary of semiotic theory, technical analyses of a subject's modes of expression, as Derrida arguably illustrates, add depth to our understanding of "the text" but may lose the actuality of the subject.

Notes

1. Hartman refers to Derrida's discussion of *Beyond the Pleasure Principle*, but the point about the illusory scientific nature of Freud's writing can be extended. Derrida writes that the theme of the essay (repetition) "must be identified not only in the content . . . but also in Freud's very writing, in the 'steps' taken by his text, in what it does, as well as in what it says" (1978, p. 115).
2. In the last part of his *The Order of Things*, Foucault (1966) announced that man would disappear like a face made of sand. He meant that the term "man" represented an historical fiction, the creation of a particular time and place.
3. Freud's 1917 essay was written prior to his revisions in the structural model and seems to refer to the topographic, conscious ego. The later model of the ego, however, moves large portions of ego function into the unconscious, further undermining the illusion of control and unity.
4. "The subject is nothing other than what slides in a chain of signifiers, whether he knows which signifier he is the effect of or not. That effect—the subject—is the intermediary effect between what characterizes a signifier and another signifier, namely, the fact that each of them, each of them is an element. We know of no other basis by which the One may have been introduced into the world if not by the signifier as such, that is, the signifier insofar as we learn to separate it from its meaning effects" (Lacan 1972–73, p. 50).
5. Lacan spoke about the real as a source of desire that can never be completely represented in the symbolic or imaginary registers. Hence his puzzling phrase, *ce qui ne cesse pas de ne pas s'écrire* (what never stops not being written) to refer to the unconscious (1972–73, pp. 144–145).

References

Althusser, L. (1996). *Writings on Psychoanalysis: Freud and Lacan: Louis Althusser*, Ed. O. Corpet and F. Matheron, trans. J. Mehlman. New York: Columbia University Press.

Amati-Mahler, J., Argentieri, S., & Canestri, J. (1993). *The Babel of the Unconscious: Mother Tongue and Foreign Languages in the Psychoanalytic Dimension*, trans. J. Whitelaw-Cucco. Madison, CT: International Universities Press.

Derrida, J. (1978). Coming into one's own, trans. J. Hulbert, in *Psychoanalysis and the Question of the Text: Selected Papers from the English Institute, 1976–77*, Ed. G. Hartman, pp. 114–148, Baltimore, MD: Johns Hopkins University Press.

Foucault, M. (1966). *The Order of Things*, New York: Pantheon Books, 1971.

Freud, S. (1917). A difficulty in the path of psycho-analysis, in *The Standard Edition of the Complete Psychological Works of Sigmund Freud, Volume XVII (1917–1919): An Infantile Neurosis and Other Works*, pp. 135–144.

Freud, S. (1937). *Constructions in Analysis, SE 23*, 257–269.

Gallese, V. (2001). The "shared manifold" hypothesis: From mirror neurons to empathy, *Journal of Consciousness Studies*, 8:33–50.

Green, A. (2002). *Idées directrices pour une psychanalyse contemporaine*, Paris: Presses Universitaires de France.

Hacking, I. (1995). The looping effects of human kinds, in *Causal Cognition: An Interdisciplinary Approach*, Ed. D. Sperber, D. Premack, & A. Premack. Oxford: Oxford University Press, pp. 351–383.

Hacking, I. (2006). Making up people, *London Review of Books*, 28:23–26.

Hartman, G. (1978a). Preface to *Psychoanalysis and the Question of the Text: Selected Papers from the English Institute, 1976–77*, Ed. G. Hartman, pp. vii–xix, Baltimore, MD: Johns Hopkins University Press.

Hartman, G. (1978b). Psychoanalysis: The French Connection, in *Psychoanalysis and the Question of the Text: Selected Papers from the English Institute, 1976–77*, Ed. G. Hartman, pp. 86–113, Baltimore, MD: Johns Hopkins University Press.

Lacan, J. (1972–73). *Encore: The Seminar of Jacques Lacan, Book XX*, Ed. J.-A. Miller, trans. B. Fink, New York: W.W. Norton, 1975.

Schafer, R. (1979). The appreciative analytic attitude and the construction of multiple histories, *Psychoanalysis and Contemporary Thought*, 2:3–24.

Schafer, R. (1983). Introduction, *Psychoanalysis and Contemporary Thought*, 6:403–404.

Schwartz, M. (1978). Critic define thyself, in *Psychoanalysis and the Question of the Text: Selected Papers from the English Institute, 1976–77*, Ed. G. Hartman, pp. 1–17, Baltimore, MD: Johns Hopkins University Press.

Chapter 8

Intersubjectivity in practice

Beyond semiosis

I use the expression "beyond semiosis" to cover aspects of the analytic relationship that operate at a different conceptual level from the communication of signs. As discussed in Chapter 1, subjectivity is not simply a function of the intersubjective, semiotic field or the inherited properties of the mammalian brain, although it depends upon both. The speaking subject is a product of semiosis, but cannot be adequately captured at that level. In this chapter, I do not attempt to develop the possible linkages between the phenomenology of the relationship of two subjects in analysis and the dynamic exchanges of signs or signifiers between them, which would be another project. Instead, I examine relational dimensions of the task of the therapist in his culturally designated role.

As my starting point for this approach to the subject, I take the notion of a private, unknowable self, as emphasized by Winnicott and Modell (following the early assertions of William James)—the realm of "what it is like to be me" or the qualia of ineffable personal experience and its physical embodiment. Psychoanalysis and the neurosciences traditionally look beyond such surface manifestations to discover the determinants of conscious feelings and the mechanisms underlying their appearance. The scientific approach favored by both disciplines bypasses the phenomenologic subject (as suggested by the common language of causality), thereby obscuring the lived reality of human experience. Yet, in practice, psychoanalysis cannot dispense with notions like agency, intention, affects, self-states, and other unscientific designations without abstracting itself from the concerns of actual life. The conceptual challenge for theory lies in preserving a humanistic perspective without idealizing or mystifying the nature of subjectivity or reducing it to impersonal operations.

As discussed in Chapters 1 and 7, critical philosophy debunked the myth of a subject conceived as the manifestation of an enduring substance or structure inside the person. Hume, modern French theorists, structuralist and analytic philosophers, and Lacan variously dismissed spiritual or metaphysical notions of an internal, core entity that expresses itself through behavior and speech, taking the converse view that what we call "the self" represents a product of these signs. Neuroscientists provided support to their critiques by reminding us that no center of agency, no directing force, can be located in the brain. Because we feel a sense of conscious control over our actions and can speak in conventional terms of "having" a self does not mean that a guiding center of initiative exists inside our heads.[1]

Peirce (1868) also made critical remarks about the concept of the individual personality as an isolated center of the person, stressing instead the intermeshing of minds in the semiotic continuum of human society. He wrote that it is necessary to distinguish the notion of self as an interpreting object from an interpreted one; as the latter, self is inseparable from the semiotic process. In his detailed summary of Peirce's remarks on this theme, however, Colapietro (1989) notes a variety of ways in which Peirce paradoxically took a developmental perspective to justify the emergence of the individual subject. At minimum, Peirce's work supports a dynamic, fluctuating, and evolving form of self-consciousness dependent on signs (thinking as an internal flow of signs). Although scholars debate what he intended by his many statements on the matter, for me they suggest a dialectical perspective on subjectivity and intersubjectivity. Salvatore (2015) describes this approach as combining the vertical (reaching down into the body and its history to discover the roots of the subject) with the horizontal (sharing a world with others who confer subjectivity). In a similar manner, André Green (2002) saw psychoanalysis working at the intersection of the intrapsychic and the interpsychic,[2] while Kaës (1993) proposed the duality of a group and an individual unconscious. Apart from the philosophical conundrums of this relationship, we are left with the ethical problem of our relationship to the subject in clinical work. What position do we take in relation to the other, our *semblable* in the clinical situation?

To think beyond the impersonality of the sign, drive, or a physiologic process in therapeutic practice requires a way to speak about a non-substantive personal self, perhaps in terms of a shifting, rebalancing movement of personal signifiers in time and space, as Peirce came to describe. The reflective speaking subject, however, possesses the peculiar property of being the product of a semiotic process that can turn on itself within a framework it has internalized (Žižek, 2006). It arises as the precipitate of formative symbols around an embodied awareness; in Lévi-Strauss's famous metaphor, the subject resembles a player who has no choice about the cards dealt him or even the structure of the game but can still choose how to play his hand. Lacan made the analogy of subjectivity to a game of dice, already thrown before birth, but with the possibility of rolling the dice once again in psychoanalysis. All these constraints (the cards, the dice, the first signifiers) describe the nature of the field open to a particular child at a specific time and place, but playing the game, which begins at birth, immediately modifies the given structure. Although adverse experiences like deprivation and trauma greatly restrict the possibility for agency and may come close to eliminating it entirely, psychotherapy ultimately relies on this human potential.[3] Hacking's concept of "looping," the reciprocity of interaction with the determining persons and institutions that shape subjectivity (see Chapter 6), portrays an existential freedom absent from the determinism of many theories. I agree with Žižek that a recognition of the autonomy of the subject as a symbolic entity, organized or precipitated within the field of signs produced by the cultural matrix, interacting with the developing brain, must be included in any understanding of human experience.

In proposing a psychoanalytic approach to a level "beyond semiosis," I build on three familiar but ambiguous terms: empathy, recognition, and responsiveness, dimensions that address the embodied dynamic subject in flux. Together, they mark out the ethical stance of an intersubjective therapist toward his patients. As presented in prior chapters, each of these concepts has important limitations, yet captures an essential feature of intimate human interactions that applies to psychoanalytic psychotherapies. I see the three as enigmatic, but necessary terms; they lack a precise referent, but convey a dispositional and affective orientation of subject to subject.

To begin, the word "empathy" includes several common connotations. By its etymology, empathy conveys a stance of feeling with the other, either sharing the other's actual affective state or feeling together with the other in some significant emotional context. Perhaps the former occurs in states of emotional contagion under heightened situations of arousal, but usually we accept the limits of joining the other's feelings except in a very approximate way. Someone in tears tells a sad story and we respond with a similar, although certainly not identical, affect. We can say that we *feel with* the other as an analogy to Widlöcher's (2004a, b) concept of the *co-pensée* (thinking with). We think and feel together with the other around a shared (but not identical) object. Often, the expression "empathic immersion" suggests identification with another person approaching sameness, as suggested by the term "mirroring," in which two subjects each reflect the image of the other by expressing iconic and index signs of closeness and identity. These two types of non-verbal, non-symbolic signs evoke joining or mimicry, at least on the level of facial expressions or gestures. They produce the illusion of our inhabiting the same space. Sharing an expressive, affective state by mirroring can be supplemented by a cognitive effort to understand the other based on our knowledge about them. Probably this effort goes along with distancing, not joining the other but seeing the person as separate in his own context. A related and useful notion is "perspective taking," in which one tries to view the world from the other's position, a kind of trial identification based on contextual and narrative knowledge. Finally, an empathic approach often suggests an affective stance of solicitude or concern without passing judgment, an effort to respond sympathetically to another's thoughts and feelings.

The limitations of taking an empathic position toward the conscious self-presentation of a patient and his current feeling state derive from its implicit endorsement of a "nuclear self," as Kohut suggested, and from the tendency of such gestures to devolve into unmediated mirroring. A naive understanding of empathy reifies the presenting self, like settling for a snapshot of the other, omitting alternative selves not actively present in the current situation and important unconscious or dissociated psychic elements. Empathic mirroring as an attempt at mutual identification and affect-sharing plays a part in therapeutic interactions by offering supportive, reassuring signs of understanding and care, but must be moved beyond to achieve the analytic goals of growth and freedom (as Peirce might have advocated). One can attempt to convey empathy for a loving, vital self one hopes the other will one day become, a potential subject in the making, as a therapeutic attitude, but whichever aspect of empathy we pursue, we are limited to an always incomplete knowledge of the other. If we conceive of the Peircian self as polyphonic, an amalgam of different voices and identities, our grasp of its feelings and ways of experiencing remains partial, and our selection of what to empathize with reflects something about ourselves and our countertransferences. Although we may try not to assume a simple complementary position to the most salient self-presentation and to sustain the multiplicity of elements in play, we are pulled toward joining the dyad as part of our engagement. If we pause to reflect, we tend to disengage, risking a too distant, bird's-eye view of the other. The tension between the extremes of mirroring sameness and distancing objectification creates a field in which our exercise of empathy operates.

Of the various forms and definitions of empathy, two aspects seem most relevant to my argument: the attitude of concern and the intention to understand. These commitments establish an intersubjective position assumed by the analyst/therapist that he will inevitably communicate (by signs) to his patient. Empathy in this sense refers to an intentional stance, a way of attending to a patient, and an openness of reception, rather than to the product of listening carefully, an identification, a capacity to imagine feelings, or any attempt to join the other's experience. The analyst attempts to be present and to seek understanding as part of his commitment to the cultural role he has chosen, without reifying the perceived other or convincing himself that he does understand.

The South African trauma scholar Pumla Gobodo-Madikizela (2015) uses psychoanalytic concepts of intersubjectivity in her discussion of witnessing from an empathic position. In her work on the Truth and Reconciliation Commission, she found "emergence of new subjectivities" in the encounter of victims and perpetrators, which might be a good definition of any successful intersubjective relationship. She emphasizes the important element of concern and care for the other as key to the empathic stance. Again, the process (and the result), rather than the content of the empathic interaction is its major feature.

The empathic intersubjective stance focuses on existential states like loneliness, joy, remorse, despair, meaninglessness, and desire that belong to the human condition and challenge the coherence of every subject throughout a lifetime. These terms resist precise symbolic definition or formulation in theoretical or scientific language. While each culture marks out important core experiences in its own manner and provides unique ways for dealing with them, Gobodo-Madikizela's example of the encounter of victims and perpetrators suggests a universal sensitivity to a few fundamental affective/ideational states. Despite important cultural differences, clinicians in many societies address similar issues, which may account in part for the wide diffusion of psychoanalytic concepts and programs across Eastern Europe, Asia, Latin America, and Africa. Analysts are concerned with the phenomenology of common human feelings and know something about them, but even within one cultural area they must continually remind themselves that they cannot fully share or understand how another subject experiences them.

The major task of the empathic intersubjective stance involves maintaining an optimal distance, oscillating between a position of conscious reflection and private associations about the other subject and the near-collapse of the affective space between them (feeling together with). This tension requires self-monitoring. At the extremes, the analyst finds himself either overly immersed in the affects of his patient through identification and complementary or wishful responses, or asymmetrically detached from the interactive field. To counter these tendencies and maintain a mobile attention, he needs regular access to a third, preferably an actual colleague or group with whom he can speak regularly about his actual practice, as discussed in Chapters 2 and 3. An internal third, like the voices of supervisors or peers in private dialogue, can also support an open empathic stance, although it is obviously less reliable than actually talking freely about one's work with another. The analyst's words and affects bring unrecognized aspects of his countertransference into the conversation with a third to be heard and worked with.

For the second mainstay of an intersubjective therapeutic approach, I propose the phenomenology of recognition. Much has been written about recognition, of which I have highlighted the contributions of Benjamin, Lacan, and Modell in Chapters 3 and 6. As an abstract concept, it shares problems with many terms we have been dealing with throughout, especially the question of who is being recognized and from what position. Just as with attempts at empathy, a reification or static image of the other imposes a limited definition of who they are, which can even have a coercive effect, as in Althusser's concept of *appellation* (a call that defines its recipient). In her elaboration of Hegel's philosophical position, Benjamin (1990) emphasizes man's basic desire to be recognized as a subject, which remains a consistent focus of her work. The principle of recognition as a subject carries important political and social implications that bear on the equality of all subjects. Using the etymology of the term, she reminds us that human beings are subjects of a social order, which confers rights and privileges. Yet this ethical, humanistic stance toward others does not fully address the demand for recognition by specific individuals.

Lacan dealt with the problem of what or who will be recognized by proposing an ethics of psychoanalysis that acknowledges the absolute alterity and unknowability of the other. In the work he considered his major accomplishment, *The Ethics of Psychoanalysis* (1959–60), his thesis culminates with the famous formula of never to cede (never give up on) one's desire (*jamais céder sur son désir*). Since desire arguably represents the most singular element in a subject otherwise shaped by extrinsic structures, Lacan made the analyst's affirmation of an individual's desire his central principle. In doing so, he posited a unique ethical position to be assumed by the analyst. He reasoned that, having learned in his own analysis to appreciate both his subjective destitution (lacking a substantial self and facing a void surrounded by fantasies) and the wish for realization of what he called the fundamental fantasy (of achieved desire), a psychoanalyst could now pass his new knowledge on to others. The process seems circular; analysis creates analysts who reproduce an ethic of their own experience. Perhaps in different versions, all analyses contend with this self-fulfilling assumption.

As noted above, analytic psychotherapists have a function that seems to be widely appreciated across many cultures. Since there are no formulae or rules that adequately cover the task, applying the method may have to be reinvented with every patient, but the general guidelines remain: the central tenet of the analyst's job concerns listening from a particular position of responsibility toward the analysand. Lacan's ethic, which proposes a hands-off policy of influencing the other's desire or pursuing normative goals, represents a form of this obligation. The notion of recognition functions in his early work as an affirmation of separateness and singularity, more like recognizing a state of affairs than something specific about the person. Recognition, like empathy, describes a position of concern without judgment.

While each analysis follows a unique course, the set-up of treatment reflects cultural models of caretaking for afflicted individuals. In Lacan's discussion, an engagement in acknowledged concern for the other or if one's impact on the other seems lacking. Acknowledgement of what transpires in the analytic interaction belongs to the process of recognition. Usually, a patient's demand for help touches on far-reaching difficulties he experiences in maintaining a sense of who he is as a desiring subject, usually the result of failures of early relationships to meet universal needs for love and affirmation, and of painful histories of trauma and betrayal. Traditional analytic technique focused on the intrapsychic management of effects of these experiences, but the source and perpetuation of the problem belong to the intersubjective domain. The unconscious drama unfolds in the present, where it takes a new shape in the bipersonal analytic field. Realization of the inadequacy of classic methods to respond sufficiently to the traumatic marks of absence (neglect or abandonment) and presence (abuse and impingement) of the primary objects led analysts to make important changes in theory and practice, especially around the handling of countertransference fears and wishes. These transformations of analytic technique have an ethical dimension. Analysts respond to major failures in fundamental human requirements for care, respect, and attention that could not be addressed adequately by traditional methods of interpretation (if such were ever literally applied) but require the assumption of a position of empathic concern, readiness to acknowledge what emerges, and recognition of a subject's history. Although Lacan's definition respects the separateness of the other and suggests an affirmative attitude, his technique tilts too much toward a detachment he himself criticized in practices of his time. Accepting the irreducibility of the other's desire conveys non-judgmental acceptance, yet does not affirm the right to being nurtured and responded to as a separate subject within a human community that trauma and deprivation can negate. Although cultures vary widely in their conception of human rights, their ideals may converge to a substantial extent around this basic value.

Of course, the analyst cannot make up for the past or provide a substitute for what was lacking. Lacan was correct that the task of coming to terms with lack falls on everyone, and the analyst makes himself available to being recruited into this struggle. Schafer (1979) introduced an important perspective on the inter-subjective process with his notion of the appreciative analytic attitude. The analyst should not approach the other as a potential adversary out to foil the analysis, but as someone whose efforts simply "to be" deserve appreciation. The patient has struggled, not always successfully, with difficult experiences and conflict-ing pressures, and the analyst must avoid judgmental or critical perceptions of these efforts. Schafer writes: "Through recall, insight, and empathy, the analyst gets to understand the extent to which the analysand has managed to continue living hopefully, lovingly, and honestly, and also in a way that is dignified, proud, talented, and constructive when, considering all the relevant adverse life circumstances, the odds against this achievement have been very great if not overwhelming" (1979, p. 5). Of course, the failures and negative features of the subject's journey cannot be ignored, but we can view them as attempted solutions. Everyone knows this, yet some formulations—for example, of resistance to treat-ment, of effects of a death drive, and of negative therapeutic reactions—can express derogatory judgments of patients. I suggest that Schafer intended his message to counteract these ungenerous conceptions, replacing them with an appreciative attitude toward a person trying to make do with the limited resources at his disposal. His attitude conveys a recognition of the subject's history and the choices he has made for better and worse to cope with it. Appreciation need not mean acceptance; confrontation and clarification may even be made easier from Schafer's position.

In the final chapters of his book, Paul Ricoeur (2004) presents a phenomenologic analysis of the problems of recognition I have raised from a relational and psychotherapeutic perspective. He addresses the potentially interminable Hegelian struggle to be recognized on both individual and social levels, commenting, "When would a subject judge himself truly recognized?" (2004, p. 337). Jean-Jacques Rousseau spoke of "the insatiable craving to secure recognition for one's person from others" (Mishra, 2016, p. 70). The negative and positive aspects of this contestation seem embedded in human nature and thereby potentially interminable, linked to the questions of identity that preoccupy modern man. Identity and alterity occupy the poles of every intersubjective encounter, creating an ineradicable tension between recognition and misrecognition. "The originary dysymmetry between myself and the other" (p. 397) cannot be resolved but only interrupted by a truce Ricoeur calls "states of peace" (p. 341), which he attempts to define through studies of the dynamics of the gift. The ritual acts of gift giving, he shows, establish reciprocity through social rules and obligations, but not a mutuality that provides assurances about recognition. He finds an example of a state of peace in the intermediary affects of gratitude and generosity, which take on a festive character of shared involvement without a demand for symmetry between subjects engaged in an exchange.

A similar gap lies at the heart of speaking and listening between persons; one cannot show that one truly understands the other or expect to be entirely understood by him. The "between" within the dissymmetric couple is the key for Ricoeur. The constitutive dissymmetry offers two advantages: first, "One is not the other; one exchanges gifts, not places," and, second, it "preserves a just distance in the heart of mutuality," against "the traps of fusional union" in love, friendship, or community (p. 401).[4] In the treatment situation, an analyst does not expect equality or reciprocity of recognition; yet striving for a "just distance" against the pulls toward imaginary sameness or alienation creates moments of mutuality that punctuate the give and take of charged interaction.

I suggest responsiveness as the third and most difficult term basic to inter-subjective psychoanalysis. Analysts have always debated when and how much to respond to an analysand's communications. Some of the differences between schools reflect these differences, although I suspect that they are exaggerated in practice. Analysts tend to be reserved, although they cannot avoid conveying reactions by facial expression, gesture, and tone—even their choice of words. The perspective of intersubjectivity includes the unavoidability of communicating unconscious or preconscious interpretations (interpretants in Peircian terms), and the analyst must rely on a patient's responses to know how he has been under-stood. The bipersonal field dominates the here-and-now of the treatment relationship and constantly shapes and contains it. Nonetheless, the intrapsychic domain (the unique subjectivity of each participant) comprises much of the content represented and enacted in the dual situation; the analyst responds as a separate subject with his own personal countertransferences.

If responsiveness is inevitable in all interactions, what does it add to a model of psychoanalytic intersubjectivity to justify its inclusion in my triad of principles? Responsiveness has been proposed by social psychologists as the active ingredient in successful human relationships, and many empirical studies have documented this hypothesis. As a construct, it incorporates the previously discussed themes of caring, understanding, and empathy. Perceived responsiveness and positive attributions to partners correlate with successful relationship outcomes, although accuracy also appears important (Reis and Gable, 2015). A study of therapeutic relationships in three cultures found that perceived responsiveness predicted satisfaction more than other measures (Reis et al., 2008). Although the authors cite few psychoanalytic references, the parallel findings across cultures are striking. Overall and Simpson (2015) summarize research showing that reactions of persons demonstrating anxious and avoidant attachment can be successfully regulated by their partners, a fundamental insight of psychoanalytically informed infant research. Mutual regulation may be the frontier of current social neuroscience and social psychology. The conclusion of Reis and Gable's review supports the funda-mental principle of the psychoanalytic model: "because it is a fundamentally interpersonal process with intrapersonal origins and consequences, responsiveness highlights the centrality of relationships for understanding individuals" (2015, p. 67).

Unlike most real-life situations, psychoanalytic responsiveness takes place in a sheltered and highly dissymmetric context. Although private expectations influence all intersubjective exchanges, the analytic concept of transference describes a persistent pressure fostered and intensified by the method (by not clarifying realities, by sustaining ambiguity, and by avoiding actions). The responsiveness studied by psychologists in intimate relationships involves overt expressions of emotional connection, physical affection, and verbal promises and reassurances, while for analysis, the deepening play of expectancies and counter-reactions becomes itself the subject matter for examination. The analyst does not pursue a positive relationship for its own sake or to cement a personal tie. Even the notion of a therapeutic alliance includes the capacity for experiencing negative feelings in the conjoint process. So analytic responsiveness operates at a different level, but nonetheless underpins the clinical process as in other forms of relatedness.

Another form of responsiveness in psychoanalysis consists in adopting a sociocultural position explicitly incorporating ethical values. Bigras (1990) has advocated a "call to order" or a statement of moral judgment in the treatment of abused patients. In cases of sexual abuse, he favors a direct statement of the evil of the behavior and a commitment to repudiate it. The analyst should not be afraid to declare that "this is wrong," even if the patient defends the perpetrator, as can be the case. He suggests that injunctions against the mistreatment of children are quasi-universal laws that failed in the families of his patients who need a symbolic representative of the society to represent a position that was absent. What position can be neutral without assuming a lawful context for behavior? Analysts extend Bigras's point by affirming to survivors of abuse that "this was not your fault," which may make it more possible for them to explore their memories.

In the psychotherapy of a young man who had been sexually abused as a child, I took a similar stance.[5] He volunteered several times that he felt no anger toward his abuser, who may have had a history of abuse himself. The patient intellectualized in probably an accurate way about the man's behavior and, moreover, seemed aware of his general posture of detachment from life, which he regretted. Yet, while explicitly grateful for the ability to talk to me about his family secrets, he remained unwilling or unable to further pursue his thoughts and feelings. At a later point, I decided to tell him that, although I understood that he was not conscious of any anger, I felt angry on his behalf. He seemed curious and surprised by my reaction. At our next meeting, he told me he had discussed my comment with his wife, whose judgment he relied on. She said that she knew he didn't express angry feelings, but instead withdrew into himself—for example, after incidents that annoyed him at work. Her validation and support may have enabled him to work with my comment, which stirred up disturbing images and emotions. Not engaging with his affects in our sessions became a paradigm for his disengagement elsewhere, along with fears of what might emerge if he let himself feel. I realized I was treading on shaky ground (because of the severity of the initial symptoms that brought him to psychotherapy), but in any event I felt that I had probably communicated my attitude and it would be better to acknowledge it directly. Had I neither known about his wife's support for his treatment, nor experienced a growing rapport with him, my decision to speak out would have been more difficult. His denial of anger also suggested to me a paradoxical acknowledgement; its appearance in the negative had become part of the field.

Although responsiveness cannot be prescribed or made into a technique, I believe it deserves to be considered as a significant part of learning to practice psychoanalytic therapy. First, as previously stressed, the analyst cannot help responding, and putting his responses into words represents a further step into self-disclosure (it says something about the speaker, as in my example). Students need to think about their implicit and explicit choices in responding to an analysand as a major element of treatment. A patient can work more productively with a verbal intervention (as opposed to a gestural or expressive one), although it may be more threatening. As such, words must be weighed as carefully as possible, although time may be lacking for extensive consideration at important moments, as when affectively charged expressions erupt unpredictably in an analysis. Of course, non-responsiveness can possess equivalent power, and the analyst must not overlook its effects in his reflective observations. Usually, the analyst should say something about not responding, like offering an explanation or acknowledgement that he has heard, but chosen to wait. Responsiveness can also be conveyed non-verbally, demonstrated by attitude and presence, similar to the intentionality of empathy and recognition I have outlined. The future analyst/therapist should be helped in training to explore how to apply all three positions as part of his ethical commitment to the work.

Summary

In Chapters 6 and 7, I presented a semiotic perspective on the therapeutic process as governed by the exchange of signs, of which words and affects comprise the basic units. Intersubjectivity depends on the conscious and unconscious reception and response to signifying communications, but the nature of actual relationships requires a conceptual level addressing the involvement of two subjects beyond the molecular level of semiotic analysis. In addition to the nuts-and-bolts interplay of signs that underlies intersubjective relationships, a vocabulary that signifies the personal dimension of interaction is necessary. I chose the three complex terms of empathy, recognition, and responsiveness to characterize the major features of this relational level. Together, they point to a nodal position for the analyst in the network of therapeutic relationships established by a sociocultural group. This position involves a commitment to quasi-universal rights that human societies accord to their subjects. In accepting this role, the analytic therapist assumes ethical responsibilities toward the other.

I recommend the formal introduction of these core elements of the therapist's role into the educational process of candidates and students in training. Apart from exploring classic texts in the literature, trainees need to pursue in-depth discussion, analysis, and working through of the unique intersubjective position they have chosen. The concepts of empathy, recognition, and responsiveness point to relational (subject to subject) responsibilities the student assumes in becoming an analytic therapist, and engaging with them is indispensable. The question of how to define and implement these concepts within a new professional identity can serve as the focal point for group and personal exploration. This is what psychoanalytic education should be about.

Within the basic frame of psychotherapy, oriented toward an intersubjective engagement with the other, clinicians employ different preferred theories to gain understanding and insight into the treatment process. Intersubjectivity does not imply adherence to any specific school, although I criticize the traditional analytic objective of making interpretations based on presumed intrapsychic dynamics or developmental formulations as tilting toward a subject to object relationship. Psychoanalytic concepts do not refer to real objects but are abstractions, although a patient can be treated wrongly as though they describe him accurately. Theory provides interesting ways of looking at the therapeutic process, but lends itself to rationalization of personal reactions and countertransference. Many contemporary schools, however, converge in highlighting the simultaneous unfolding of the intrapsychic and the interpsychic in the intersubjective field, which functions as an open system, rather than one with fixed contents like theoretical objects.

The ultimate goal of psychoanalysis consists in expansion of freedom of thought and action in a patient's inner psychic life and the emergence of a new subjectivity in the encounter. A flowing analytic dialogue opens the possibility for a patient to speak polyphonically from many subjective positions, rather than being trapped in a rigid set of responses. Yet we know that the therapist inevitably participates in repetitive sequences by enacting complementary roles and mirroring dyads. I emphasize the importance of the analyst's monitoring his responses as much as possible, preferably by speaking regularly to a third person, and I encourage more institutional support for this aspect of his work. Receptivity to how a patient experiences his participation represents the most effective way for an analyst to learn about his countertransference. The issue is not so much that the analytic therapist has created the patient's problem as that he should take responsibility for unconsciously joining it. The engagement of the analyst shapes the therapeutic process from beginning to end, making each clinical experience unique.

The application of intersubjectivity to psychoanalytic theory and practice has brought about a paradigm shift calling for changes in our training methods and clinical theory. By bridging psychoanalysis with neuroscience, phenomenology, and infant research, the new perspective brings with it an opening to interdisciplinary collaboration and research, freer from the theoretical jargon that has isolated our discipline from fruitful dialogue. We can study intersubjectivity on many levels, although no approach can claim priority without leading to reductionism. I argue that no explanatory system can disregard the complex symbolic nature of human interaction. Causal theories, whether neurophysiologic, psychoanalytic, or semiotic may give a misleading sense of explaining behavior, but personal desires, motives, and meanings in constant interplay with their relational and social contexts remain the foundation of human relations. By affirming this level of human connection, the intersubjective turn establishes psychoanalysis on a firmer and more effective conceptual foundation.

Notes

1. In *Having a Life*, I tried to shed light on the psychological basis of subjectivity by discussing patients who complained of lacking a self (Kirshner, 2004).
2. "We have concluded that the articulation of intrapsychic . . . and the intersubjective points of view is irrefutable, the couple henceforth indissociable" (Green, 2002, p. 77, translated by author).
3. Gobodo-Madikizela gives powerful examples of this process in her work with victims and perpetrators from the period of apartheid (2003).
4. Author's translations.
5. I have written at length about this man in a previously published article (Kirshner, 2007).

References

Benjamin, J. (1990). An outline of intersubjectivity: The development of recognition, *Psychoanalytic Psychology*, 7:33–46.
Bigras, J. (1990). Psychoanalysis as incestuous repetition: Some technical considerations, in *Adult Analysis and Childhood Sexual Abuse*, Ed. H.B. Levine, pp. 173–196, Hillsdale, NJ: The Analytic Press.
Colapietro, V. (1989). *Peirce's Approach to the Self,* Albany, NY: SUNY Press.
Gobodo-Madikizela, P. (2003). *A Human Being Died that Night: A South African Story of Forgiveness*, New York: Houghton Mifflin Co.
Gobodo-Madikizela, P. (2015). Psychological repair: The intersubjective dialogue of remorse and forgiveness in the aftermath of gross human rights violations, *Journal of the American Psychoanalytic Association*, 63:1085–1123.
Green, A. (2002). *Idées directrices pour une psychanalyse contemporaine*, Paris: Presses Universitaires de France.
Kaës, R. (1993). *Le groupe et le sujet du groupe: Éléments pour une théorie psychanalytiques des groupes*, Paris: Dunod.
Kirshner, L. (2004). *Having a Life: Self-Pathology after Lacan*, Hillsdale, NJ: The Analytic Press/Routledge.
Kirshner, L. (2007). Figurations of the real, representation of trauma in a dream, *The American Journal of Psychoanalysis*, 67:303–311.
Lacan, J. (1959–1960). *The Seminar of Jacques Lacan: Book VII. The Ethics of Psychoanalysis*, Ed. J.-A. Miller, trans. D. Porter. New York: W.W. Norton, 1992.
Mishra, P. (2016). Down with elites: Roussaeau in the age of Trump and Brexit, *The New Yorker*, August 1, 2016.
Overall, N. & Simpson, J. (2015). Attachment and dyadic regulation processes, *Current Opinion in Psychology*, 1:61–66.
Peirce, C.S. (1868). Some questions concerning certain faculties claimed for man, in *The Collected Papers of Charles Sanders Peirce*, Ed. C. Hartshorne, P. Weiss, & A. Burks. 8 vols. Cambridge, MA: Belknap Press of the Harvard University Press, 1931–35, 1958.

Reis, H. & Gable, S. (2015). Responsiveness, *Current Opinion in Psychology*, 1:67–71.

Reis, H., Clark, M., Gray, P.F., Brown, J., Stewart, M., & Underwood, S. (2008). Measuring responsiveness in the therapeutic relationship: A patient perspective, *Basic and Applied Social Psychology*, 30:339–348.

Ricoeur, P. (2004). *Parcours de la Reconnaissance*, Paris: Éditions Stock; *The Course of Recognition*, trans. D. Pellauer, Cambridge, MA: Harvard University Press, 2005.

Salvatore, S. (2015). *Psychology in Black and White: The Project of a Theory-driven Science*, Charlotte, NC: Information Age Publishers.

Schafer, R. (1979). The appreciative analytic attitude and the construction of multiple histories, *Psychoanalysis and Contemporary Thought*, 2:3–24.

Widlöcher, D. (2004a). The third in mind. *Psychoanalytic Quarterly*, 73:197–213.

Widlöcher, D. (2004b), Dissection de l'empathie, *Revue française de Psychanalyse*, LXVIII (3), 981–992.

Žižek, S. (2006). *The Parallax View*, Cambridge, MA: MIT Press.

Index